700 ASL
SENTENCES

Talk in Sign Language

Donald Cabbage Ph.D.

700 ASL Sentences

Copyright © 2025 Donald Cabbage Ph.D.

ISBN (Paperback): 979-8-89672-147-5
ISBN (Ebook): 979-8-89672-148-2

Printed in the United States of America.

PROMINENT
BOOKS
EDGE

5830 E 2nd St, Ste 7000 #9983
Casper, WY 82609
USA

Introduction

With fifty years of experience and fluency in thirteen different sign languages, Don Cabbage, Ph.D. is an expert in writing and teaching sign. For those wishing to learn the basics of American Sign Language, they now can with Dr. Cabbage's English 700 ASL Sentences. Follow along as beginners will learn the basics of the alphabet and numbers before venturing on to full sentences. After the 700 exercises found in this book, beginners will have a better understanding of this incredible language and have the ability to carry on simple conversations with others.

ASL Fingerspelling Alphabet

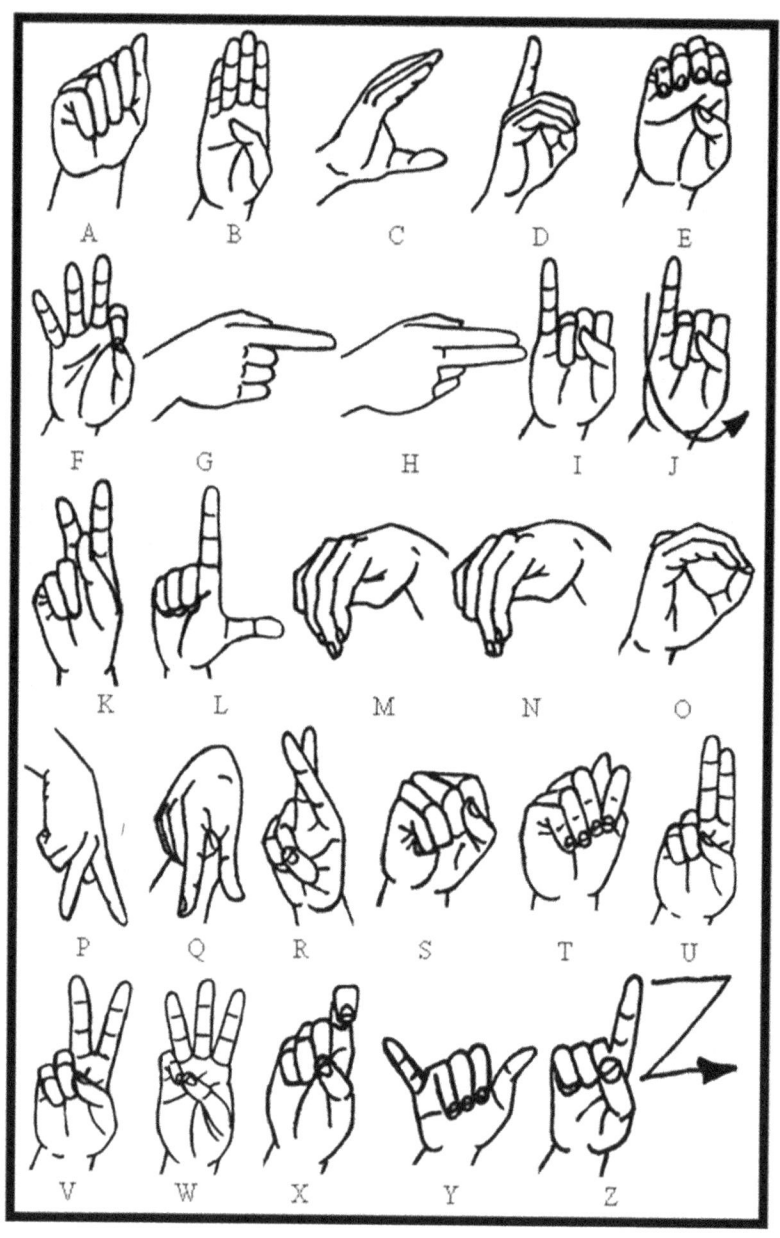

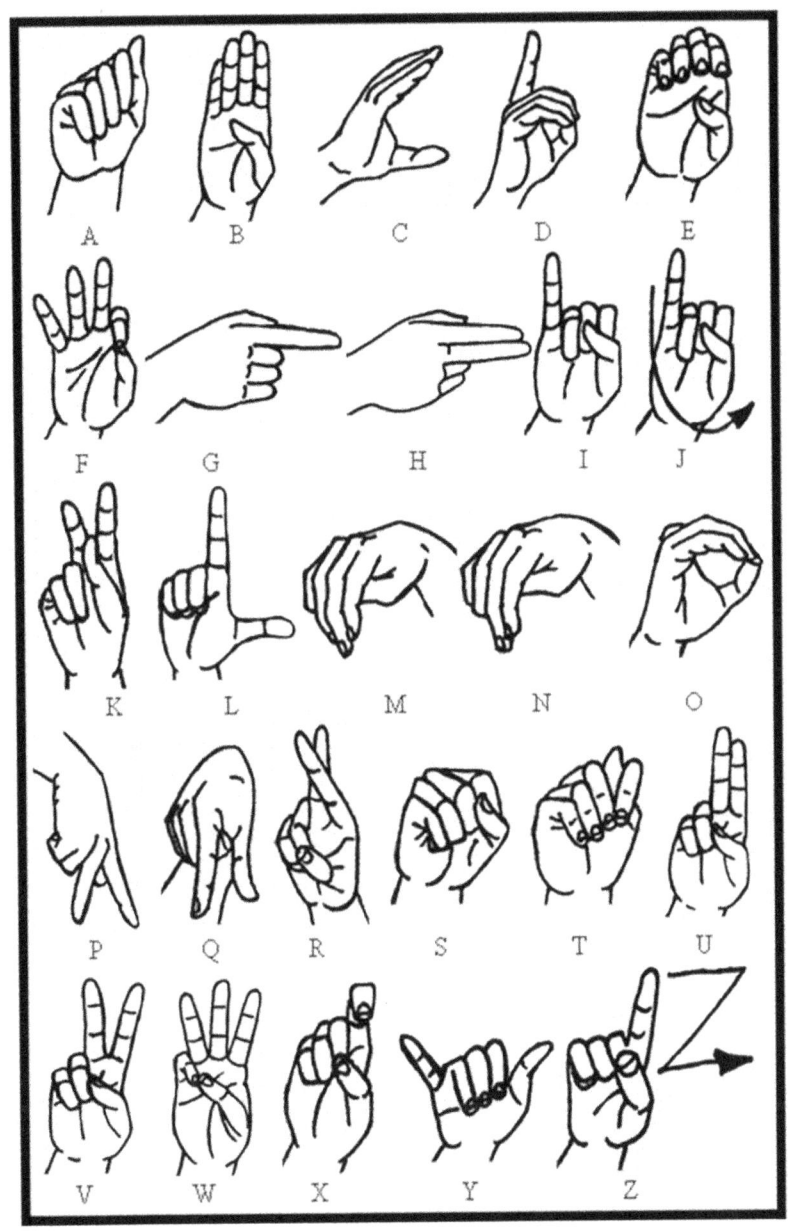

ASL Numbers

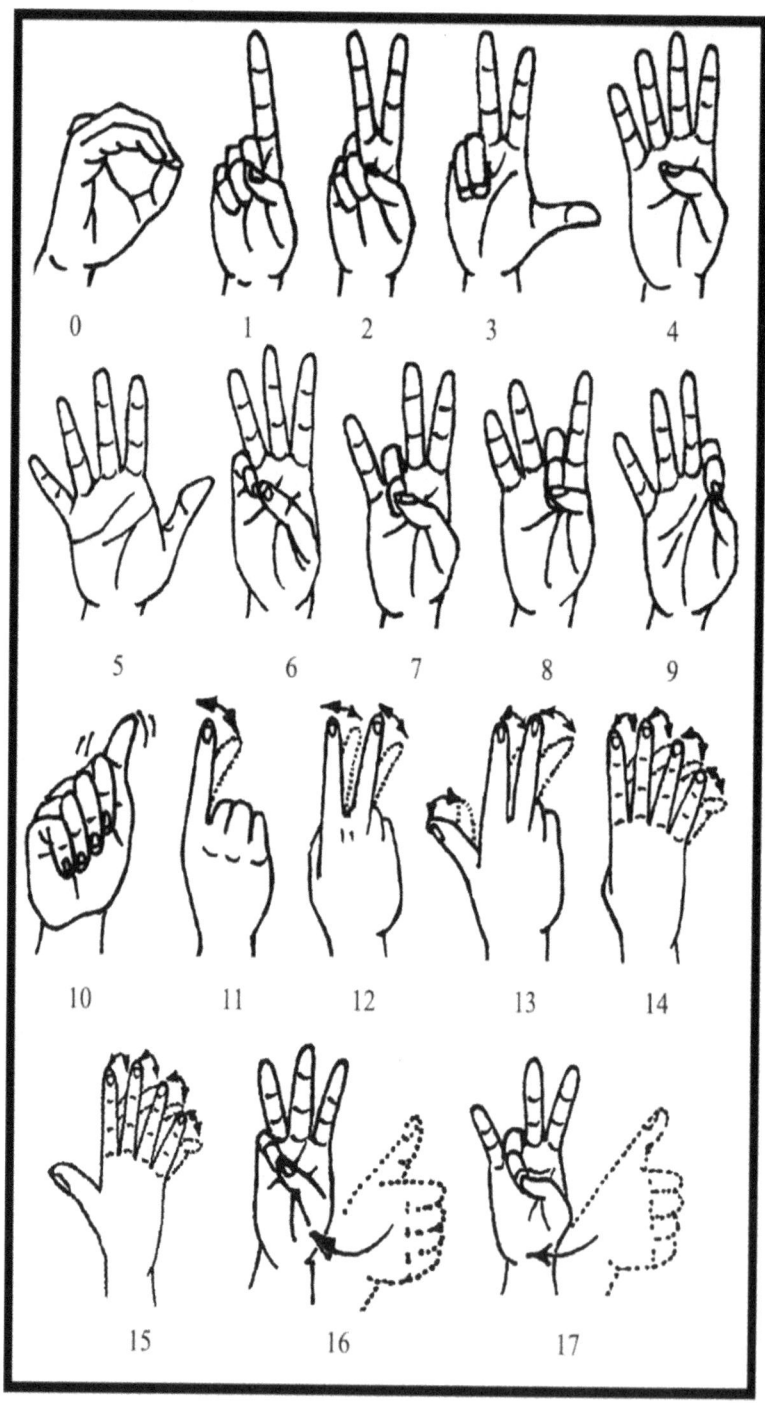

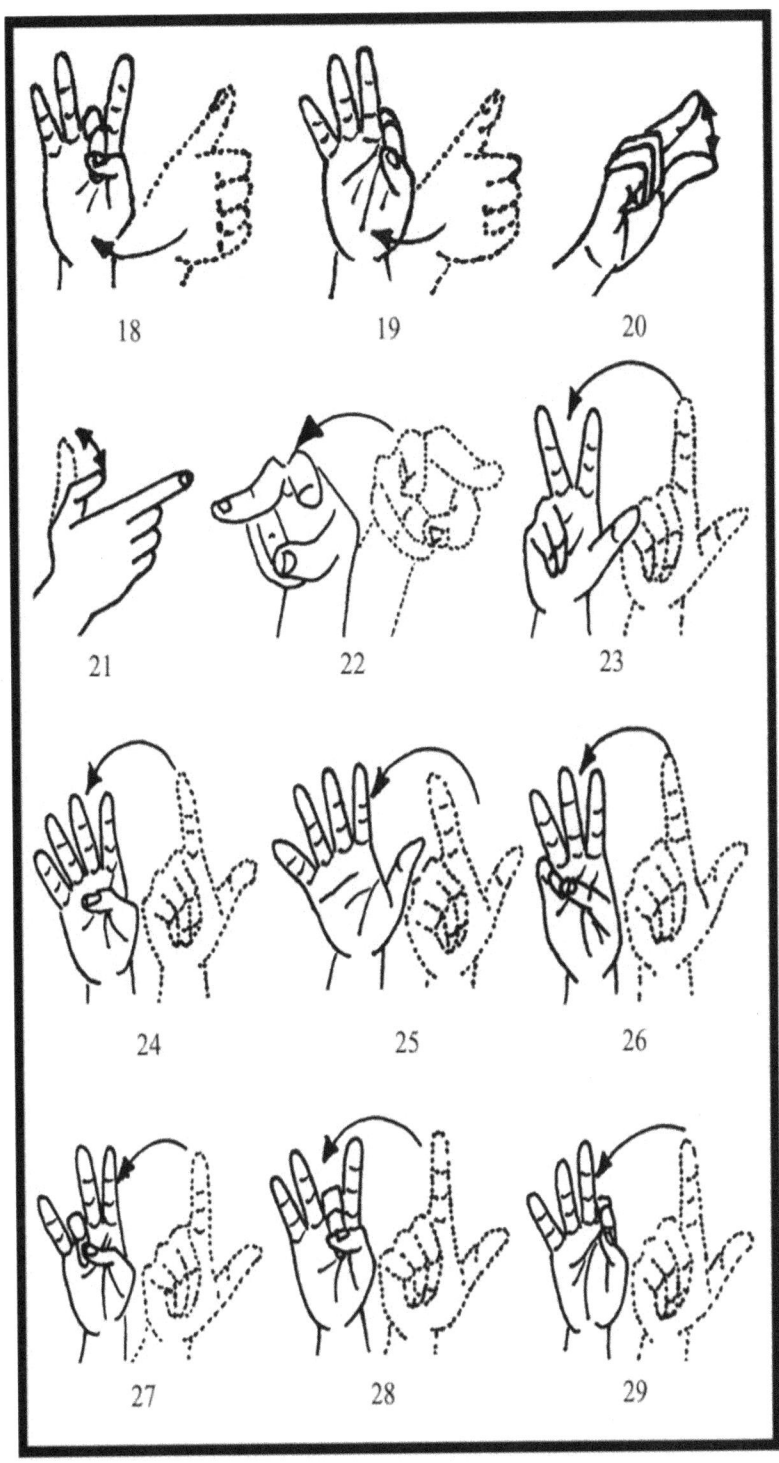

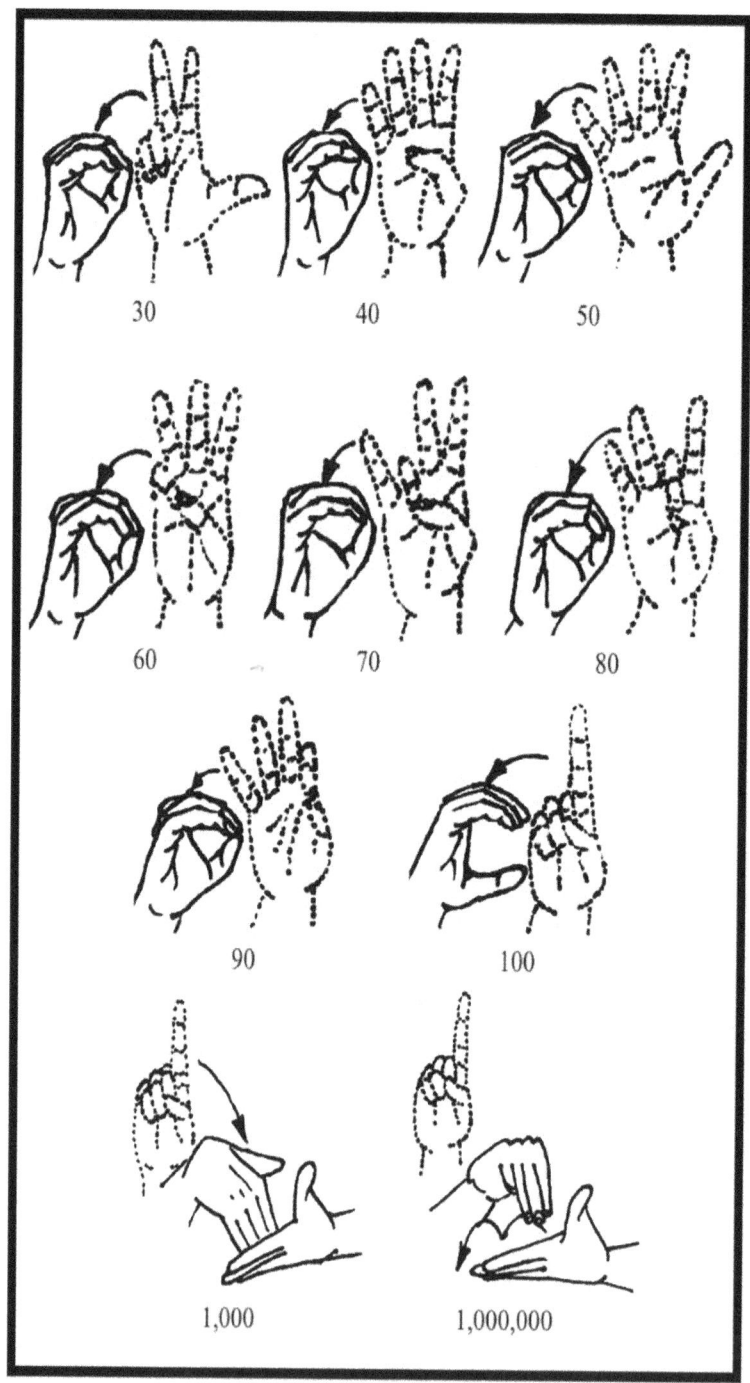

#1.   Hello.

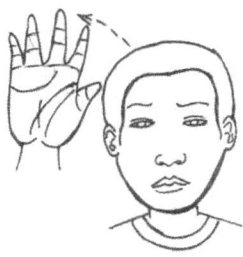

#2   Good   morning.

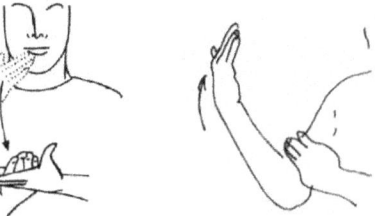

#3   I   am   John

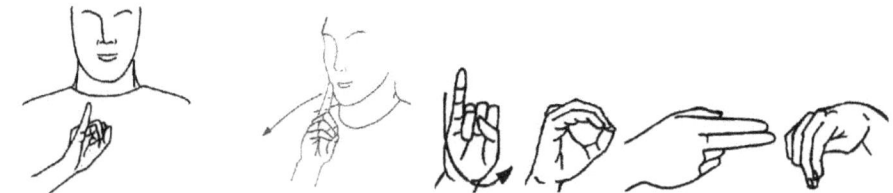

Smith.

#4. Are   you   Bill   Jones   ?

#5.   Yes,   I   am.

#6.   How   are   you   ?

#7.   Fine,   thanks.

#8.   How   is   Helen   ?

#9.   She   is   very   well,   thank   you.

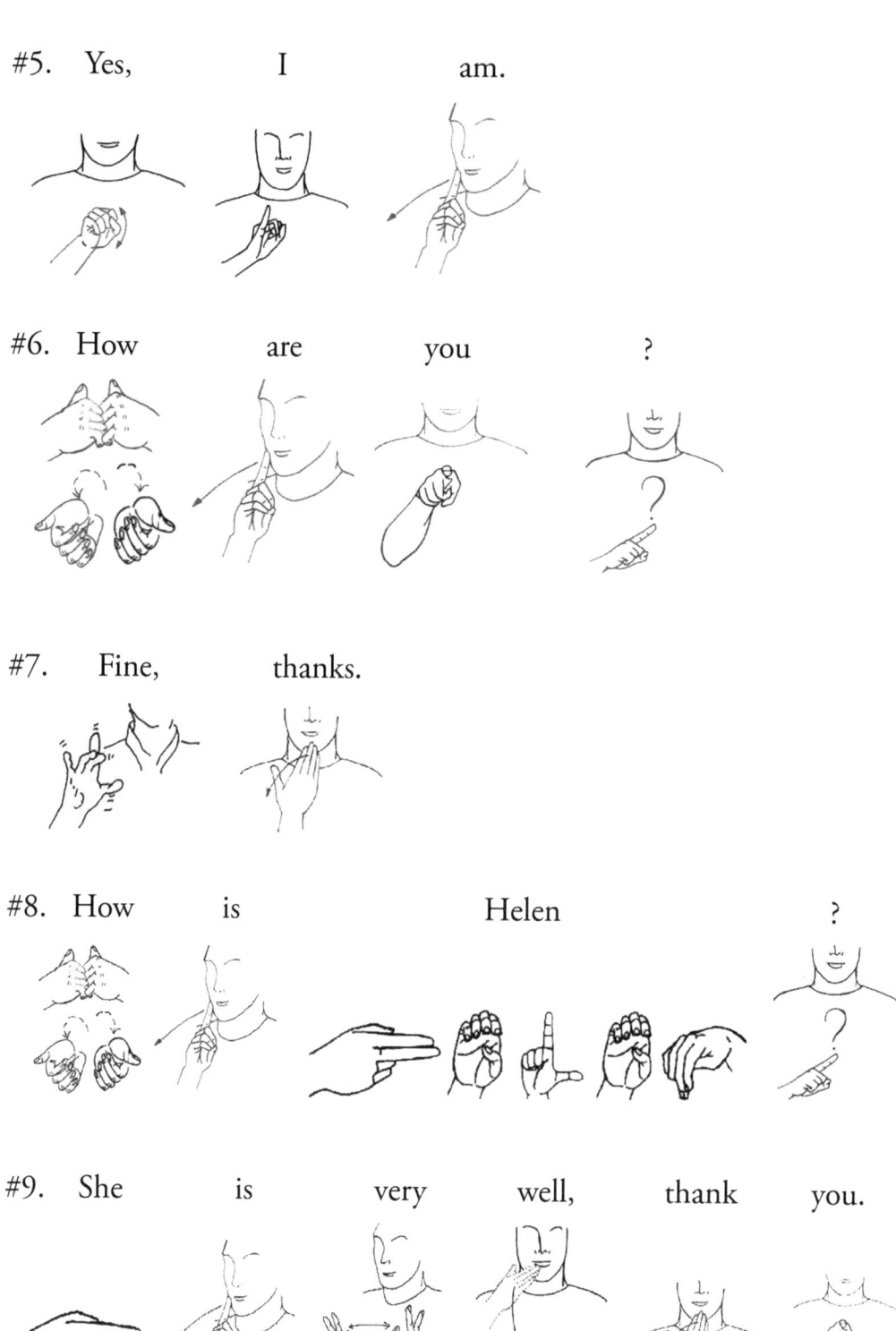

#10.   Good   afternoon,   Mr.   Green.

#11.   Good   evening,   Mrs.   Brown.

#12.   How   are   you   this   evening   ?

#13.   Good   night,   John.

#14   Good-bye,   Bill.

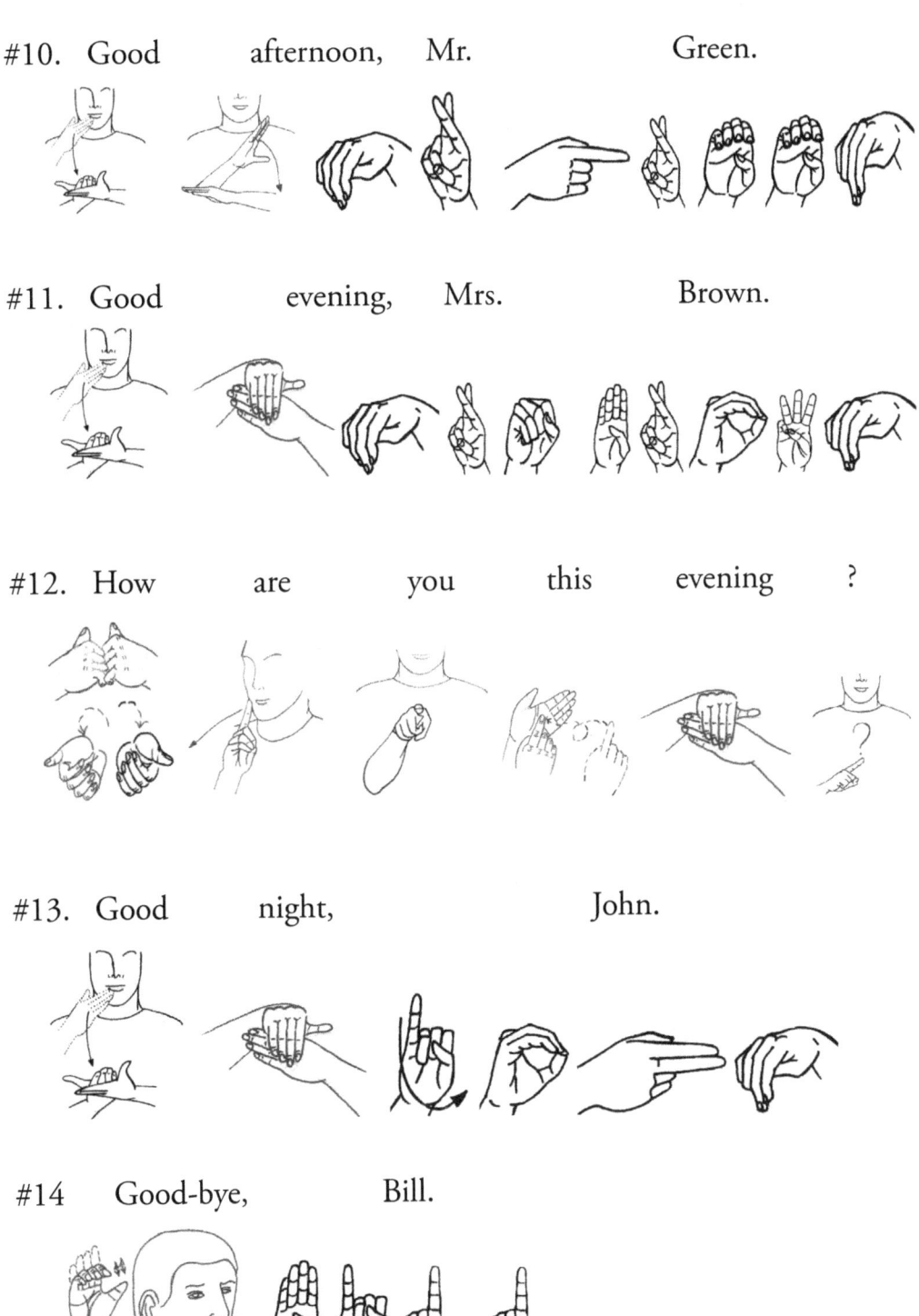

#15   See   you   tomorrow.

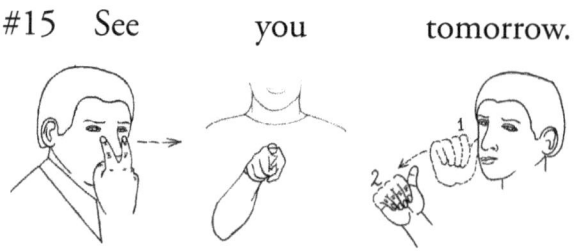

#16.   Come   in,   please.

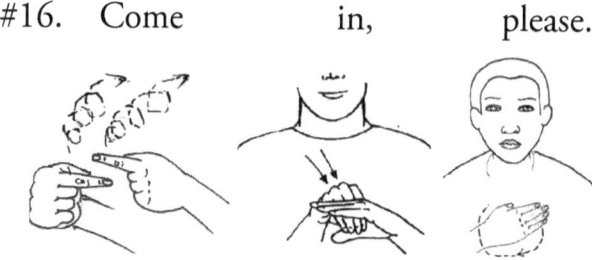

#17. Sit down

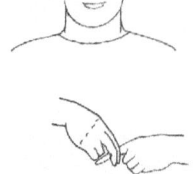

#18. Stand up,   please.

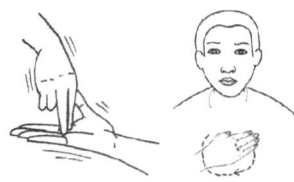

#19   Open   your   book,   please.

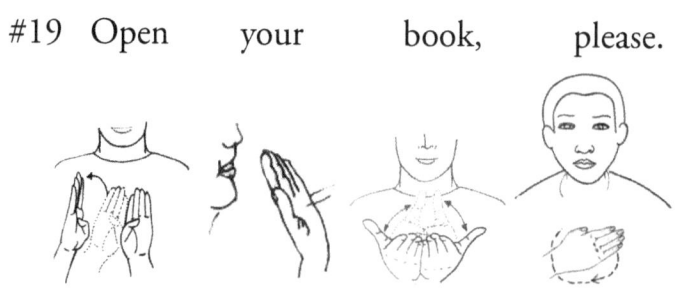

#20   Close   your   book,   please.

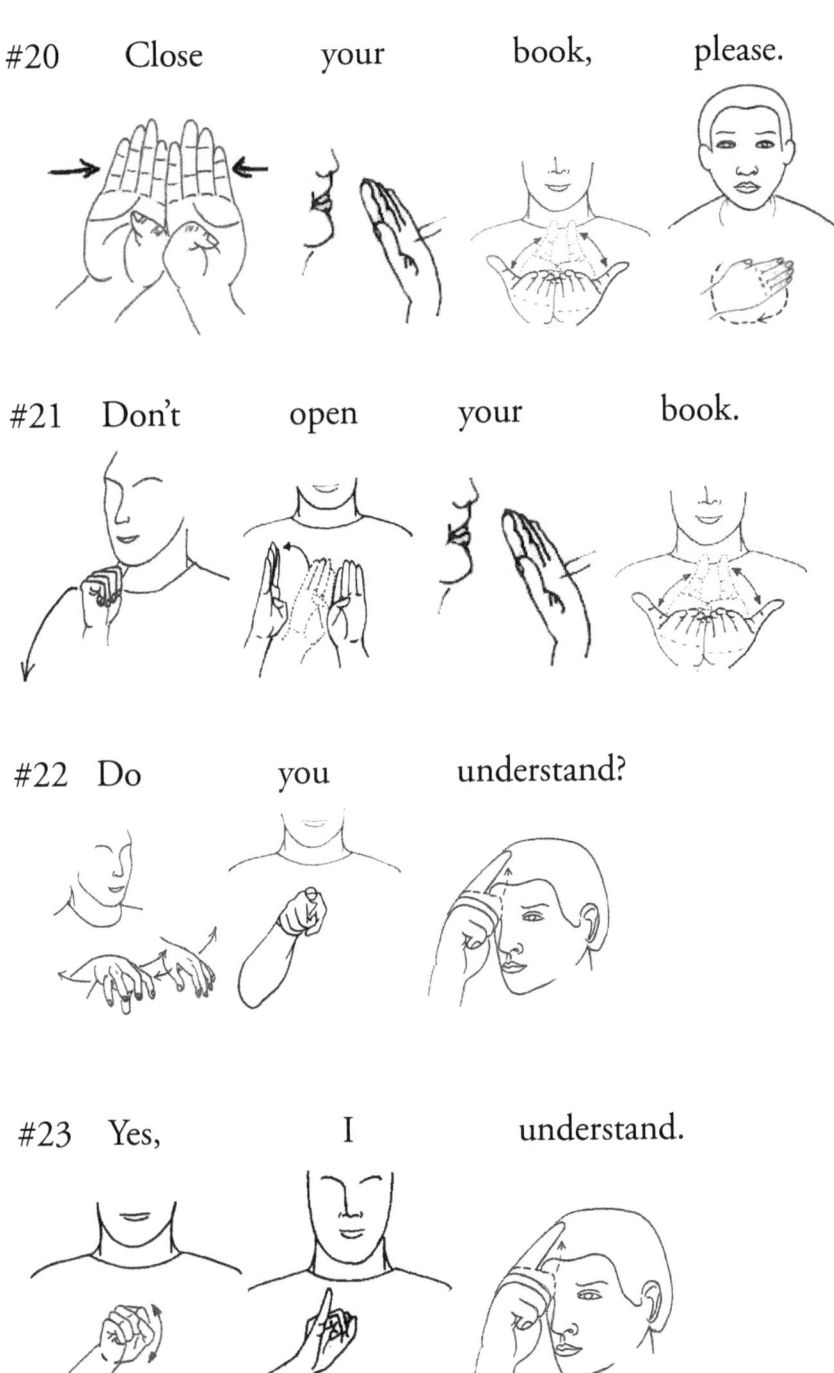

#21   Don't   open   your   book.

#22   Do   you   understand?

#23   Yes,   I   understand.

#24.   No,   I   do not   understand.

#25   Listen   and   repeat.

#26   Now   read,   please.

#27 That   is   fine.

#28   It   is   time   to   begin.

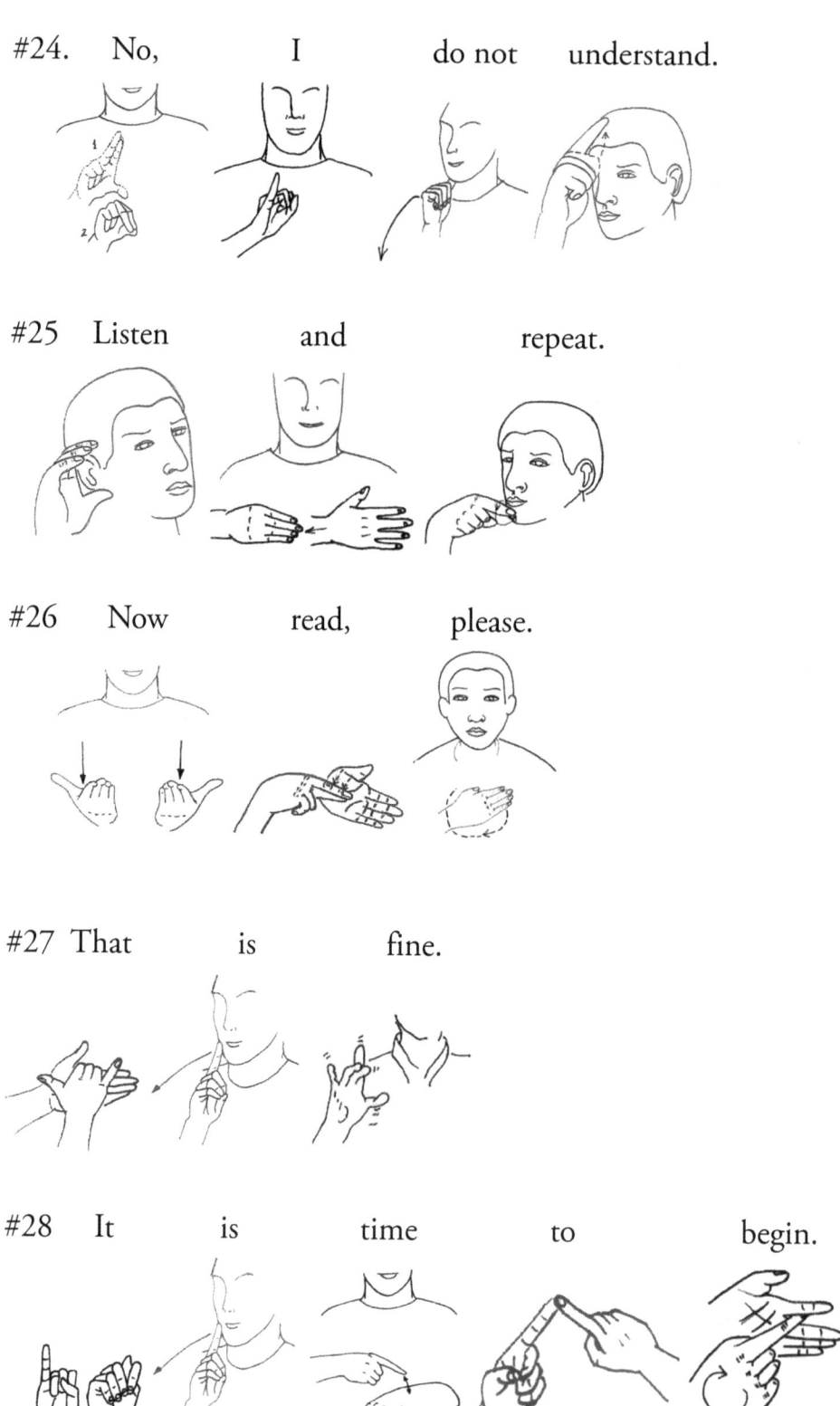

#29   Let   us   begin   now.

#30   This   is   lesson   one.

#31   What   is   this   ?

#32   That   is   a   book.

#33   Is   this   your   book   ?

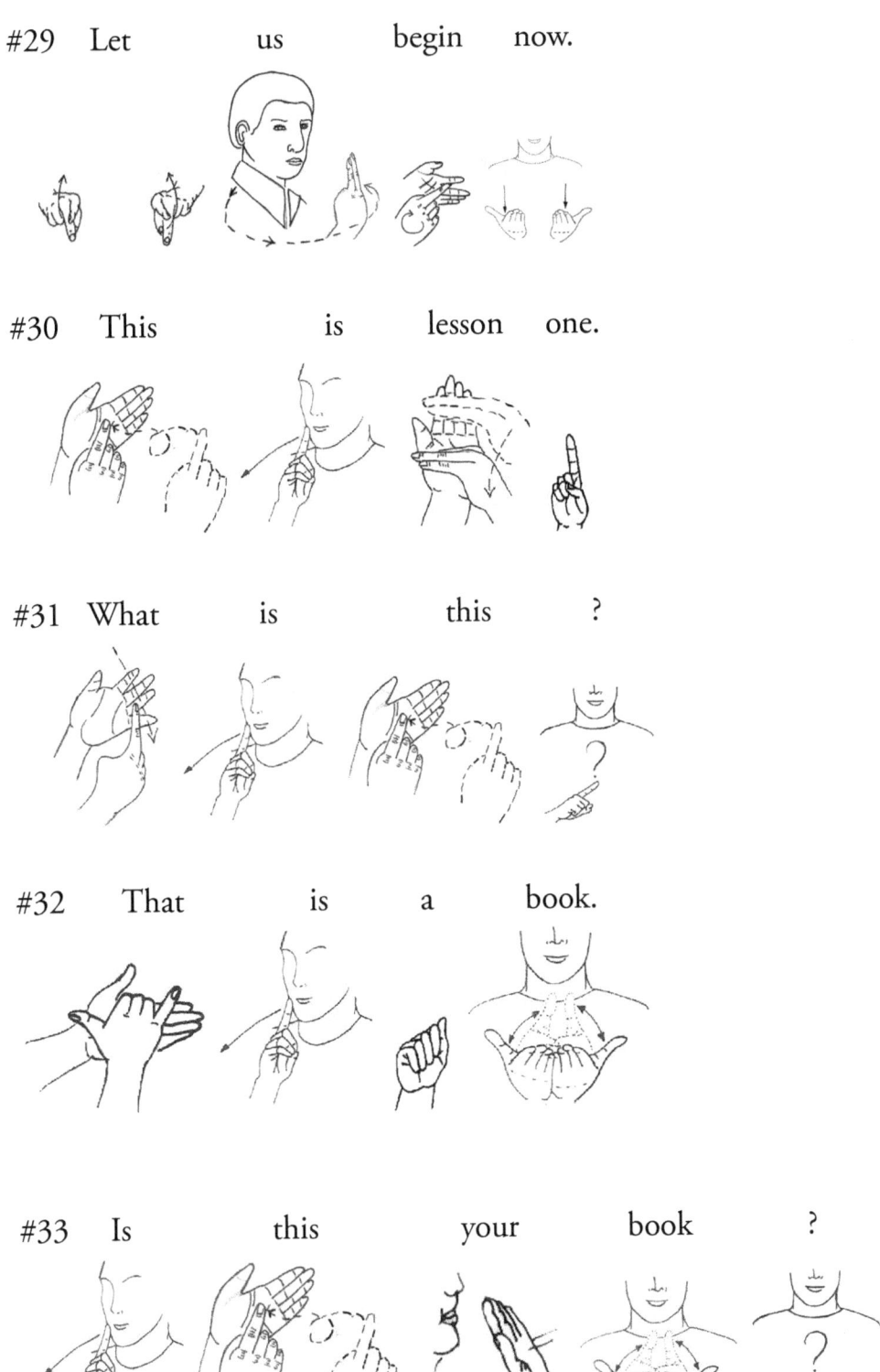

15

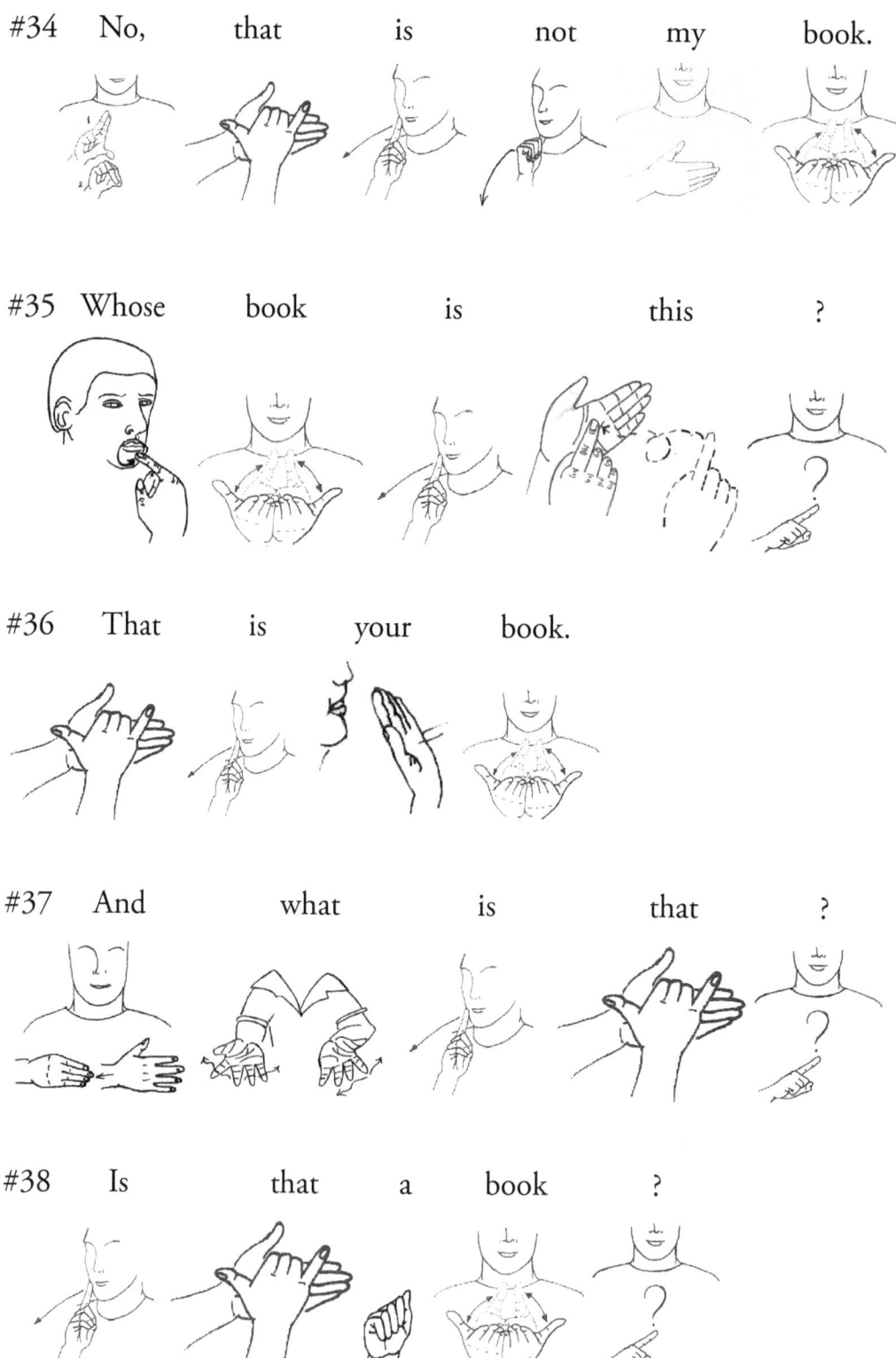

#34   No,   that   is   not   my   book.

#35 Whose   book   is   this   ?

#36   That   is   your   book.

#37   And   what   is   that   ?

#38   Is   that   a   book   ?

#39   No,   it   is not

#40   It   is   a   pencil.

#41   Is   it   yours   ?

#42   Yes,   it   is   mine.

#43   Where   is   the   door   ?

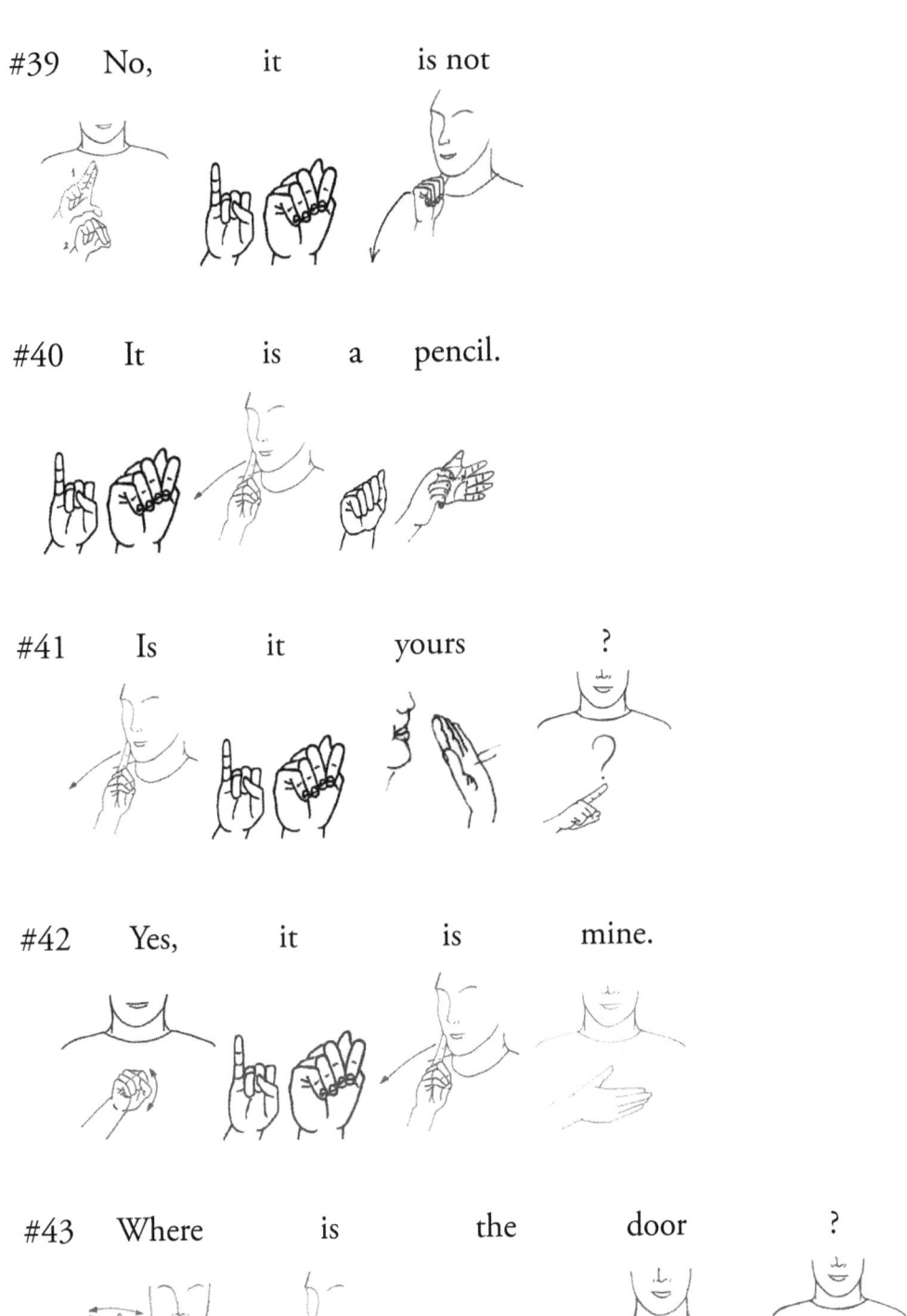

#44   There   it   is.

#45   Is   this   book   his   ?

#46   What   are   these   ?

#47 Those   are   books.

#48.   Where   are   the   books   ?

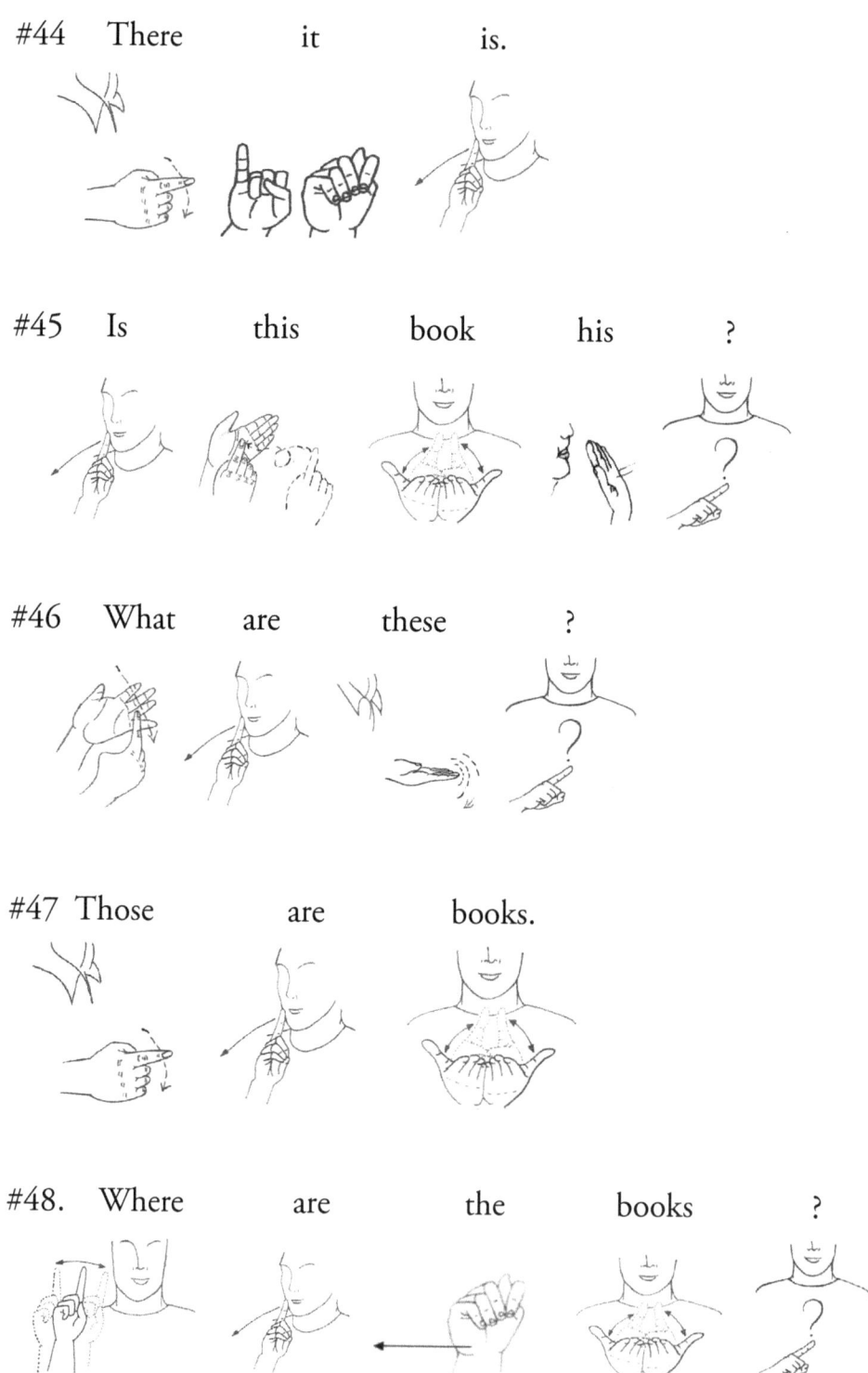

#49.   There   they   are.

#50.   These   are   my   pencils.

#51.   Where   are   your   pens   ?

#52.   They   are   over   there.

#53.   Are   these   your   pens   ?

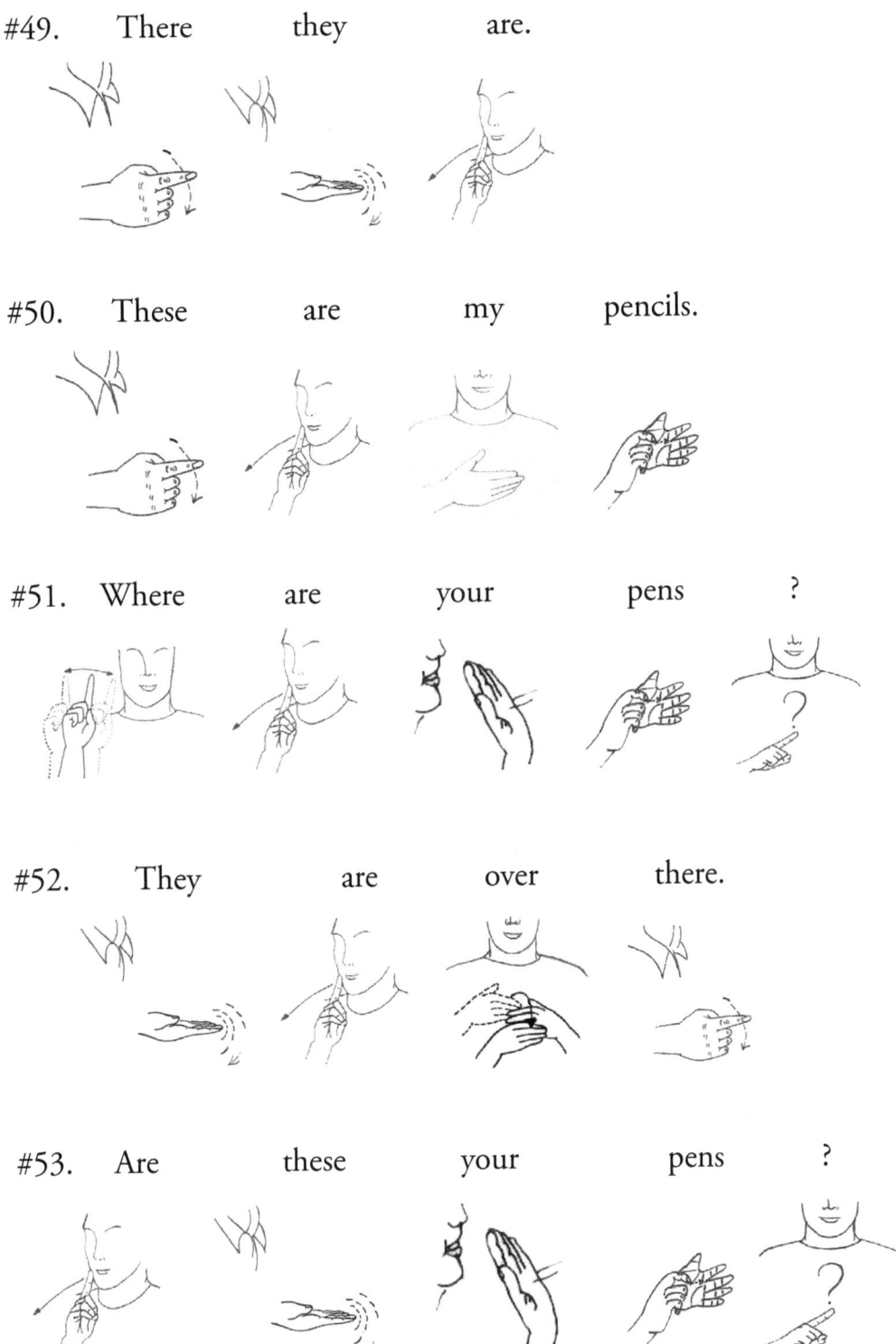

#54.   Yes,   they   are.

#55.   Those   are   mine.

#56. These   are   your   books,   aren't they   ?

#57.   No,   they   aren't.

#58.   They're   not   mine.

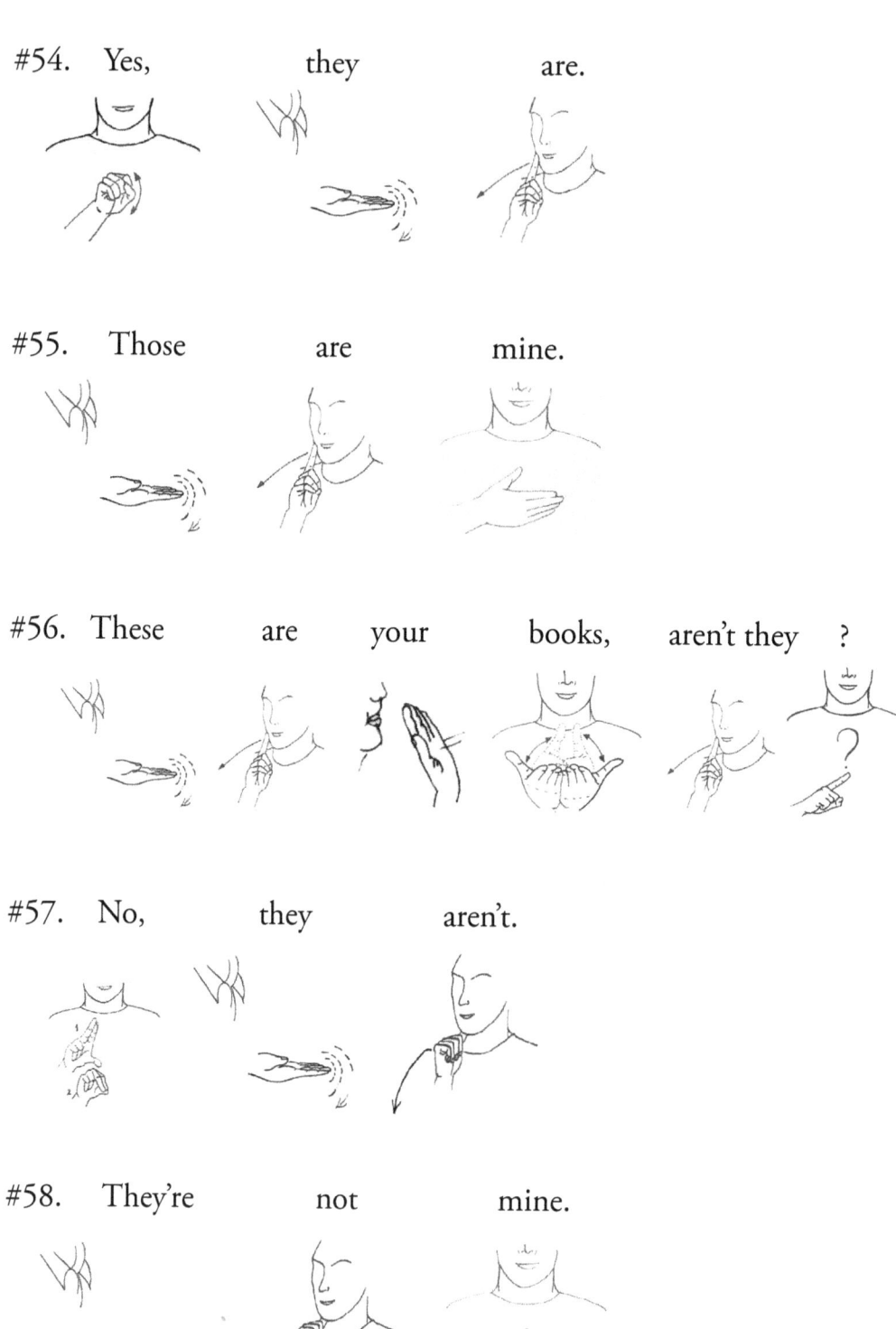

#59.   These   are   mine,   and

those   are   yours.

#60.   Those   aren't   your   pens,   are they   ?

#61. Who   are   you   ?

#62.   I   am   a   student.

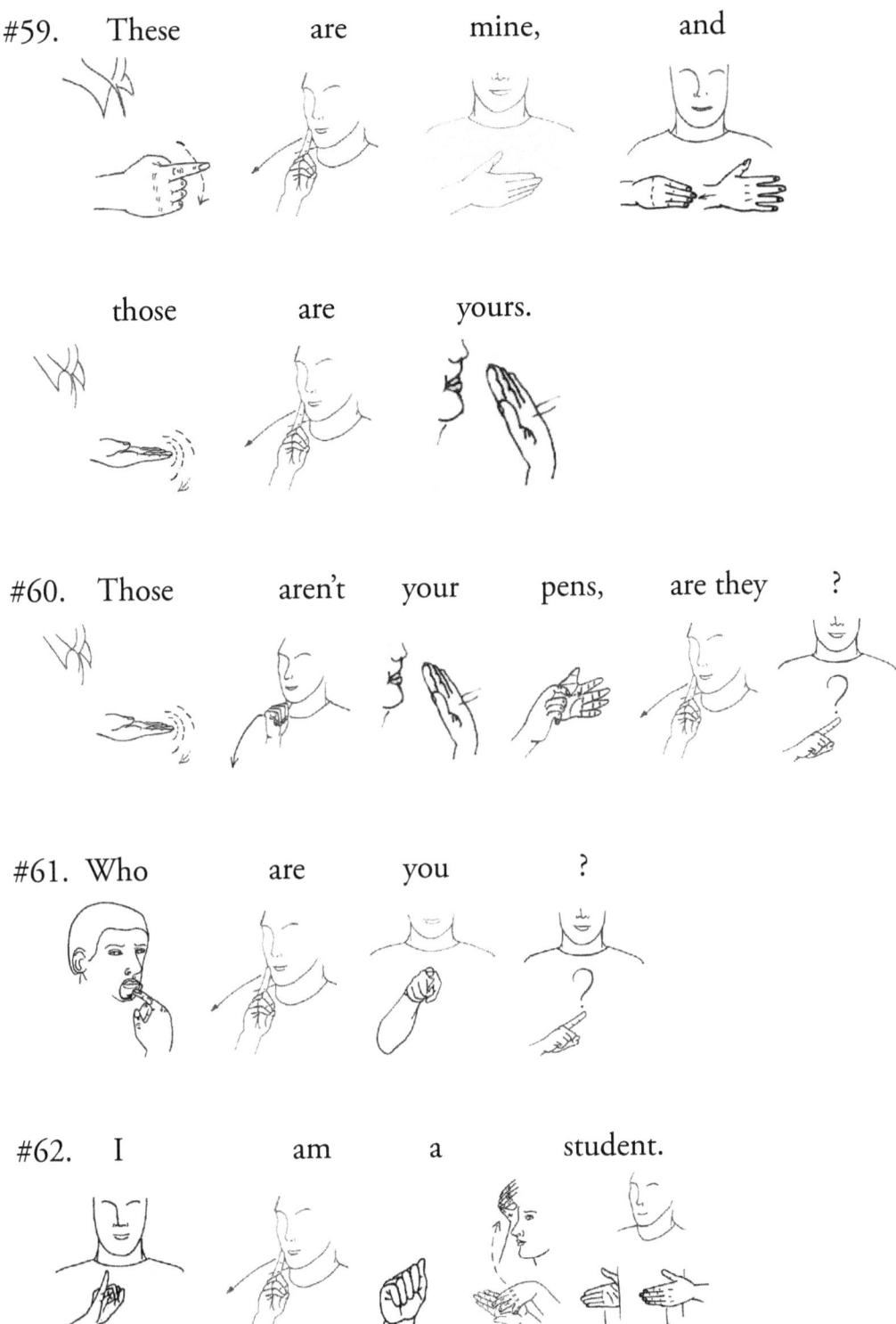

#63. Who   is   that   over there   ?

#64. He   is   a   student,   too.

#65. Is   that   lady   a   student   ?

#66. No,   she   isn't.

#67 Those   men   aren't   students, either.

#68.   Am   I   your   teacher   ?

#69.   Yes,   you   are.

#70. That   man   is   a   teacher,

isn't he   ?

#71. Yes,   he   is.

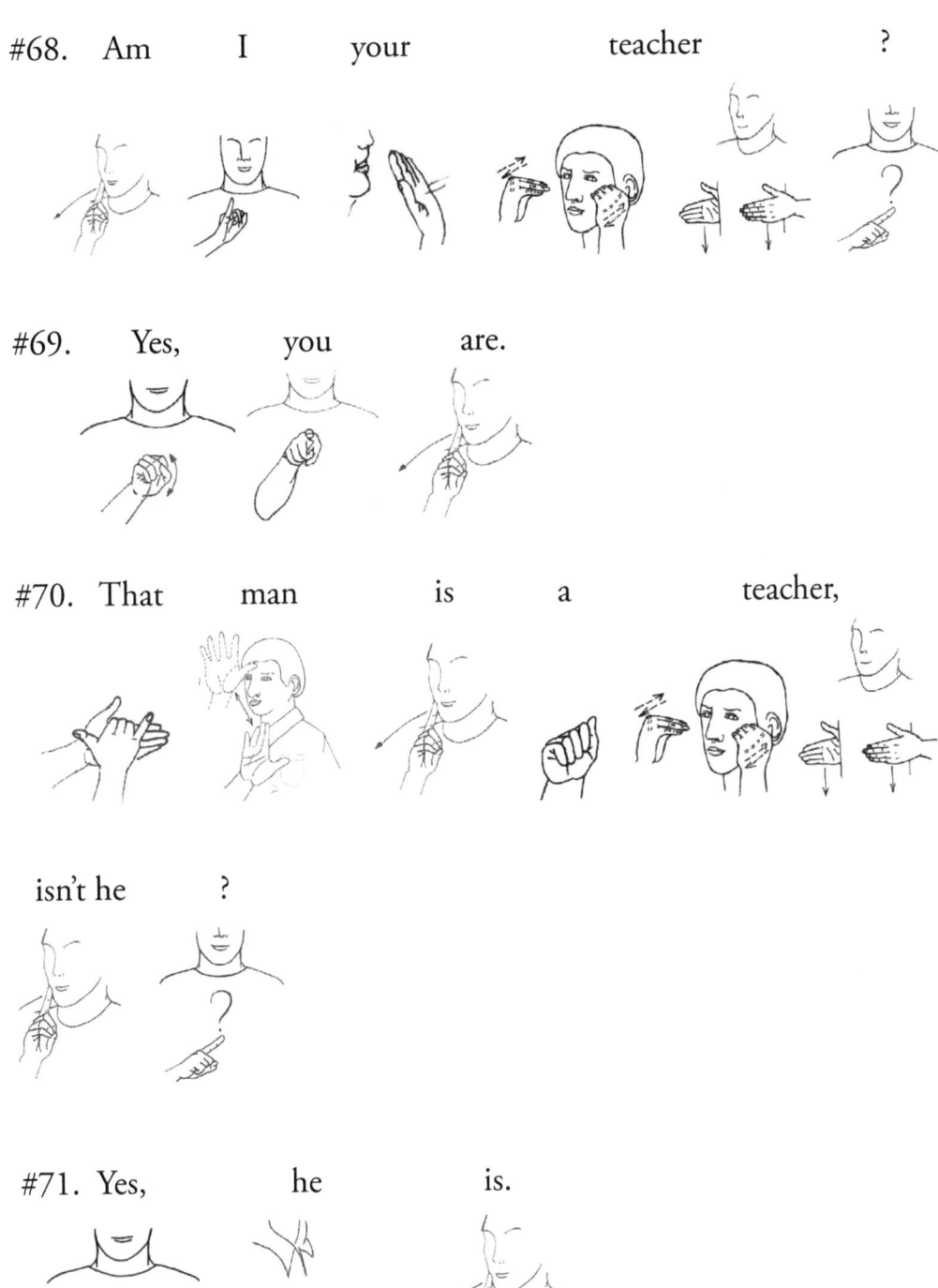

#72. Who   are   those   people   ?

#73. Maybe   they   are   farmers.

#74. Aren't   they   students   ?

#75. I   really   don't know.

#76. What   is   your   name   ?

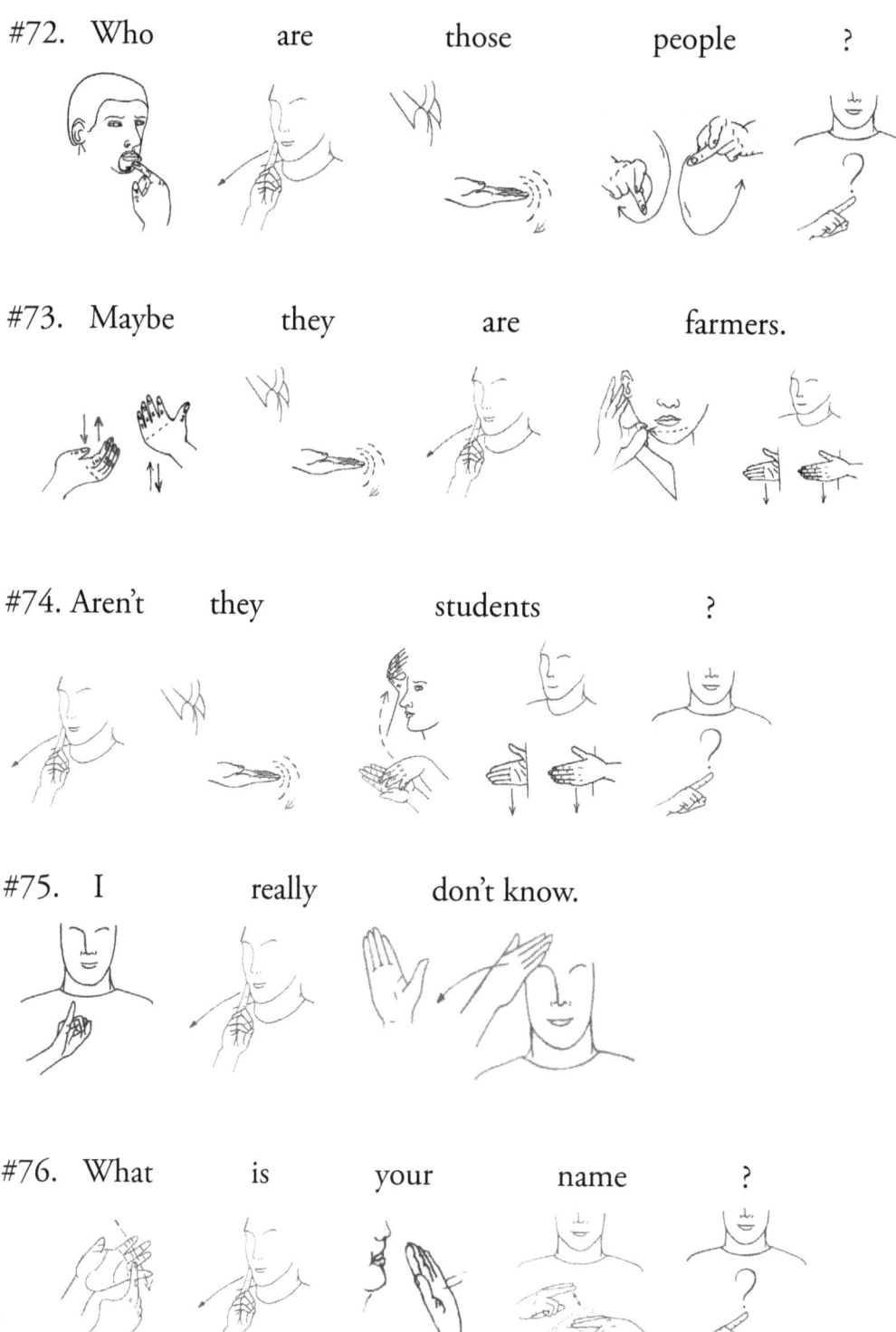

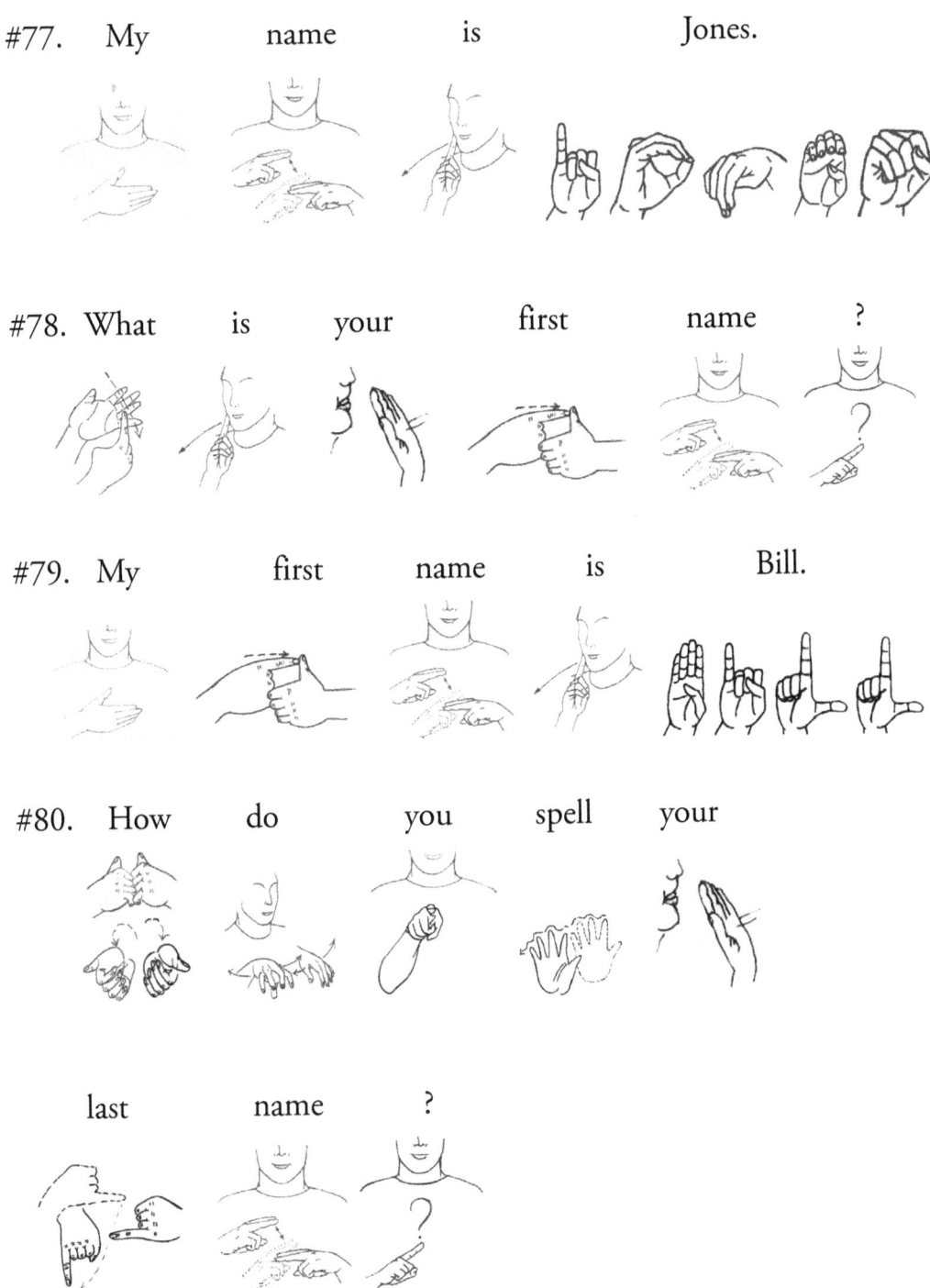

#77.   My   name   is   Jones.

#78. What   is   your   first   name   ?

#79. My   first   name   is   Bill.

#80. How   do   you   spell   your

last   name   ?

#81. J   O   N   E   S.

#82. What   is   your   friend's   name   ?

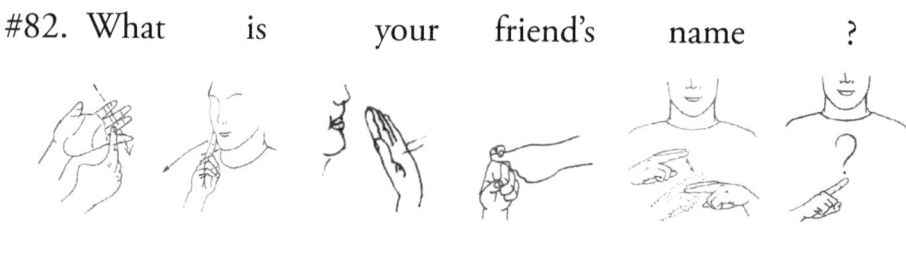

#83. His   name   is

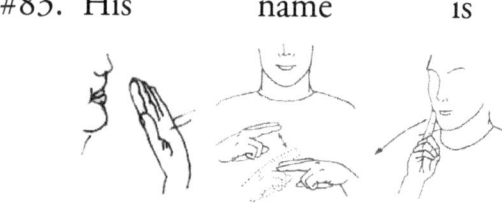

J   o   h   n   S   m   i   t   h.

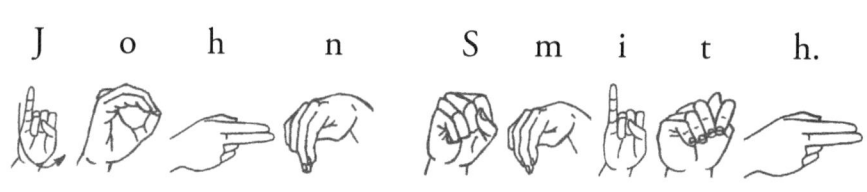

#84. J   o   h   n   and   I   are   old   friends.

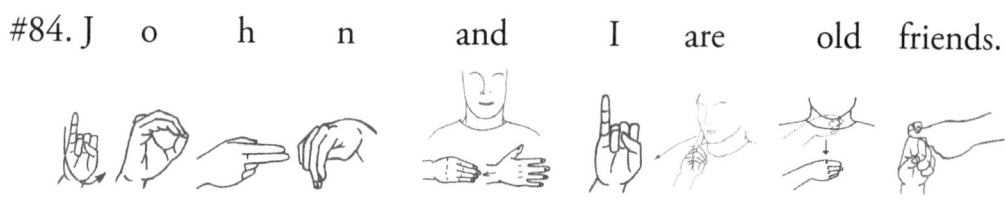

#85. Are   you   J   o   h   n's   brother   ?

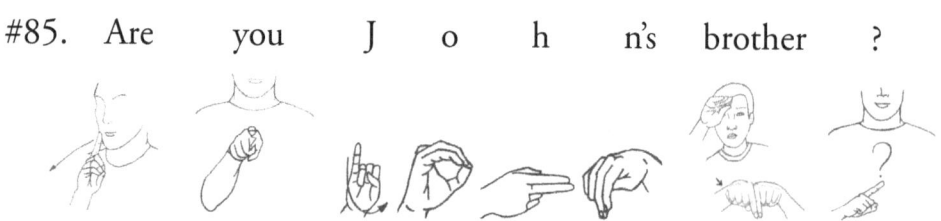

26

#86.　No,　　I'm　　not.

#87　This　　is　　Mr.　　Jones.

#88.　How　do　you　do　?

#89.　Mrs.　　Jones,　　this　is

Mr.　　John　　Smith.

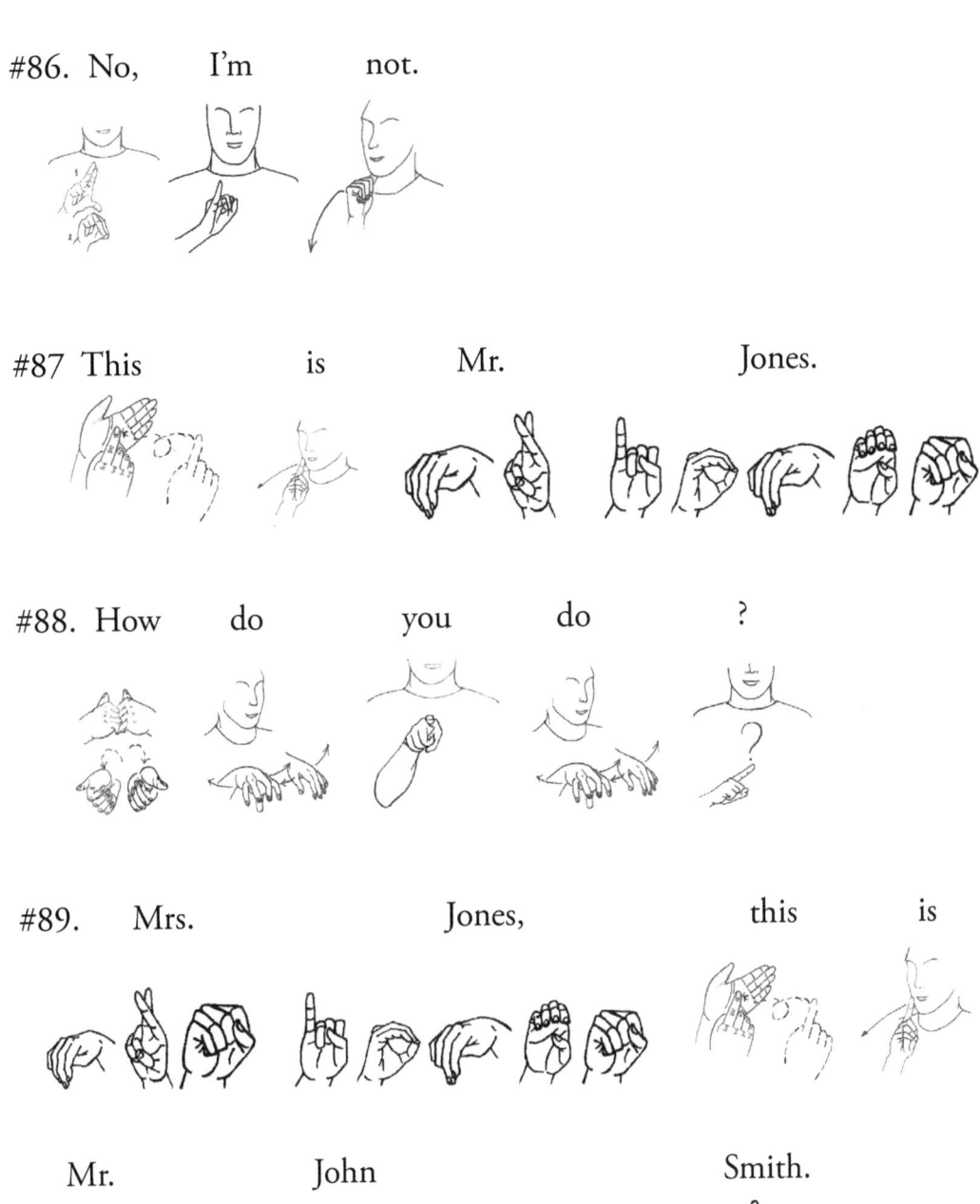

#90. Very   pleased   to   meet   you.

#91. What   day   is   today   ?

#92.   Today   is   Monday.

#93. What   day   was   yesterday   ?

#94.   Yesterday   was   Sunday

#95. What   day   is   tomorrow   ?

#96. What   month   is   this   ?

#97. This   is   January.

#98. Last   month   was   December,   was it   ?

#99. Yes,   it   was.

#100. What   month   is   next   month   ?

101.   I   was   in   the   hospital

for   several   weeks.

#102. Where   were   you   on   Tuesday   ?

#103. You were here   in   February,   weren't you   ?

#104.   No,   I   wasn't.

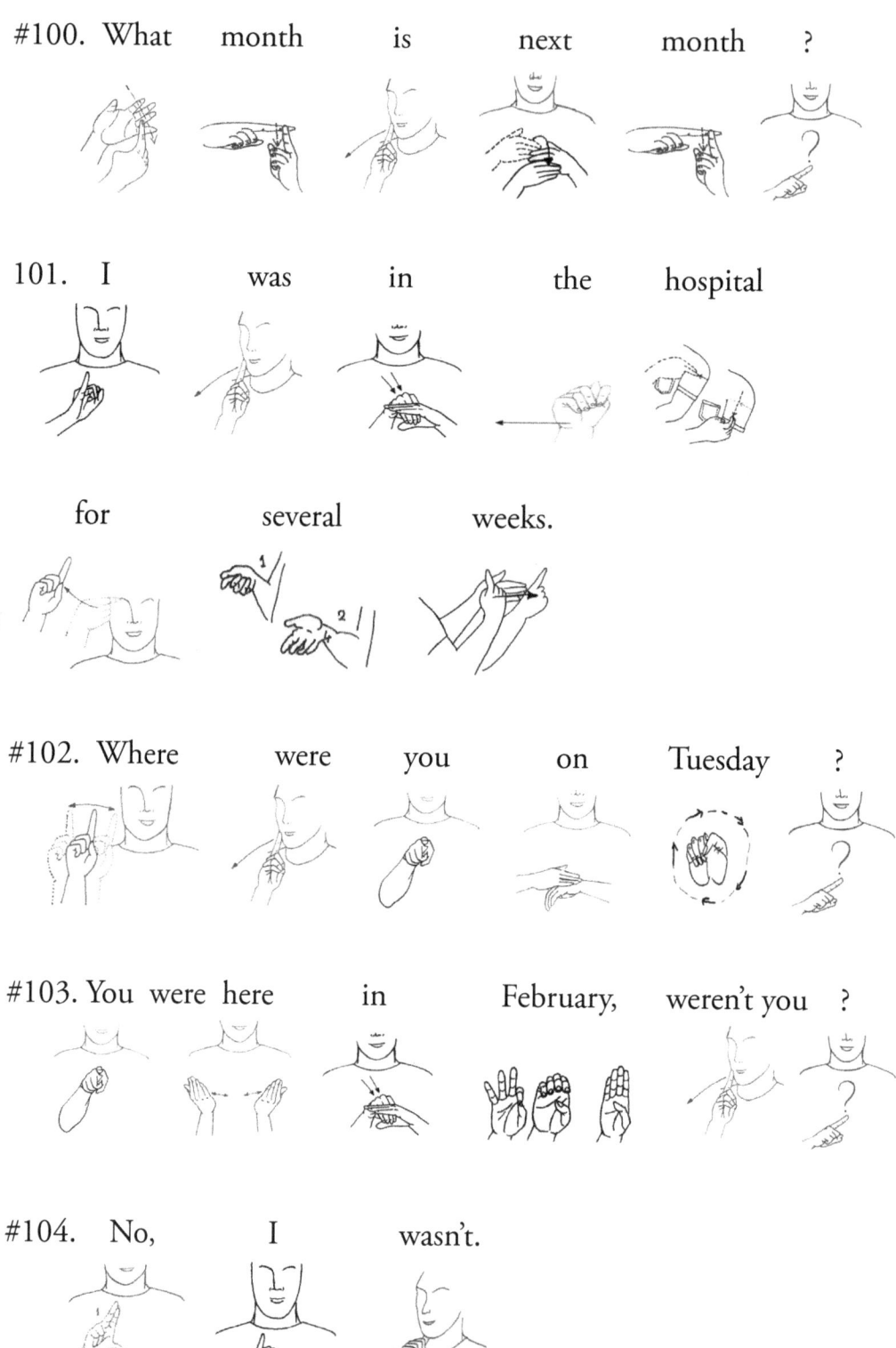

#105. Your   friend   was   here   a week   ago,

wasn't he   ?

#106. Do   you   have   a   book   ?

#107. Yes,   I   do.

#108. You   have   a   radio,   don't   you   ?

#109. No,   I   don't.

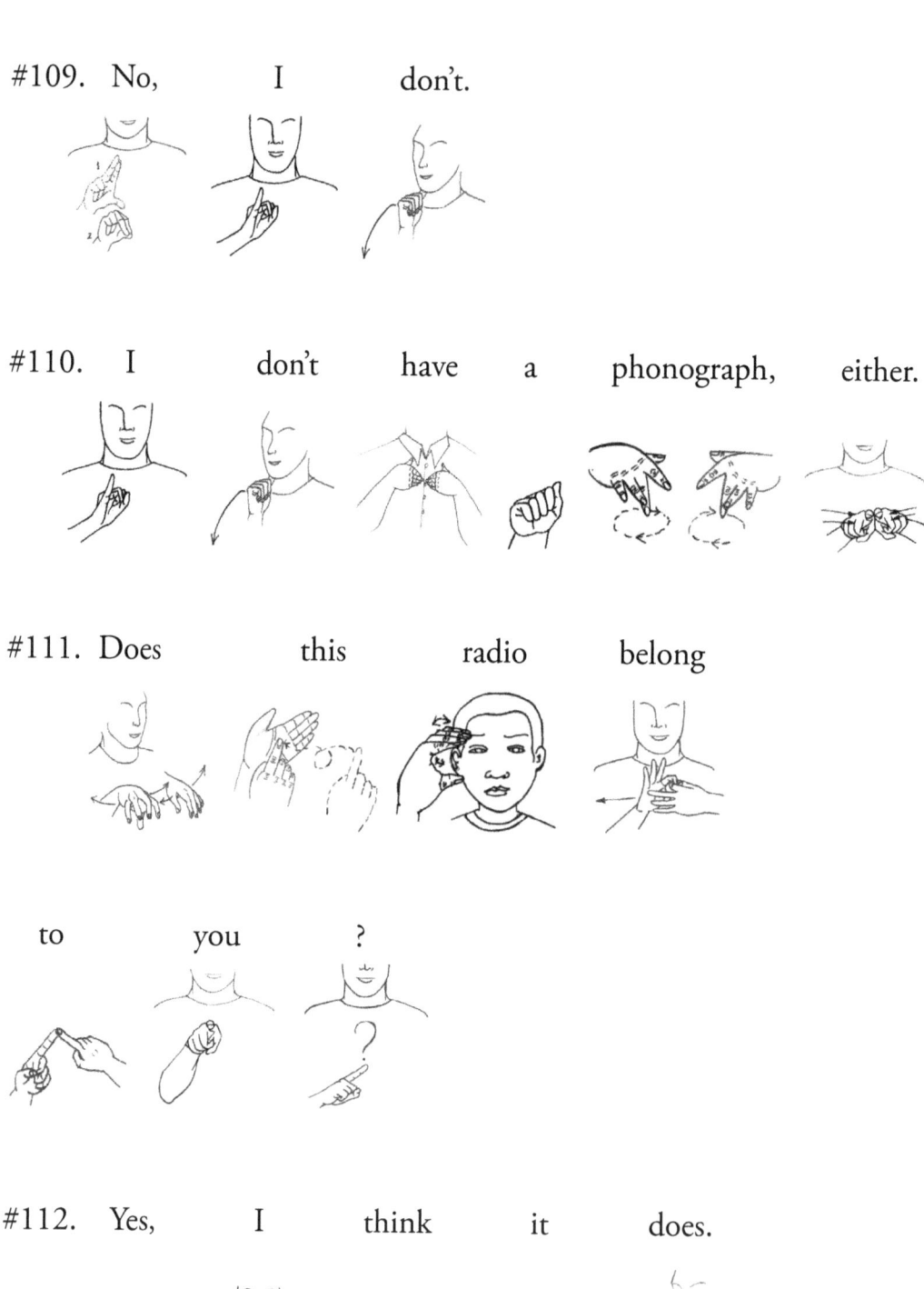

#110. I   don't   have   a   phonograph,   either.

#111. Does   this   radio   belong

to   you   ?

#112. Yes,   I   think   it   does.

#113. How many sisters and brothers do

you have ?

#114. Don't you have my hat ?

#115. Yes, I have both your

hat and your coat.

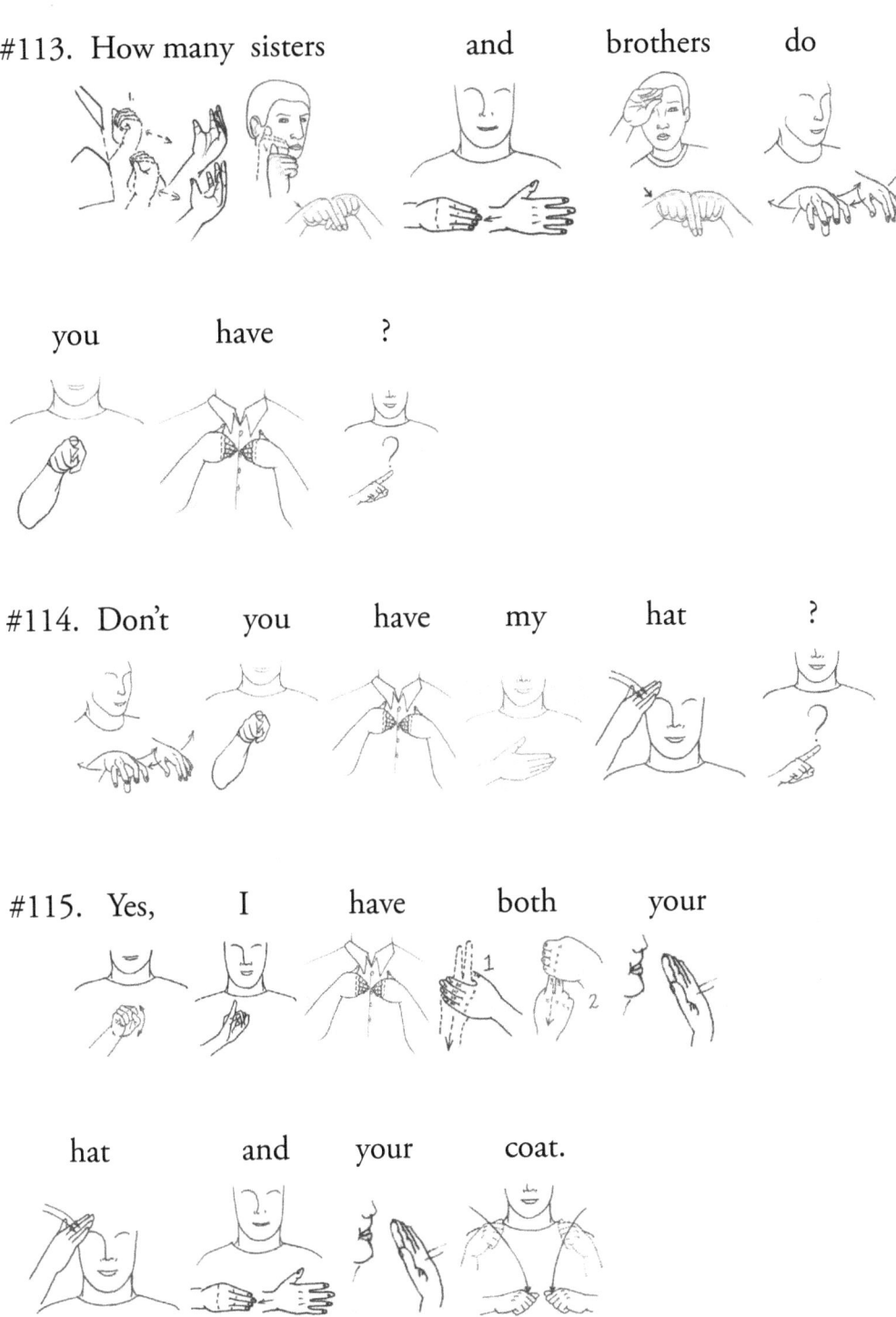

#116. Does   John   have   a

yellow   pencil   ?

#117. Yes,   he   does.

#118. He   has   a   radio,   doesn't   he   ?

#119. No,   he   doesn't   have   one.

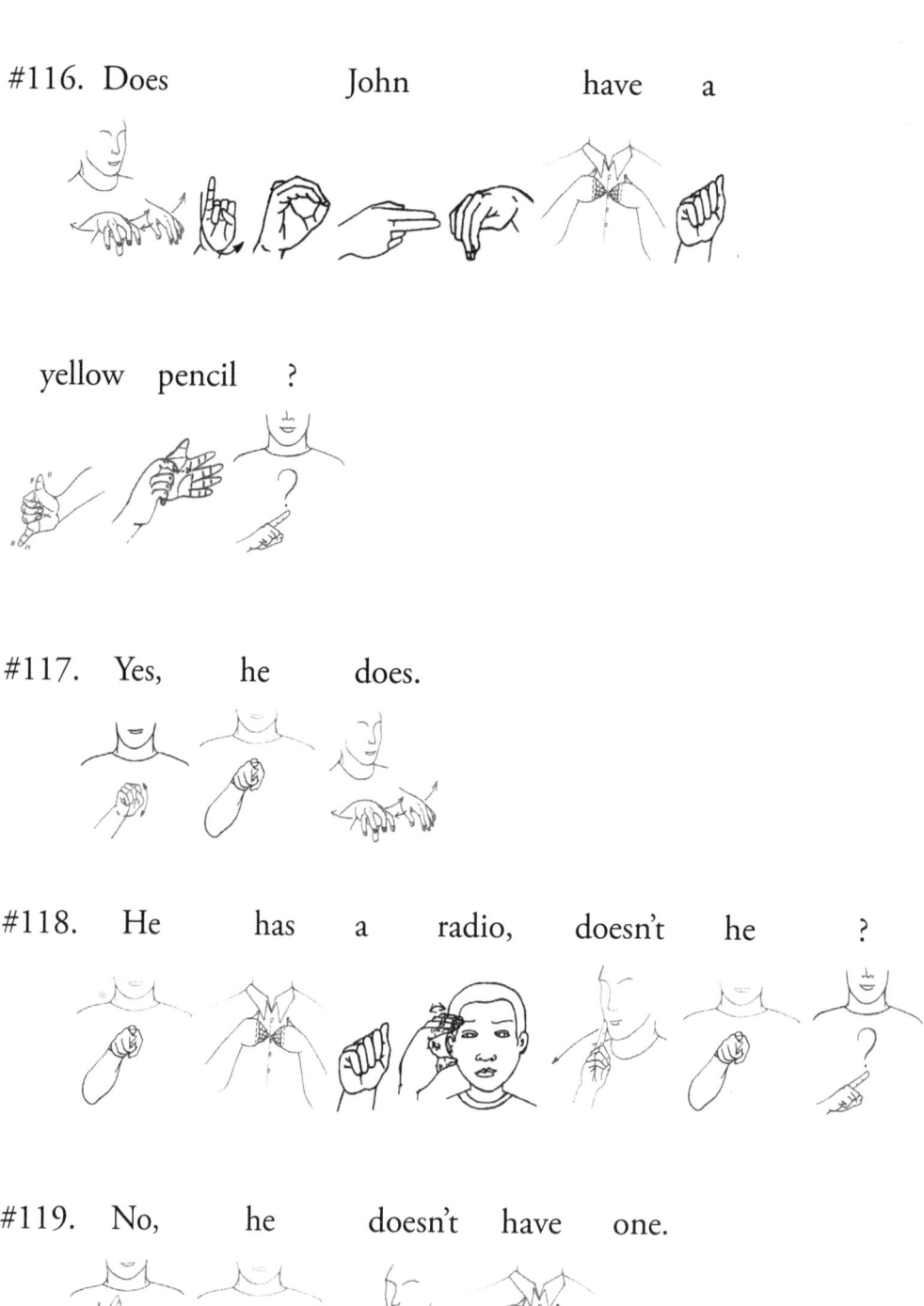

#120. He   already   has   a   phonograph,   but

he   doesn't   have   a   radio   yet.

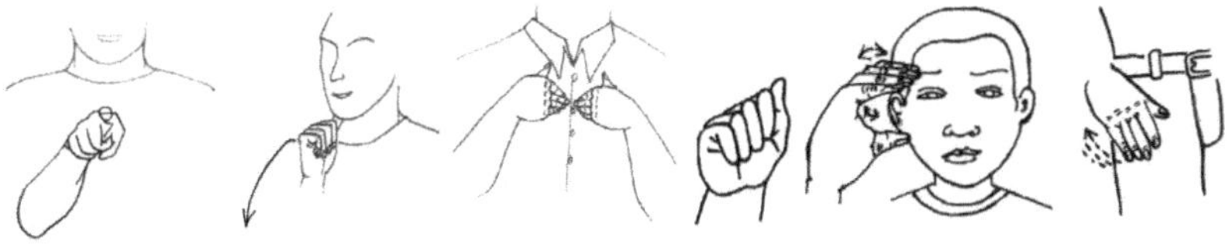

#121. What   time   is   it   ?

#122.   It   is   two   o'clock.

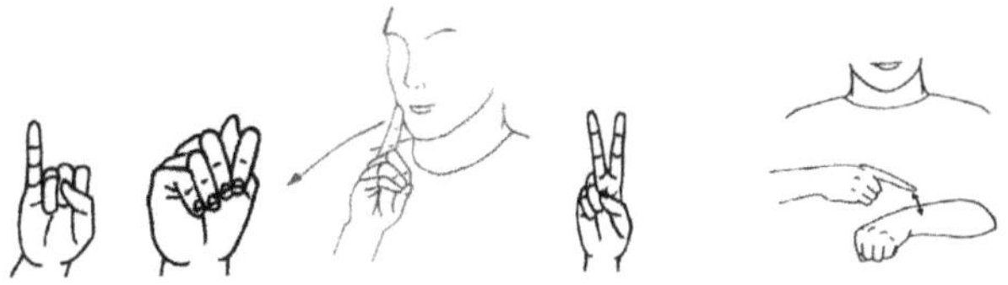

#123.   It   is   few   minutes   after   two.

#124.   My   watch   is   fast   and

your   watch   is   slow.

#125.   Excuse   me,   can

you   tell   me   the   correct   time   ?

#126.   No,   I   can't.

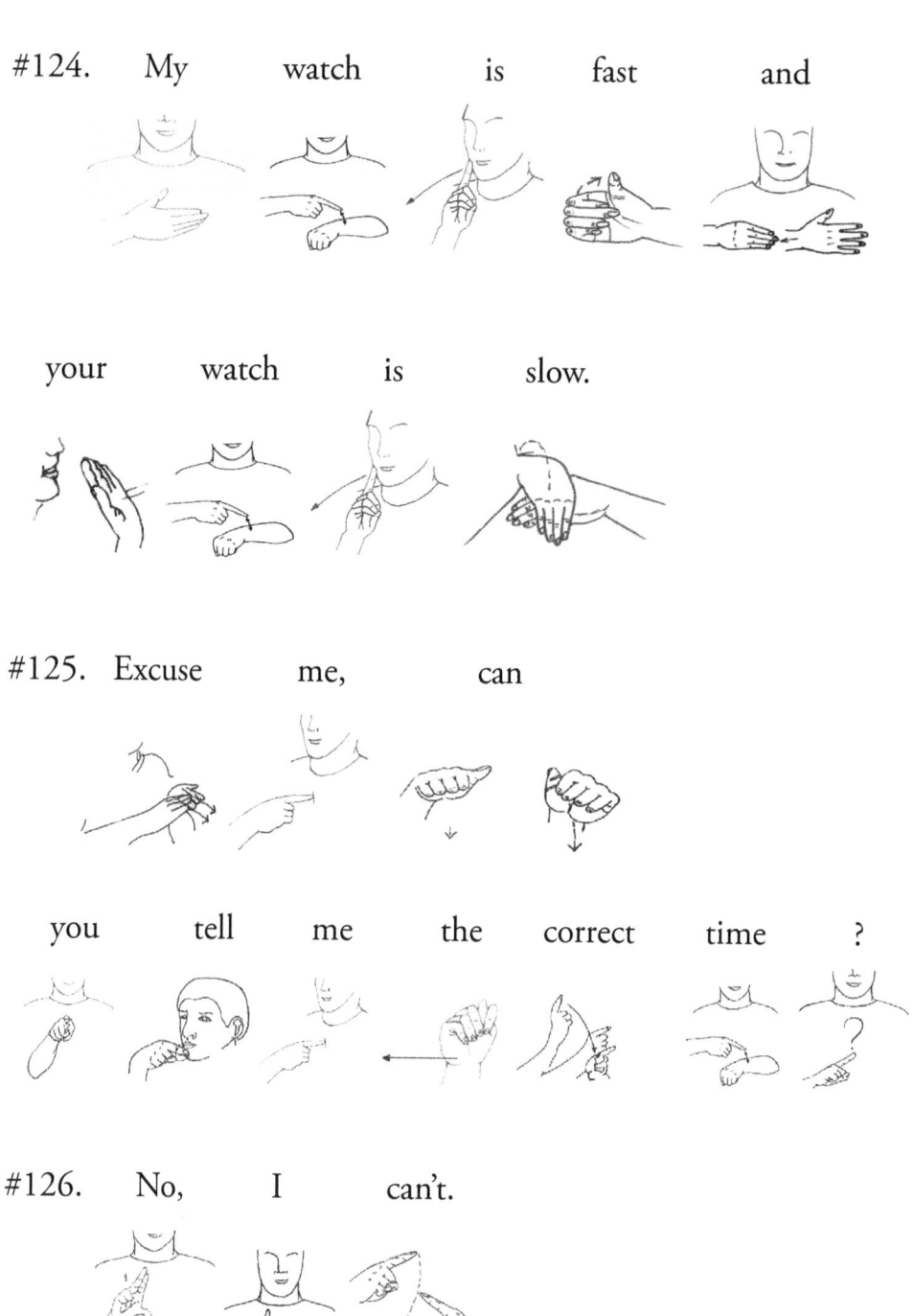

#127. I   don't know   what   time   it is   now.

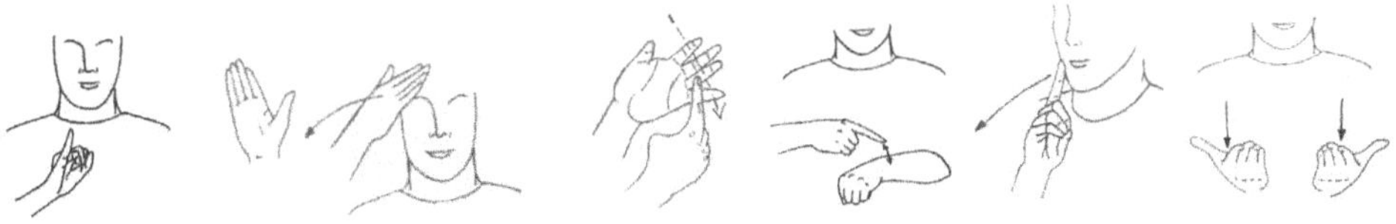

#128. I   don't   think   it's   4   yet.

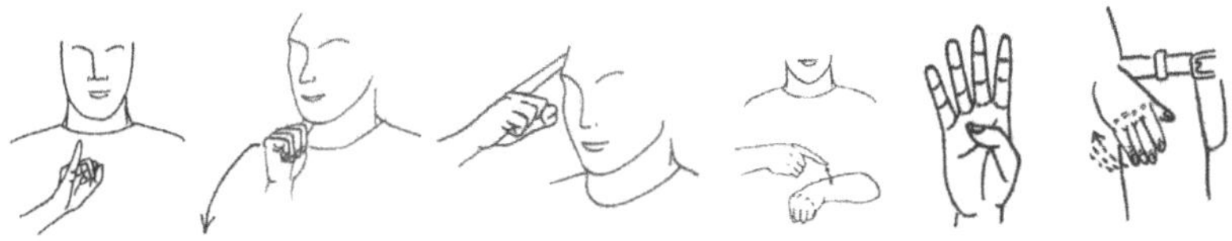

#129. It   must   be   about   three   thirty.

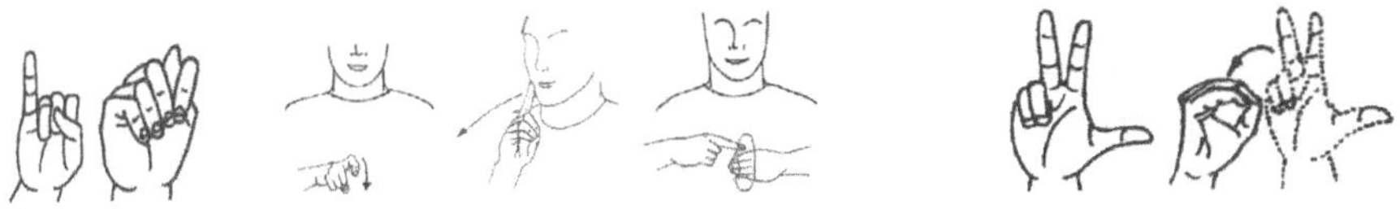

#130. I   get up   before   time   six   every   day.

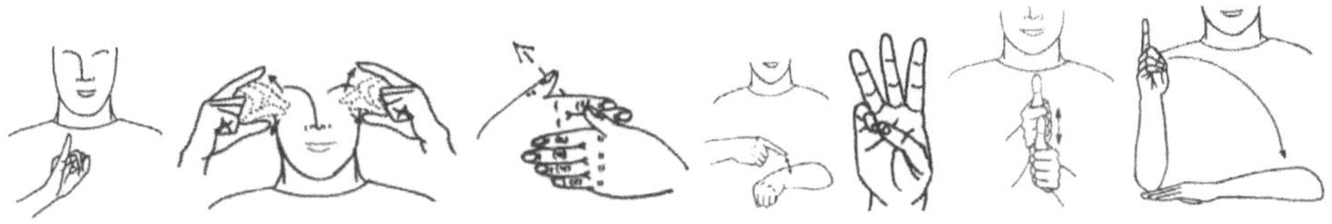

#131. The   restaurant   doesn't   open

until   seven forty-five.

#132. Will you be here at ten tomorrow ?

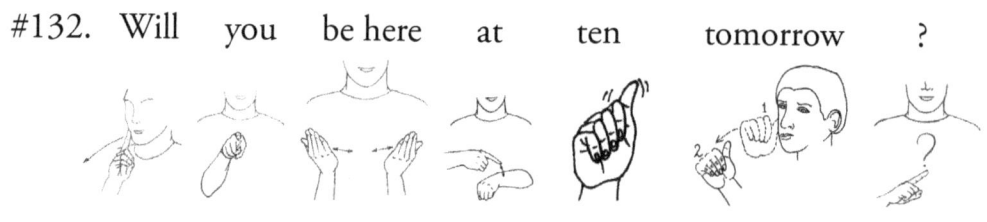

#133. Yes, I will.

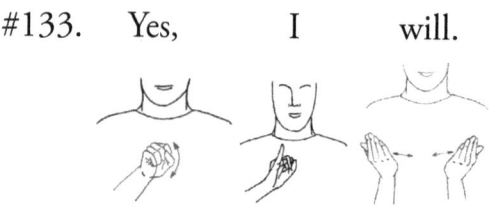

#134. We'll be on time, won't we ?

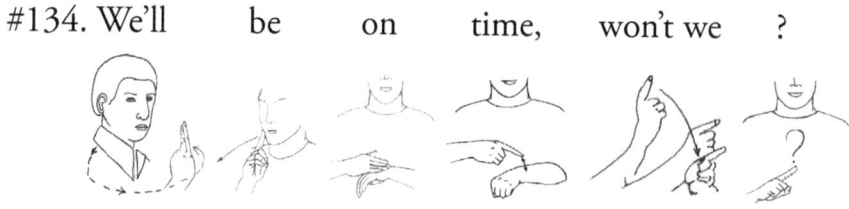

#135. I hope so.

#136. What's the date today ?

#137.   Today   is   Nov   first,

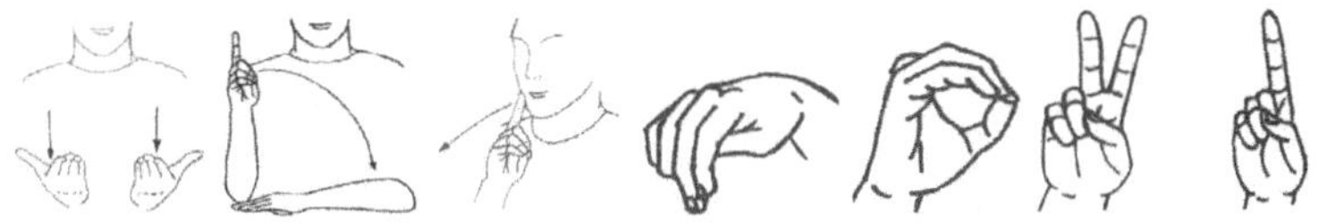

nineteen sixty-three.

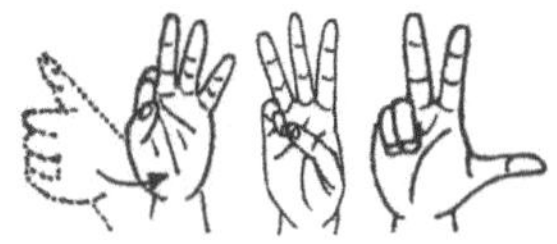

#138.   When   were   you   born   ?

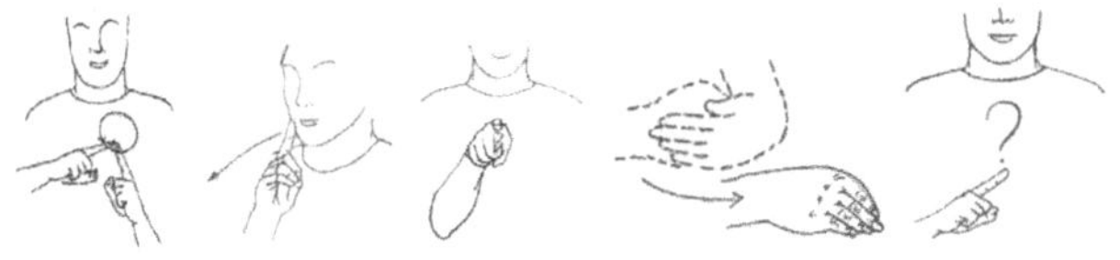

#139.   I   was   born   Nov   first,

nineteen thirty-five.

#140.   Today   is   my   birthday.

#141. My   sister   was   born   in

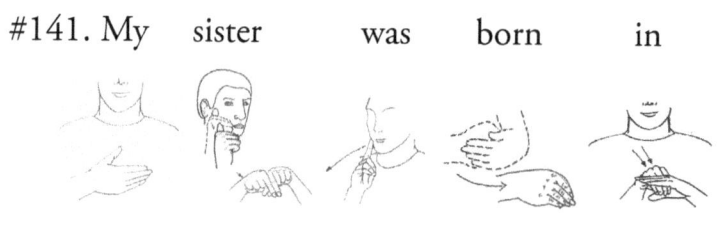

nineteen thirty-eight.

#142. I   don't know   the   exact   date.

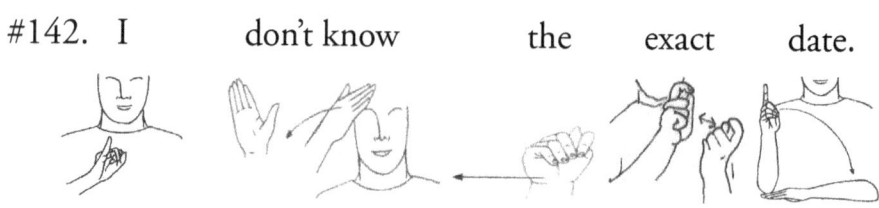

#143. Where   were   you   born   ?

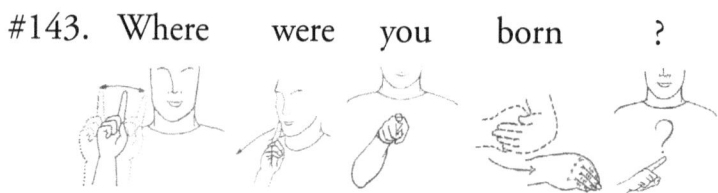

#144. I   was   born   in   a   little   town

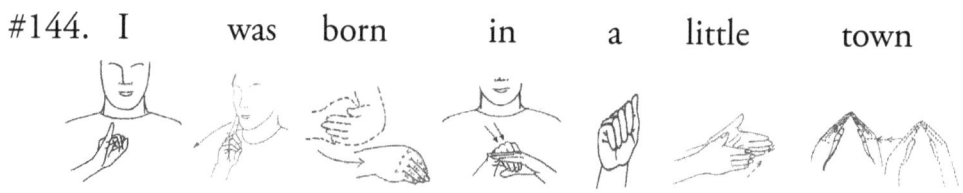

not   far   from   here.

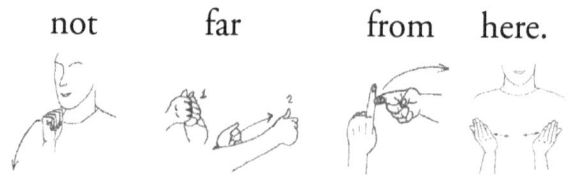

#145. What   do   you   know   about   the

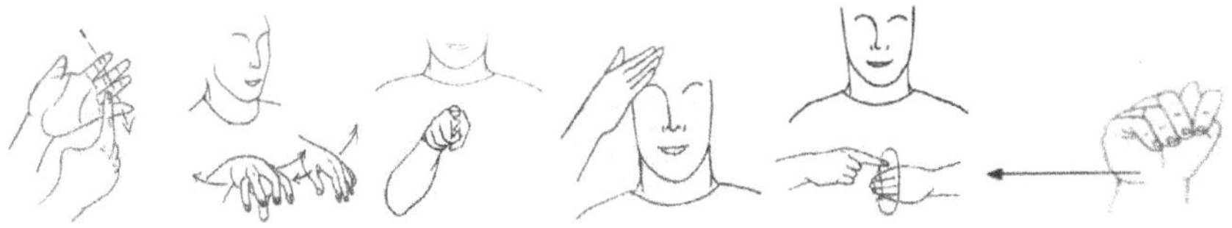

tenth   century   ?

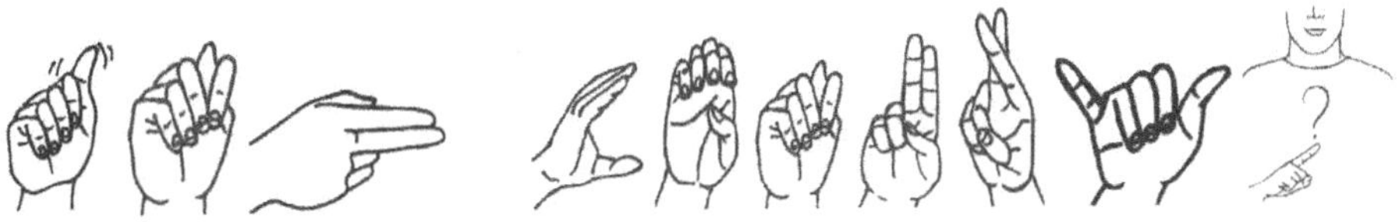

#146. I   don't know   anything   about   that.

#147. Let's   talk   about   something   else.

#148. Where   were   you   during   the   month   of

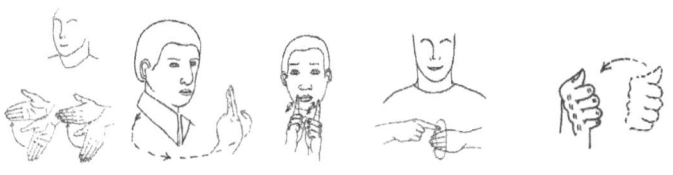

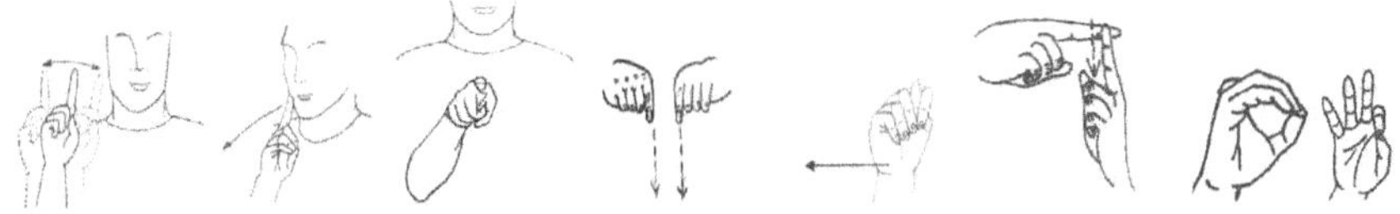

April   last   year   ?

#149. I   don't remember   where   I   was then.

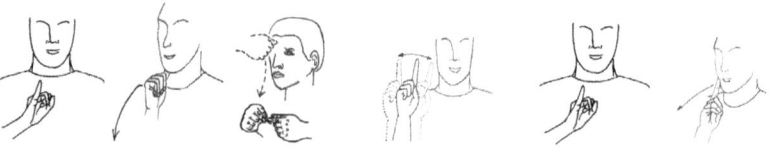

#150. Where   will   you   be   next   year   at

this   time   ?

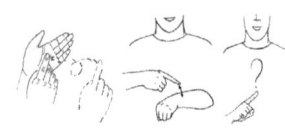

#151. What   do   you   want   ?

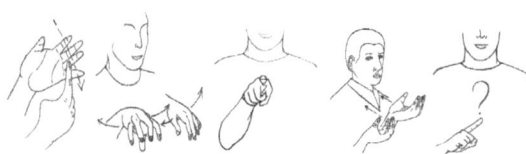

#152. I   want   a   cup   of   coffee.

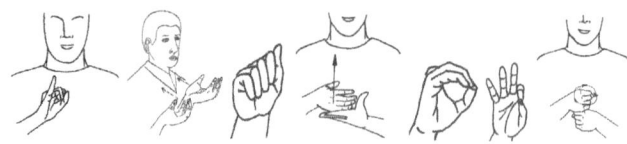

#153.   What   would   you   like   to   eat   ?

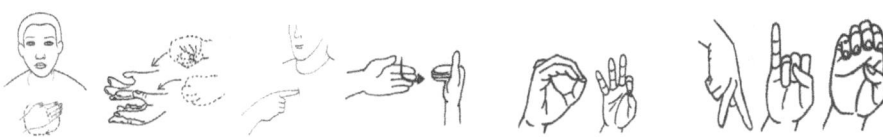

#154.   Please   give   me   a piece   of   pie.

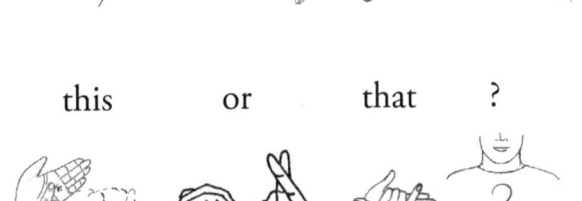

#155.   Which   would   you   like

      this   or   that   ?

#156.   It   doesn't matter   to   me.

#157.   I   want   to   talk   with   Mr.

Jones   or   Mr.

Smith.

#158.   I   am   sorry,   but   both

are   busy   right now.

#159. Would   you   like   some   coffee   ?

#160. I   would rather have   some   tea

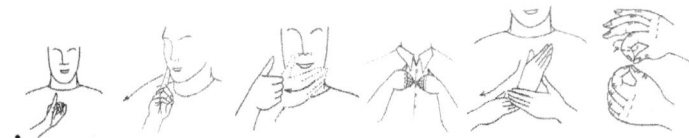

       if   you   don't mind.

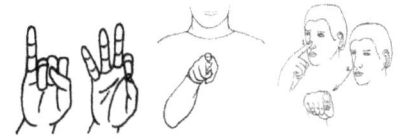

#161. Do   you   know   any   of   those   people   ?

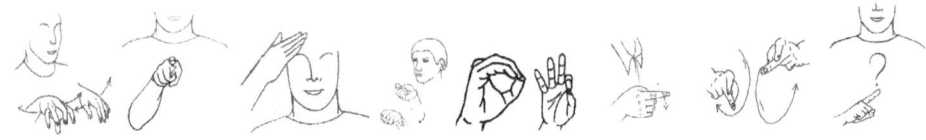

#162. Two   or   three   of   them   look   familiar.

#163. All   of   those people   are   friends   of   mine.

#164. Which   one   of   those   men   is

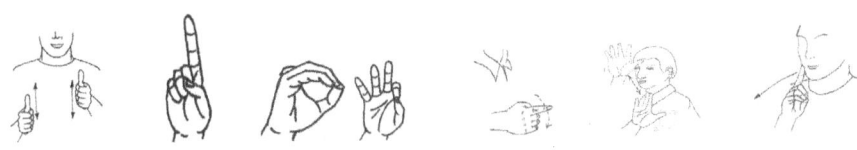

Mr.   Taylor   ?

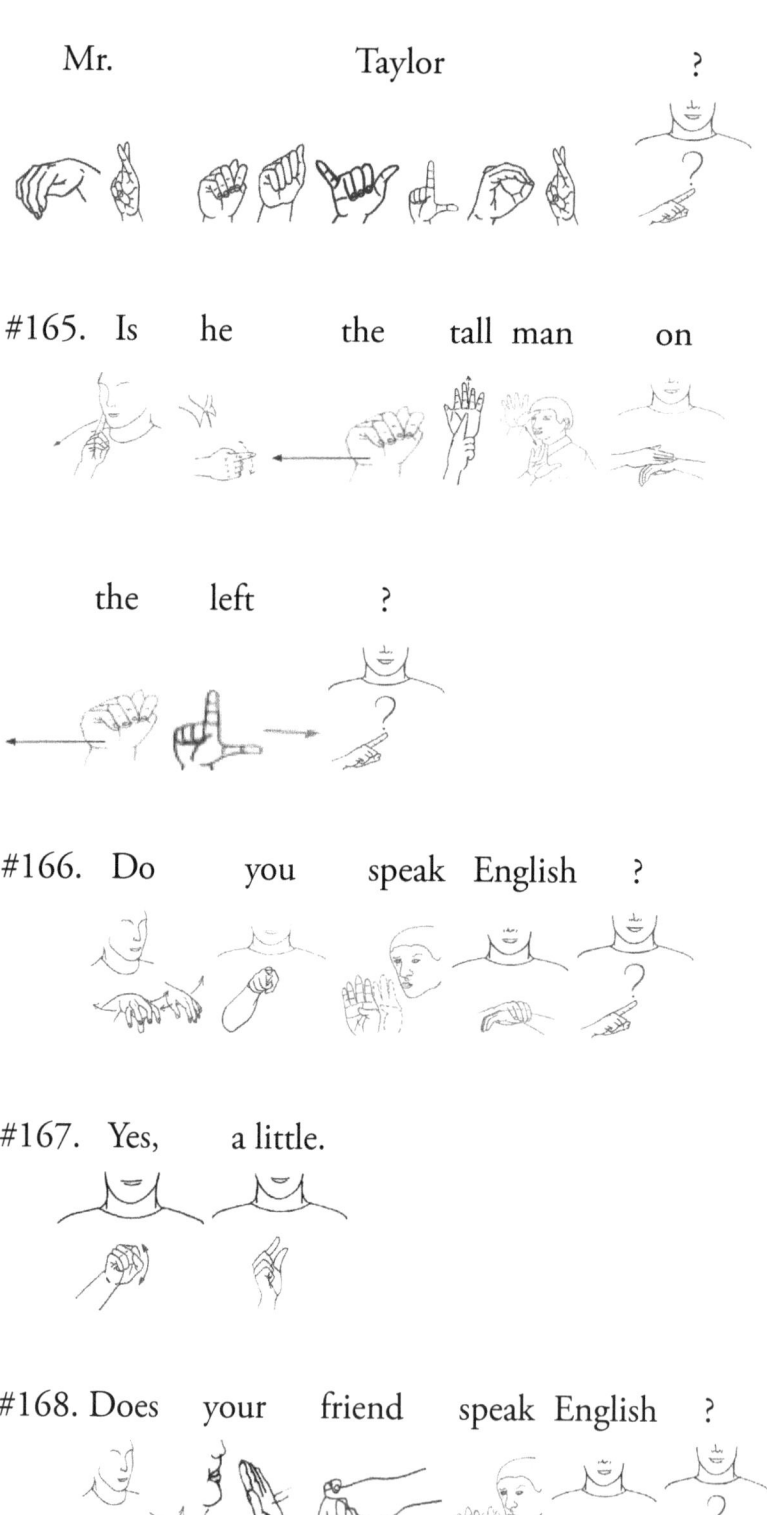

#165. Is   he   the   tall man   on

the   left   ?

#166. Do   you   speak English   ?

#167. Yes,   a little.

#168. Does   your   friend   speak English   ?

#169. Yes,   he   speaks English perfectly.

#170. What   is   his native language ?

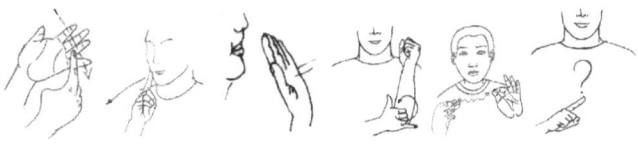

#171. I don't know what his native language is.

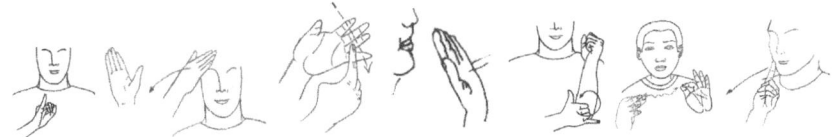

#172. How many languages do you speak ?

#173. My   friend   reads   and   writes

several languages.

#174. How   well   do   you   know   French   ?

#175. He   speaks   French   with

American   accent.

#176. My   parents   speak English fluently.

#177. Mr.   Jones   can   read

French   pretty well.

#178. Sometimes   I   make   mistakes   when   I

I

speak English.

#179. I   have   a lot of trouble with pronunciation.

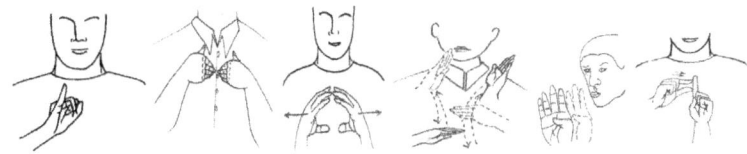

#180. How   is her   accent   in   French   ?

#181. What are   you   doing   ?

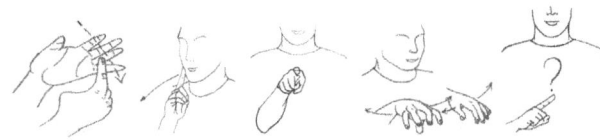

#182.   I   am   reading a book.

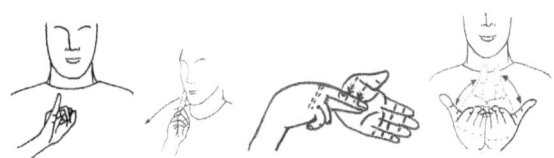

#183.   What   is   your   friend   doing   ?

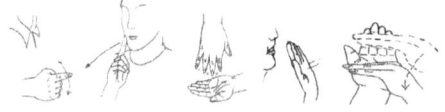

#184. He   is   studying his lesson.

#185.   I   am   not doing anything right now.

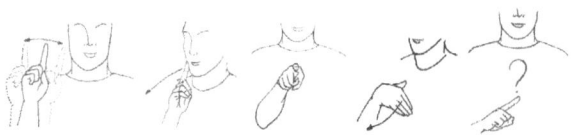

#186.   Where   are   you   going   ?

#187.   I   am   going home.

#188. What   time   are   you coming back   ?

#189.   I   am not sure what time I   am coming back.

#190. What   are   you   thinking   about   ?

#191.   I   am   thinking   about   my   lesson.

#192. Who   are   you   writing   to   ?

#193.   I   am   writing   to   a friend   of   mine

in   South   America.

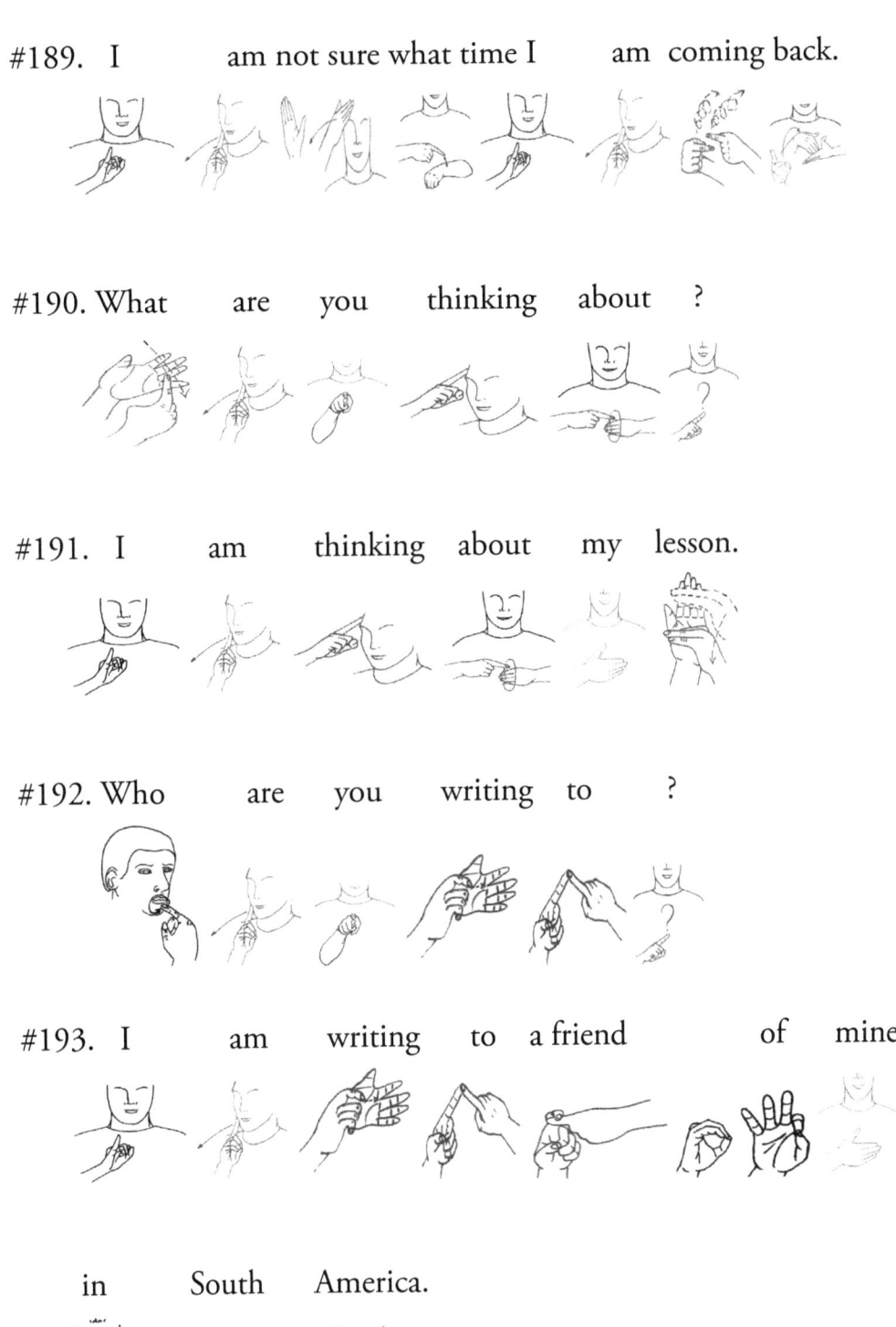

#194.   Who   are   you   waiting   for   ?

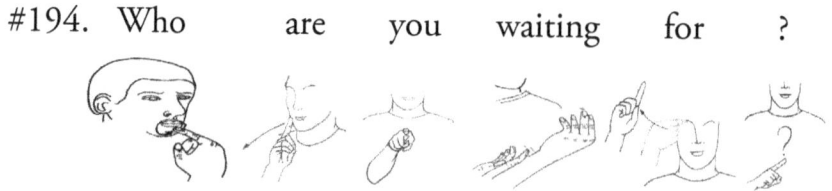

#195.   I 'm   not   waiting   for   any   body.

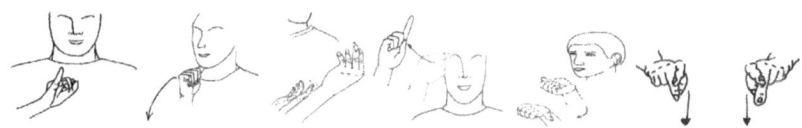

#196.   How   old   are   you   ?

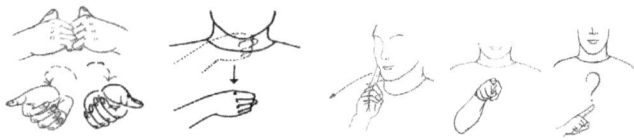

#197. I   am   twenty-one years   old.

#198. My brother is   not quite twenty-five.

#199.   John   is   not   forty-five

          yet,   is   he   ?

#200. Mr.   Smith   is   still in his   fifties.

#201. I   am   two   years   older   than   you are.

#202. My   brother   is   two   years younger   than

          I   am.

#203. How   many   are   in   your   family   ?

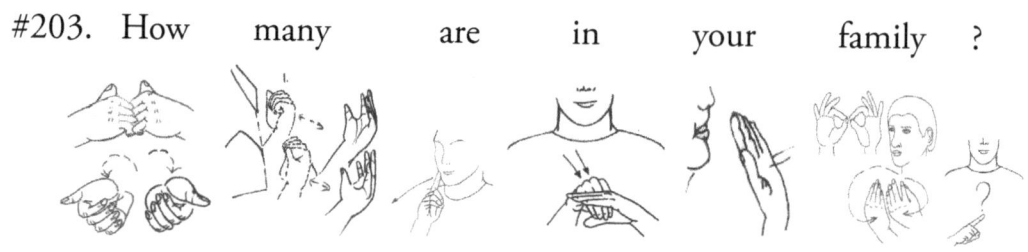

#204. There   are   seven   of   us   altogether.

#205. My   sister   is   oldest.

#206. I   am   the   youngest.

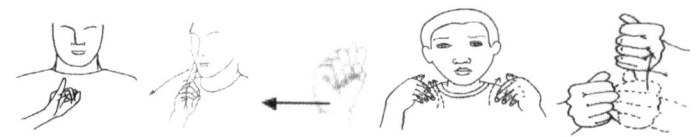

#207. Guess   how   old   I   am.

#208. I   say   you   are   about   twenty-three.

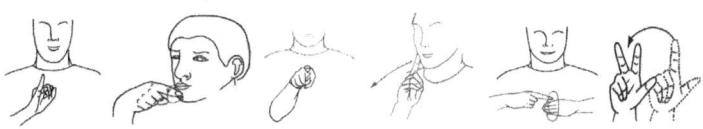

#209. I   was   thirty   on   my   last   birthday.

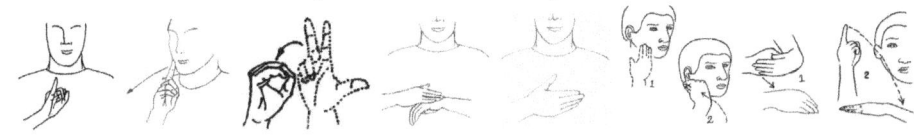

#210. I   will   be   sixty-one   next Tuesday

#211. What   time   do you   get up   everyday ?

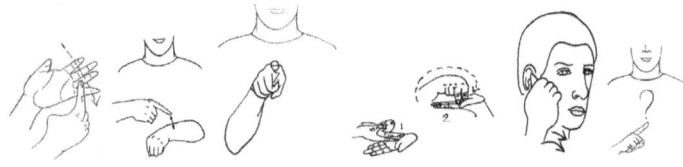

#212. I   usually   wake   up   early.

#213. I   get   up   at   6 o'clock everyday.

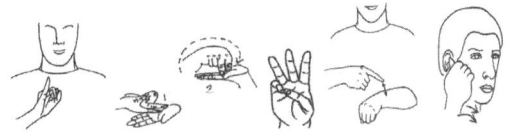

#214. My   brother   gets up   later   than I do.

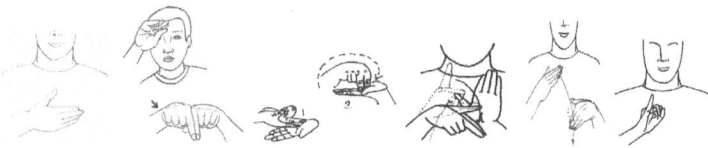

#215. After I   get dressed,   I   have   breakfast

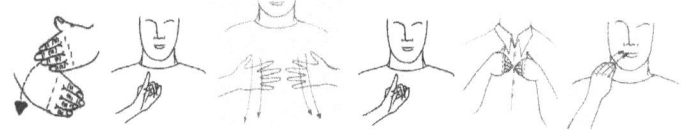

#216. Usually,   I   have   big   breakfast.

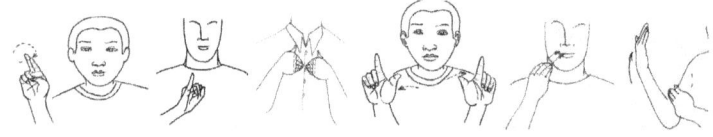

#217. I   have   juice,   cereal,

toast,   and coffee   for   breakfast.

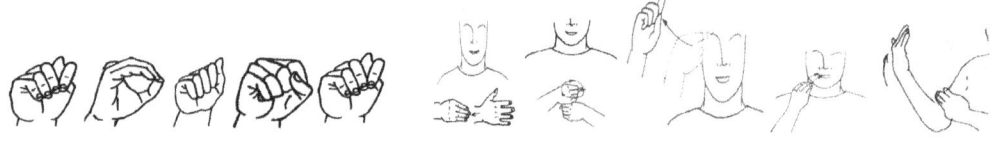

#218. I   leave the house   eight a.m.   each   day.

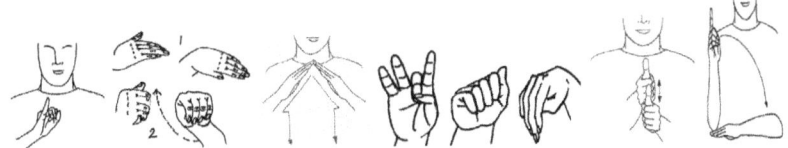

#219. I   get   to   work   at   nine   every   morning.

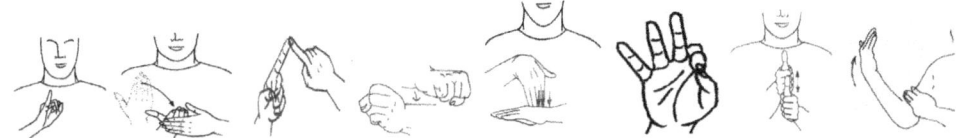

#220. I   work   hard   all   morning.

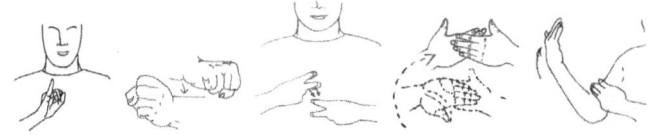

#221. I   go   out   for   lunch   about   12:30.

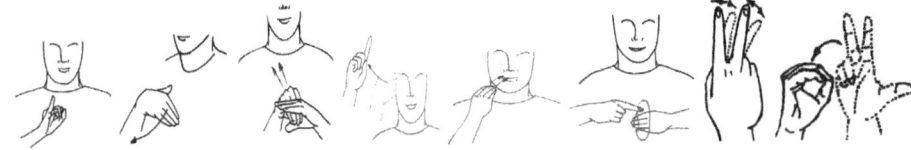

#222. I   finish   working   at   5:45

#223.   I   eat   dinner about   7

#224. Before   I   eat   dinner,   I   read

the newspaper for awhile.

#225.   I   usually   go   to   bed   about   midnight.

#226. What   time   did   you   get up   yesterday   morning?

#227. I   woke   up   early   and   got up   6 o'clock.

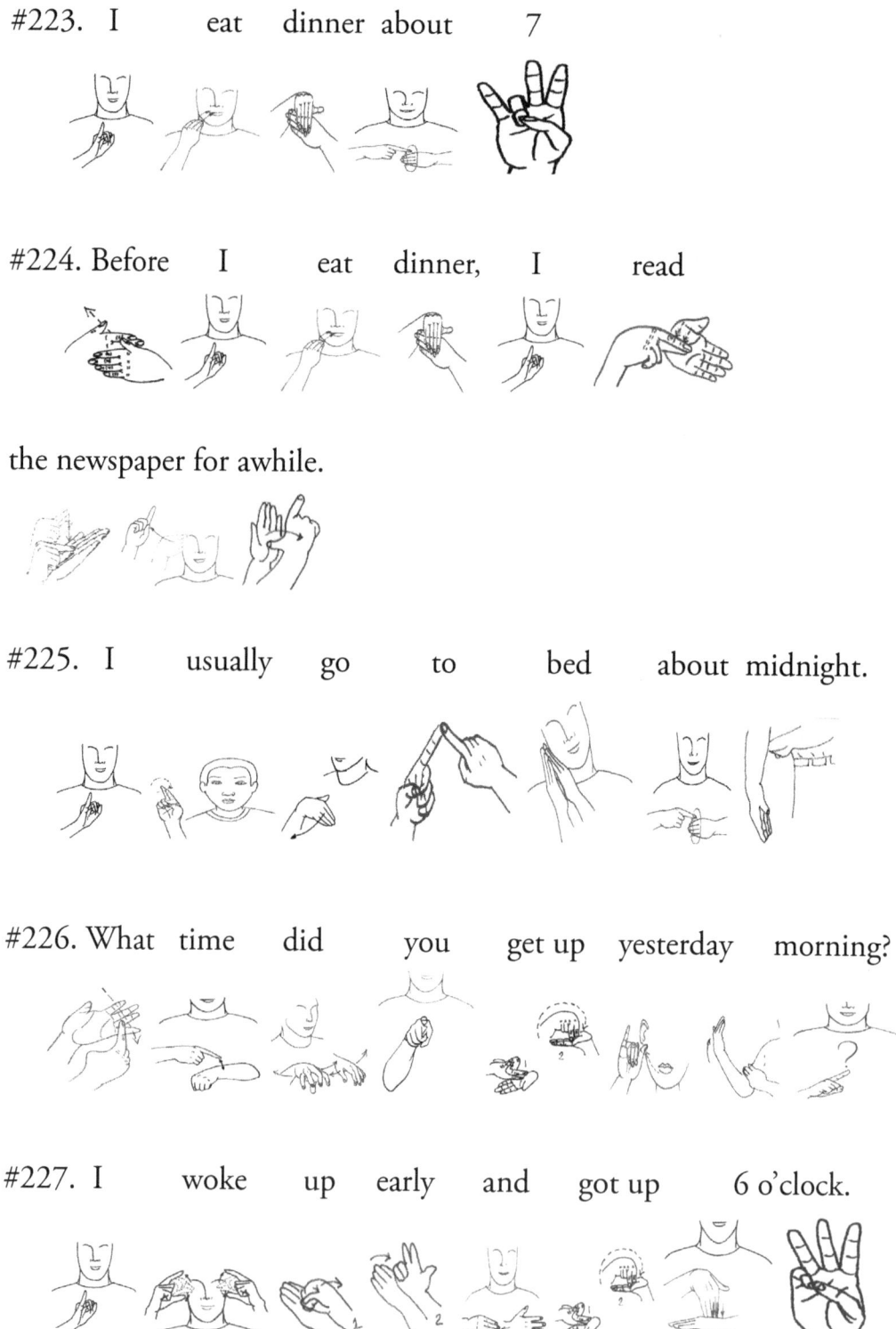

#228. My brother got up earlier than I did.

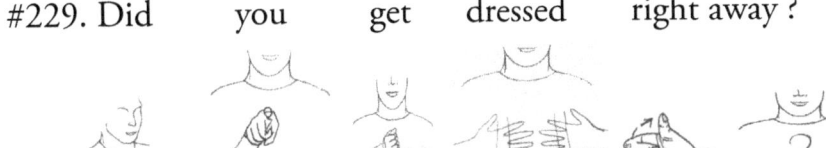

#229. Did you get dressed right away ?

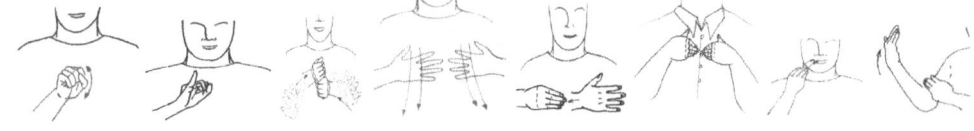

#230. Yes, I got dressed and had breakfast.

#231. What kind breakfast did you have ?

#232. What time did you get to work yesterday morning ?

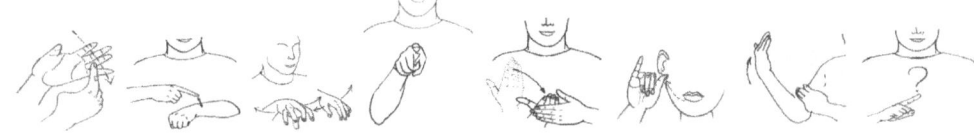

#233. I   left   the   house   at   8 o'clock

and   got   to   work   at   8:30.

#234. Did   you   work   all   day   ?

#235. Yes,   I   worked from   early   morning until

late   at   night.

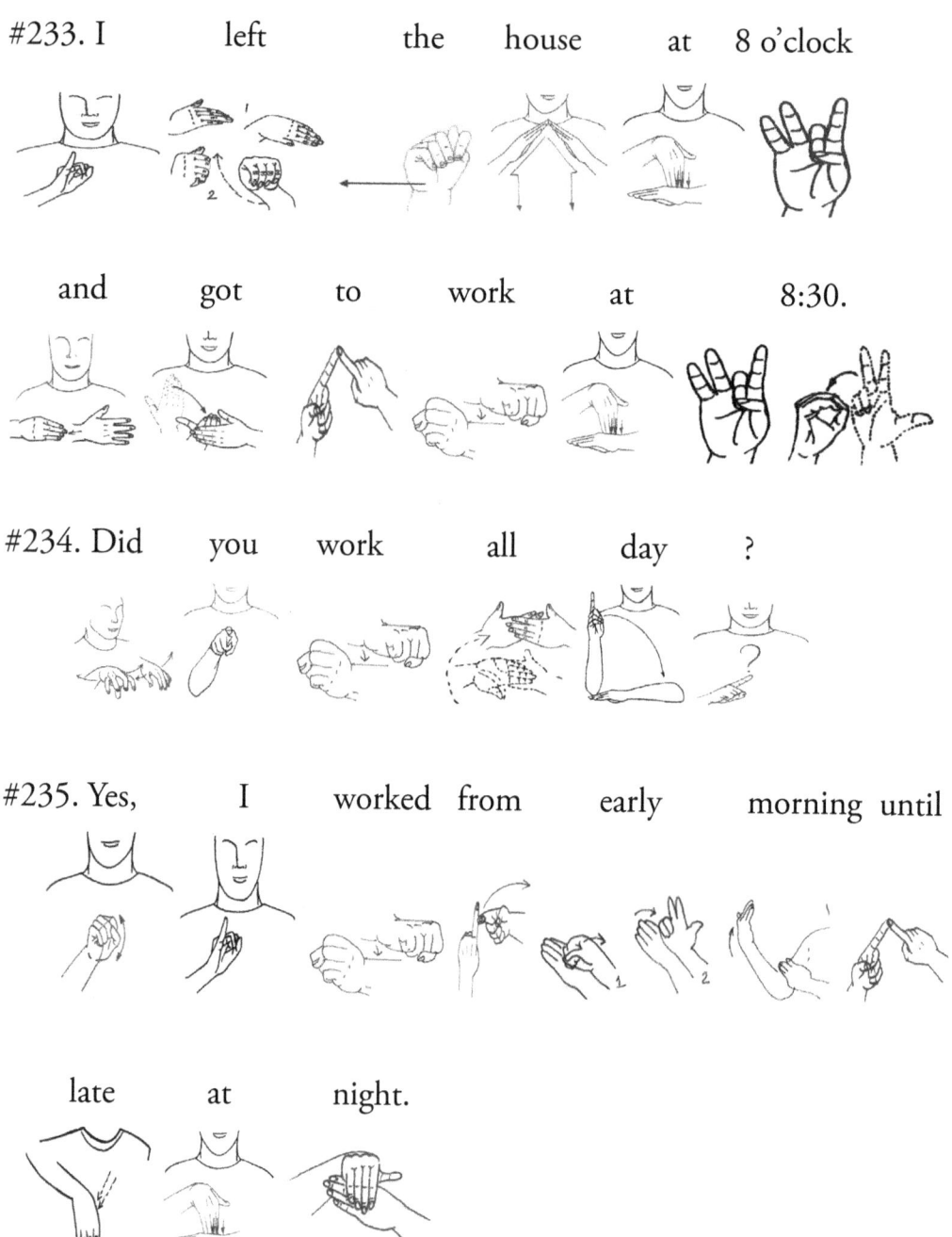

#236.   At   noon   I   had   lunch   with

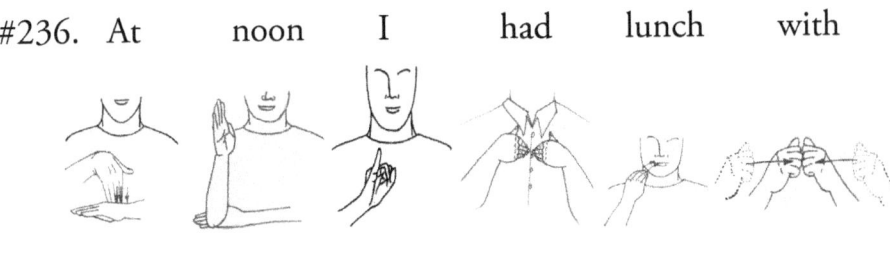

a   friend   of   mine.

#237. I   finished   working   at   5:30   and

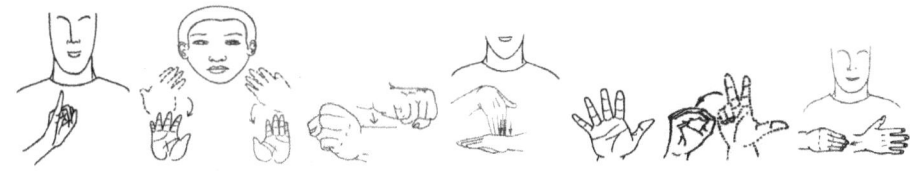

went   home.

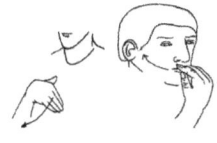

#238. After   dinner   I   read   a   magazine and

made   some   telephone calls.

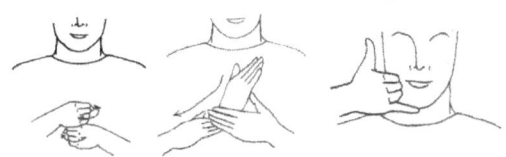

#239. I went to bed   at   11:30   p.m.

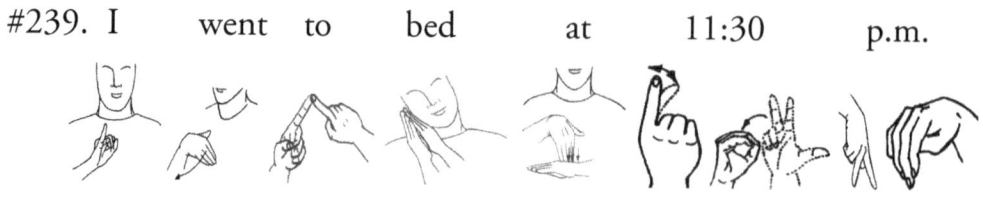

#240. I went to   sleep immediately and slept

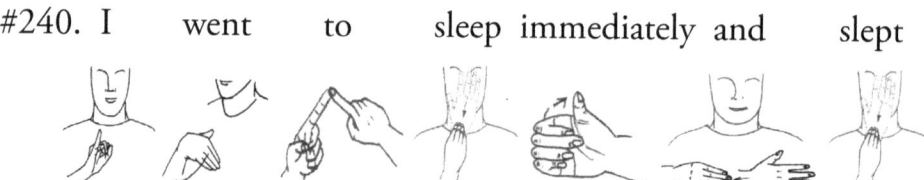

soundly all   night.

#241. Where did   you   go yesterday ?

#242. I went to see a friend of mine.

#243. Did   you   see   Mr.

Jones   ?

#244. I   didn't   see   Mr.   Jones,

but   I   saw   John   Smith.

#245. What   did   you   talk   about   ?

#246. We   talked   about   a lot   of things.

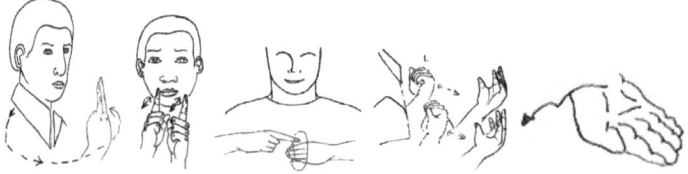

#247. I   asked   him   lot of questions.

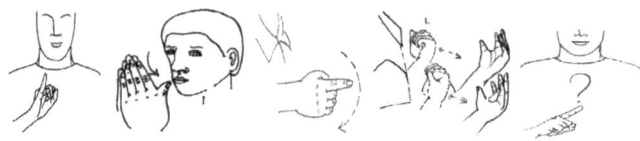

#248. What did   you   ask   him   ?

#249. I   asked   him   if   he   spoke   English.

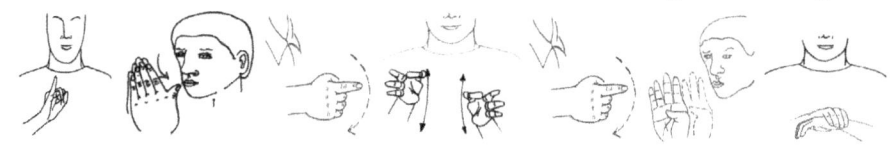

#250. He   said he   spoke   a little   English.

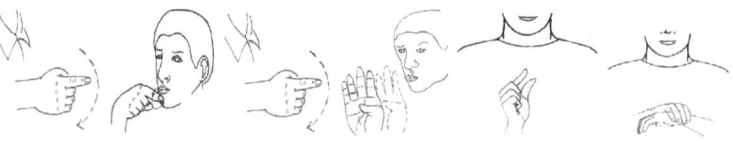

#251. Then   I   asked   him   if   he   knew

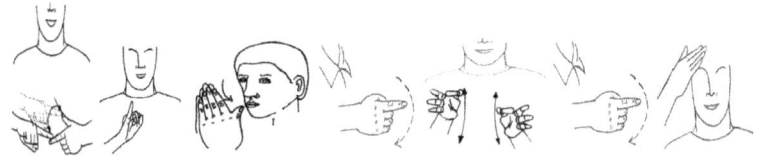

anybody in   New York.

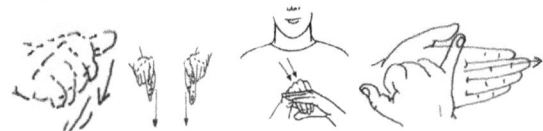

#252. He   said   he   knew   a lot people there.

#253. Finally,   I   asked   him   how   old   he was.

#254. He   said   he   rather   not   tell   his   age.

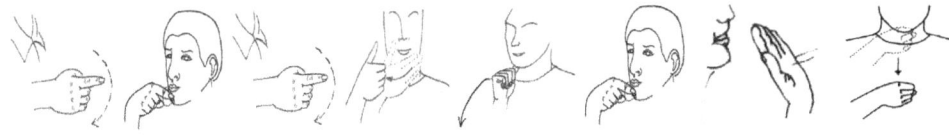

#255. He   answered almost   all   my   questions.

#256. What time did you use get up

last year ?

#257. I used to wake up early and

get up at 7 o'clock

#258. I used to set my alarm for exactly

7 a.m.

#259. I　　never　　used　　to　　oversleep.

#260. I　　used to　　get dressed　quickly　every　morning.

#261. I　　always　　used to　　leave　　for

work　　　at　　　8:30.

#262. I　　used　　to　　start　working　at

9:00　　everyday.

#263.   I   used   to   lunch   at the same time.

#264.   I   used   to   work   until   nearly

6:00 o'clock   each   day.

#265.   I   used   to   have dinner at   7:30

and   go   to   bed   early.

#266. Brother   and   I   used   to   go to

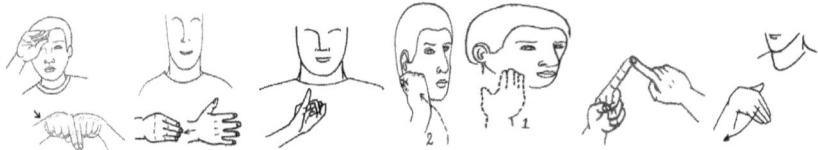

many   places   together.

#267. We   used to   go   to   movies   once   a week.

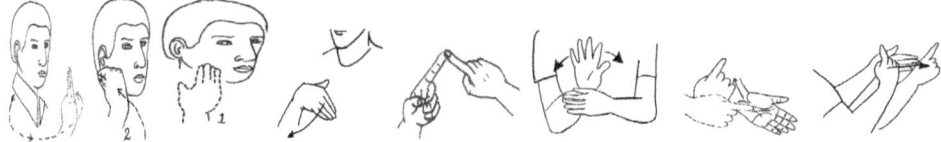

#268. We   used   to   have many   interesting   friends.

#269. My   brother   used   to   speak   French

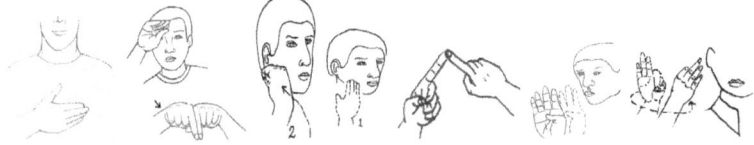

to   me.

#270. I   always   used to   ask   him   lot of questions.

#271. Where   do   you   live   ?

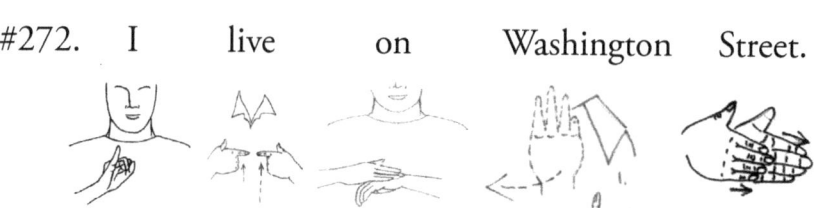

#272.   I   live   on   Washington   Street.

#273.   What's   your   address   ?

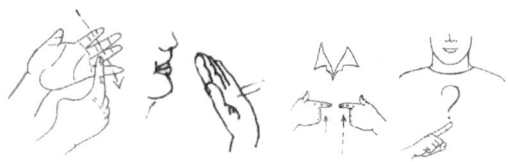

#274.   I   live   at   203   Washington Street.

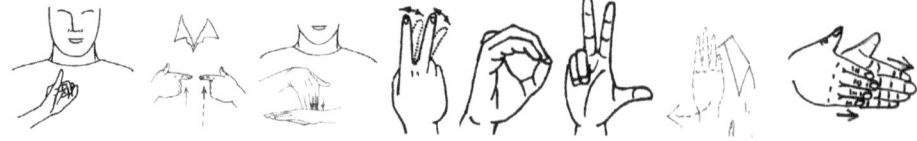

#275.   I   am   Mr.   Smith's

next   door   neighbor.

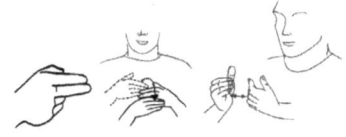

#276. You   live   here   in   the   city,

don't you   ?

#277.   I   am   from   out   of   town.

#278.   How   long   have   you   lived   here   ?

#279.   I   have   lived   here   for   five   years.

#280. He's   known   me   for   over   ten   years.

#281.   I   have   spoken English   all   my   life.

#282.   I   already   read   that   book.

#283. Has   he   studied   French   very   long   ?

#284.   Have   you   had   breakfast   ?

#285.   Yes,   I   had   breakfast

two   hours   ago.

#286. Where   were   you   yesterday afternoon   ?

#287.   I   was   at   home   all   afternoon.

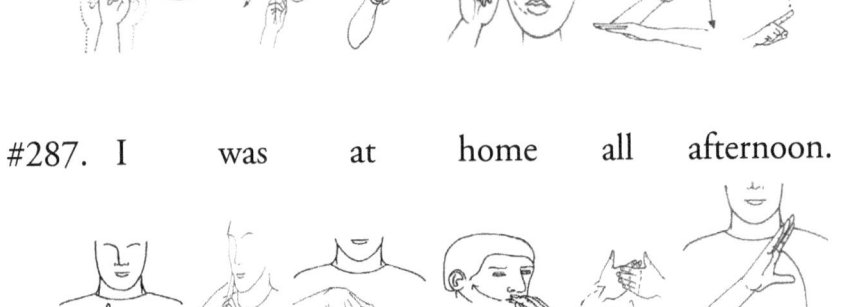

#288. I   was   writing   some letters   to   friends

of   mine.

#289. What   were   you   doing   at   about   4 o'clock

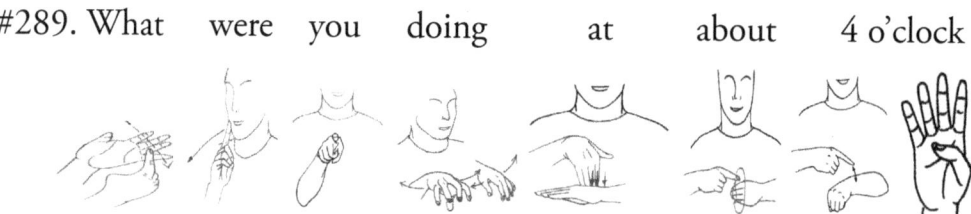

yesterday afternoon ?

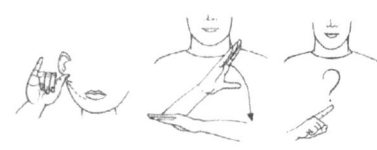

#290. I   was   listening   to   the radio.

#291. What were you doing when I telephoned

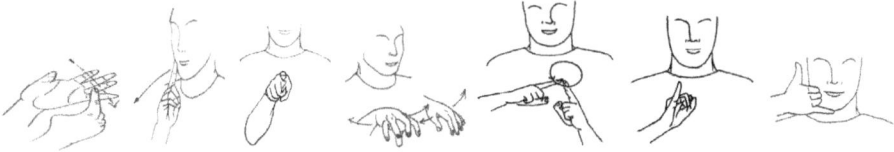

you ?

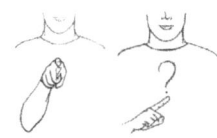

#292. When you called me, I was eating dinner.

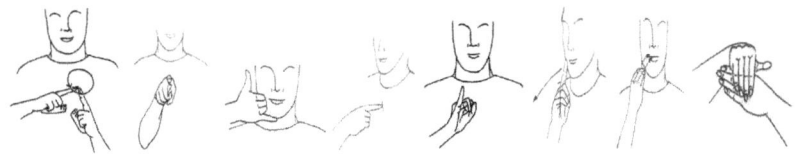

#293. When I saw Mr. Jones,

he was talking with John

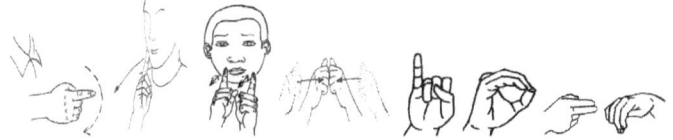

Smith.

#294. While   you   were   writing letters,   I   was

reading   a book.

#295. While   you   having breakfast,   John

was talking on the telephone.

#296. Can   you   guess   what   I   was   doing this

morning   ?

#297.　I　　　can't　　remember　what　　　　　John

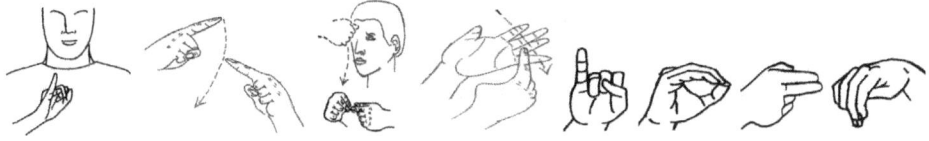

was　doing　yesterday　afternoon.

#298. I've　forgotten　what　　he　　　said　　his

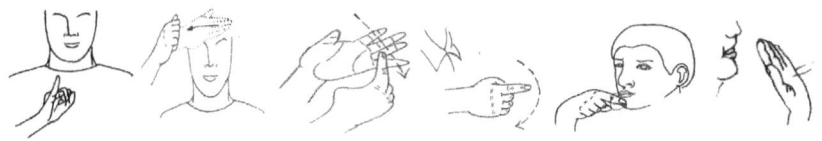

address　was.

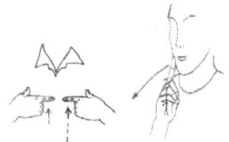

#299. I've　forgotten　what　time　he　　　said　　he

had dinner　last　　night.

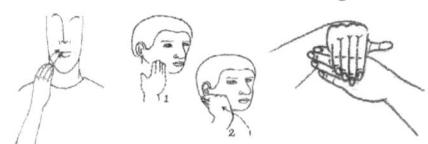

#300. They   called   just as   we   were

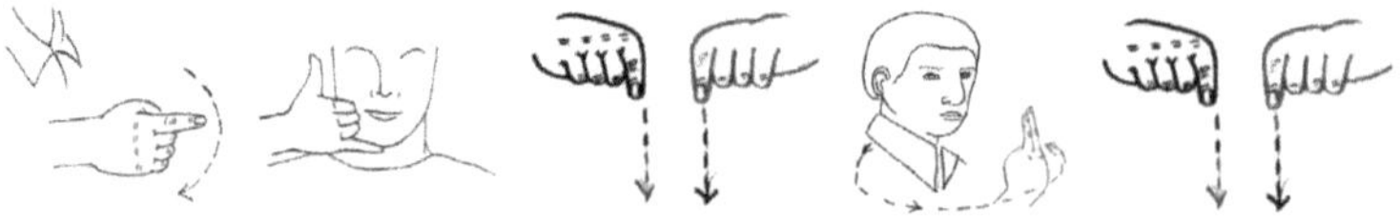

having   dinner.

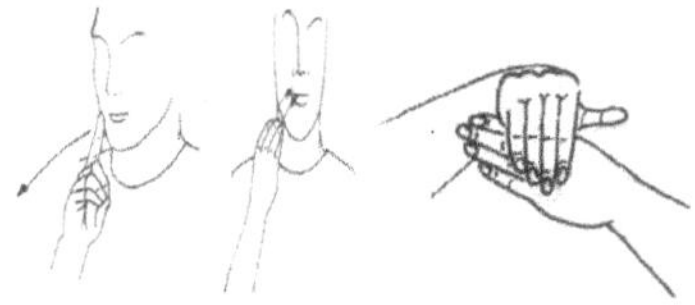

#301. What   color   is   your   book   ?

#302. My   book   has   a dark   blue

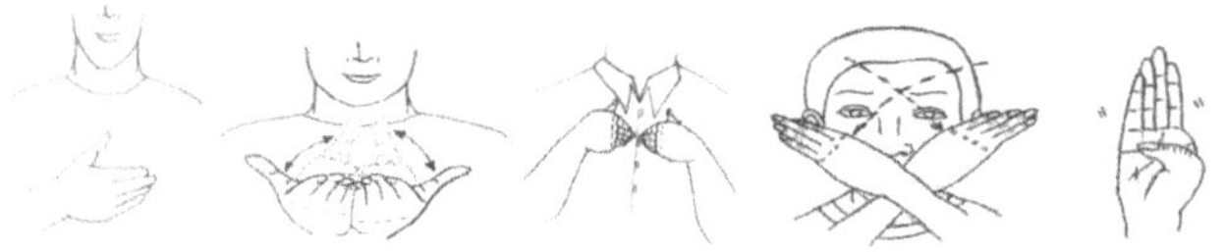

cover.

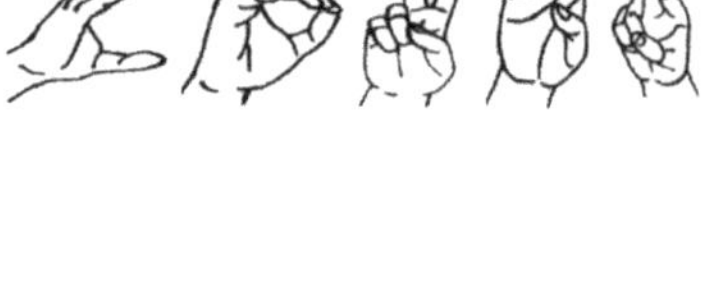

#303. How much does   that   typewriter

weigh   ?

#304. It   is   not   too heavy,   but

I   don't   know   the exact weight.

#305. This   round   table   weighs   about

forty-five   pounds.

#306. What   size   suitcase do   you   own   ?

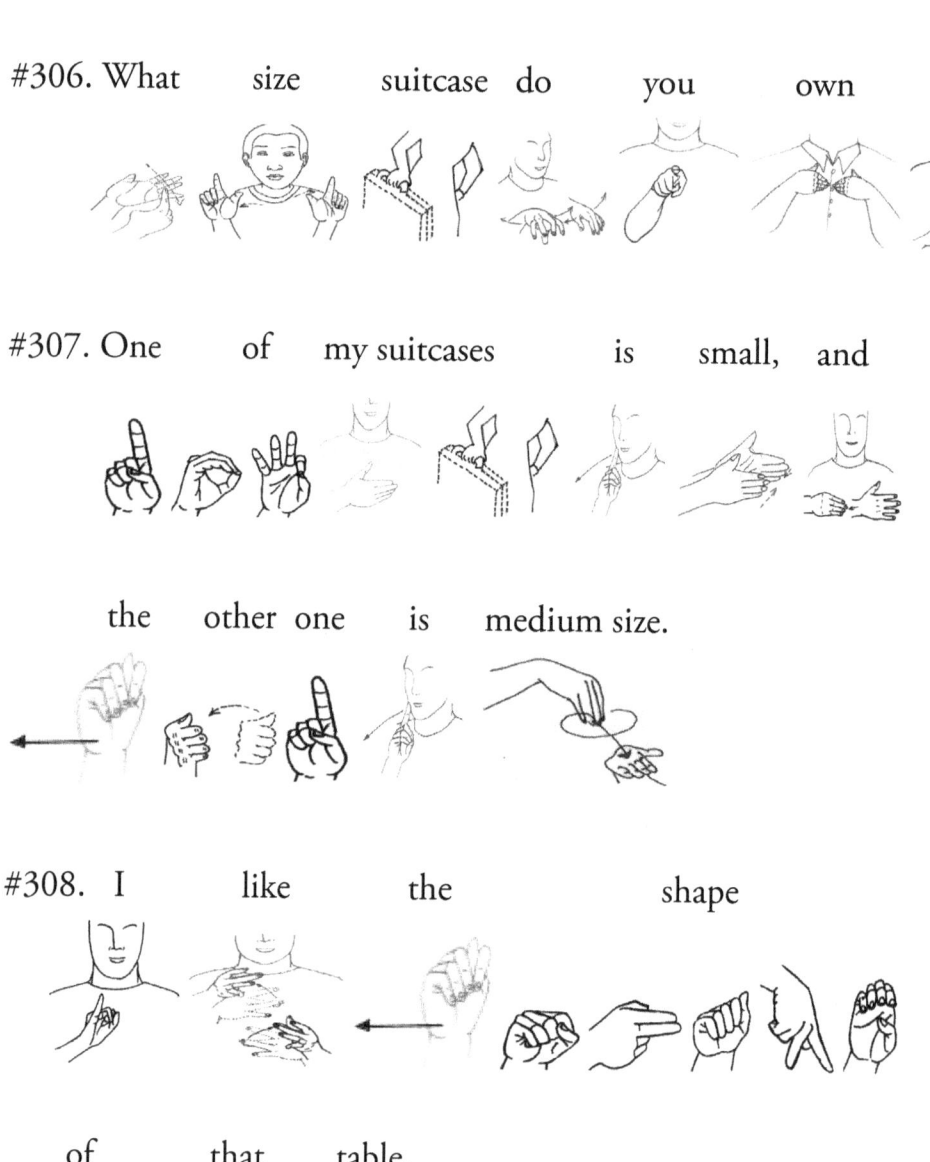

#307. One   of   my suitcases   is   small,   and

the   other one   is   medium size.

#308. I   like   the   shape

of   that   table.

#309. How   long   is   Jones

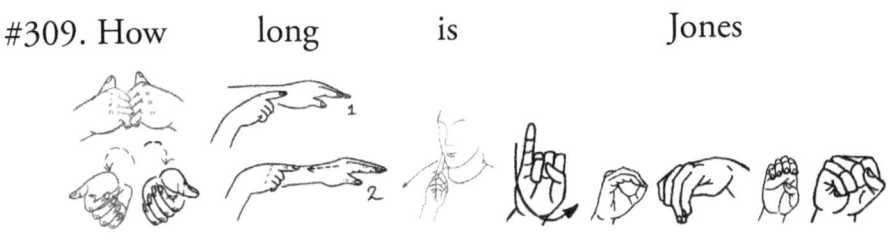

Boulevard ?

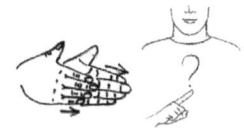

#310. That   street   is   only   two   miles.

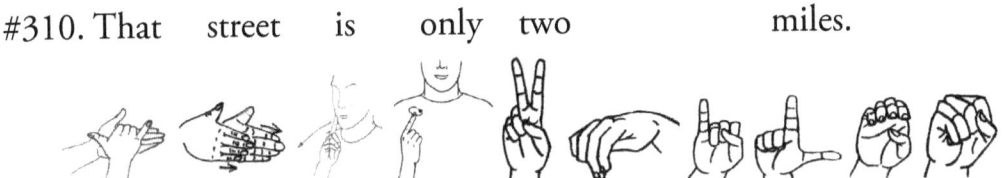

#311. Will   you   please   measure   this   window   to

see   how   wide   it   is   ?

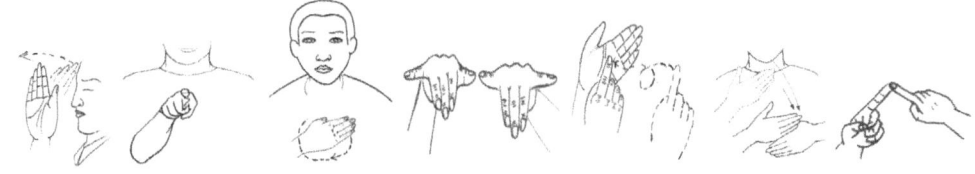

#312. This   window   is   as   wide   as that one.

#313. The   walls   are   three   inches   thick.

#314. This   material   feels   soft.

#315. This   pencil   is   longer   than   that one.

#316. Would   you   please   tell   Mr.

Cooper   I'm   here   ?

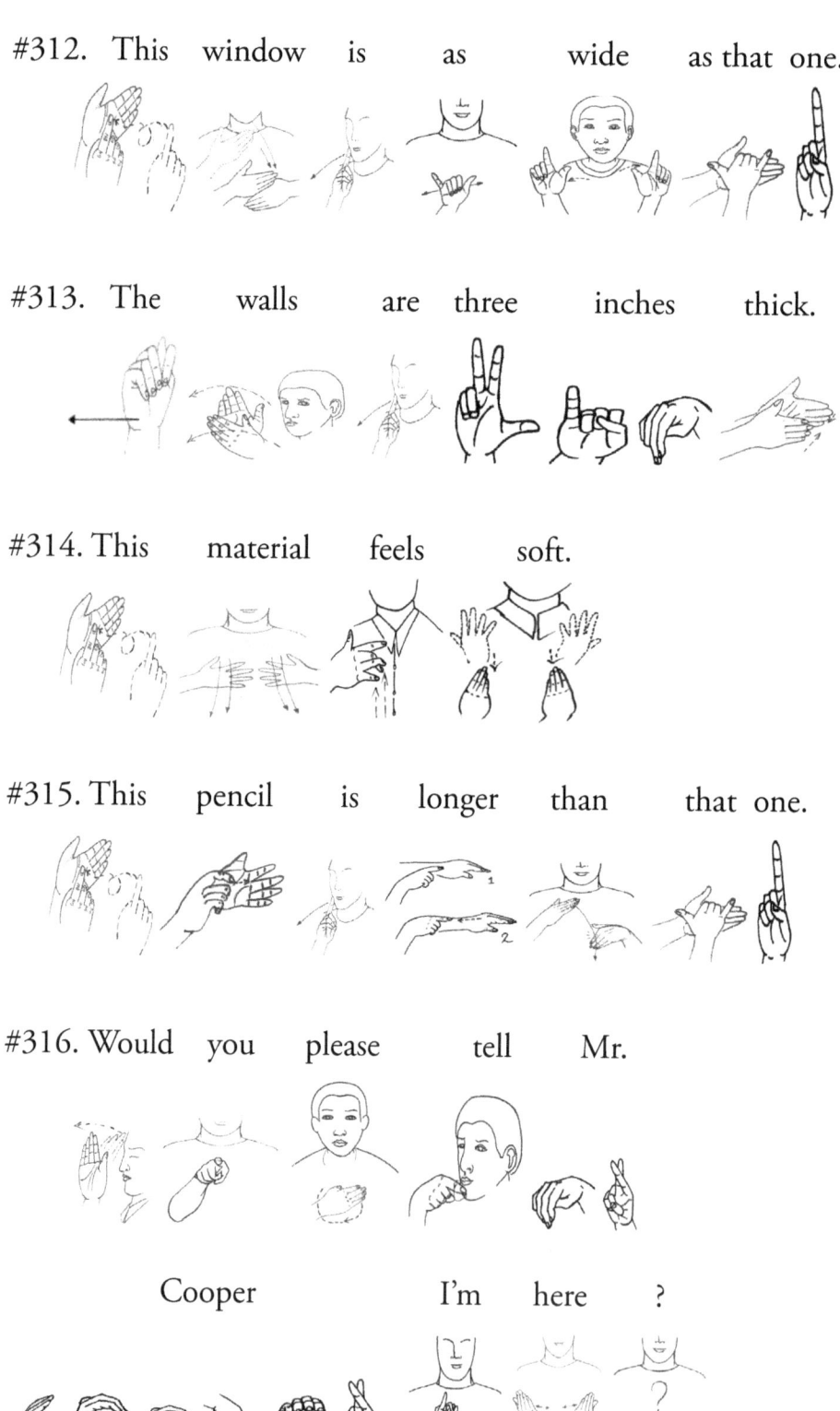

#317. Take these   books home   with   you   tonight.

#318. Please   bring   me those magazines.

319. Would   you   help   me   lift   this

heavy   box   ?

#320. Please   ask   John   to   turn off the lights.

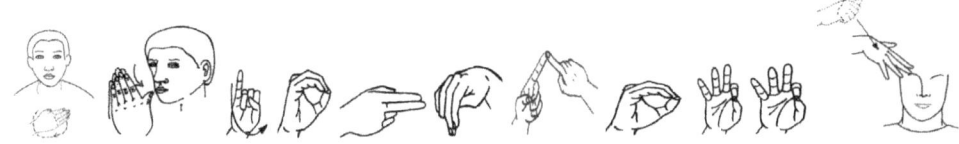

#321. Put   your   books down on   the table.

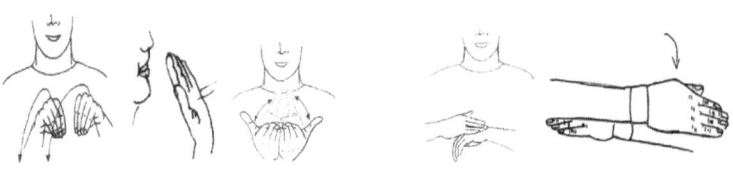

#322. Get   me   hammer   from   kitchen,   will   you   ?

#323. Hang   my   coat   in   closet,   will   you   please   ?

#324. Please don't   bother   me   now   I'm   very   busy.

#325. Would   you   mind   mailing   this   letter

for   me   ?

#326. If   you   have   time,   will   you   call

me   tomorrow   ?

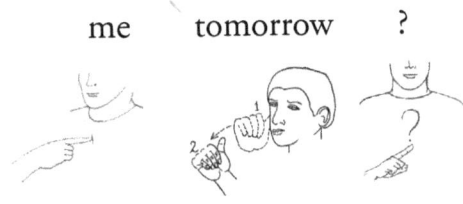

#327. Please,   pick up   those   cups   and   saucers.

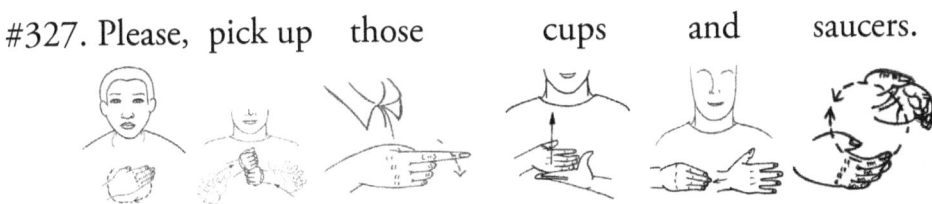

#328. Will   you   do   me   a favor   ?

#329. Please   count   the   chairs   in   that   room.

#330. Please   pour   this   milk   into   that   glass.

#331. Excuse me,   sir   Can   you   give   me

some   information   ?

#332. Can   you   tell   where   is

Peach Street   ?

#333.   It   is   two blocks straight ahead.

#334. Which direction   is   to   movie   theater ?

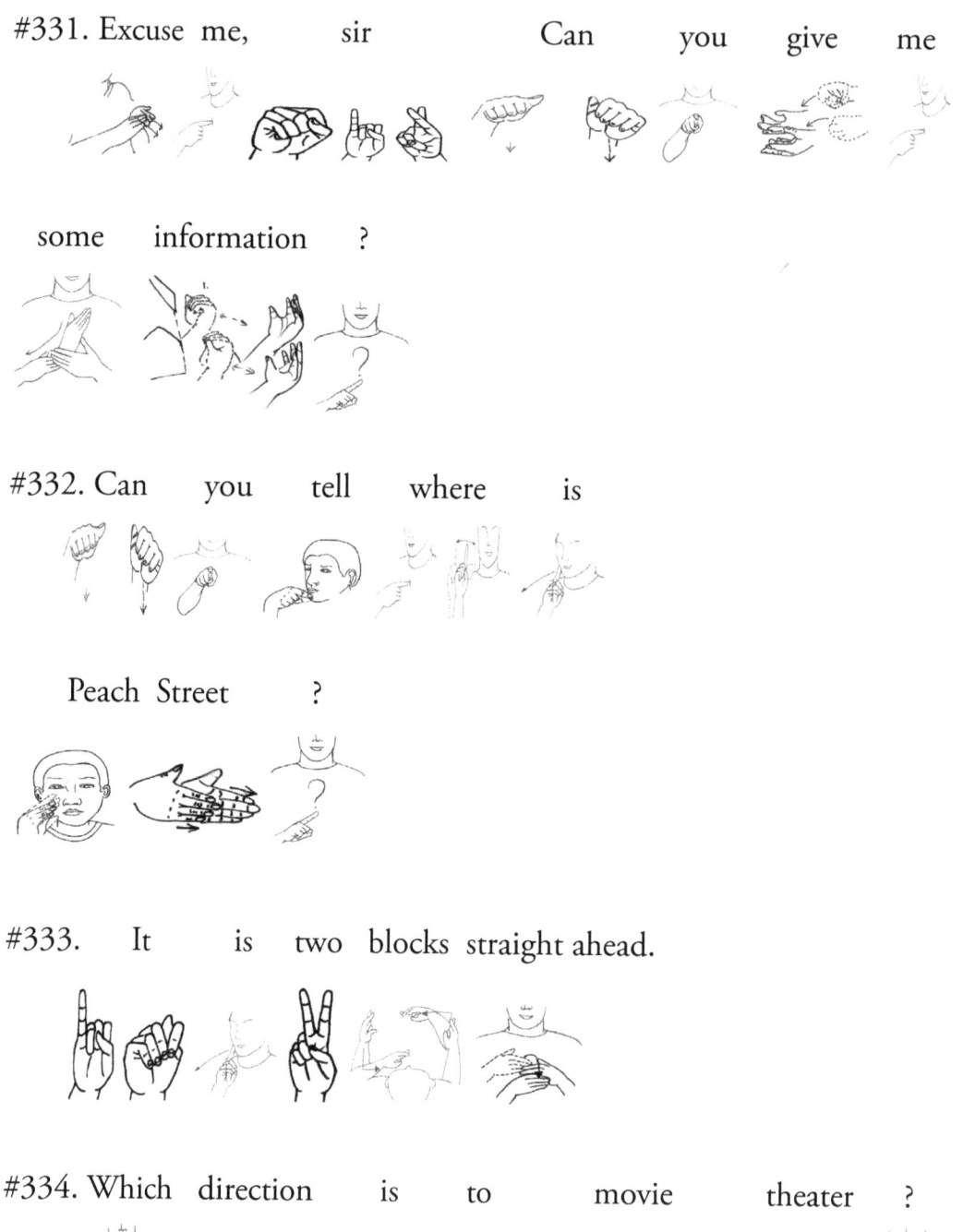

#335. Turn right at next corner.

#336. How far is it to the university ?

#337. It is a long way from here.

#338. The school is around the corner.

#339. The restaurant is across the street from the hotel.

#340. You can't miss it.

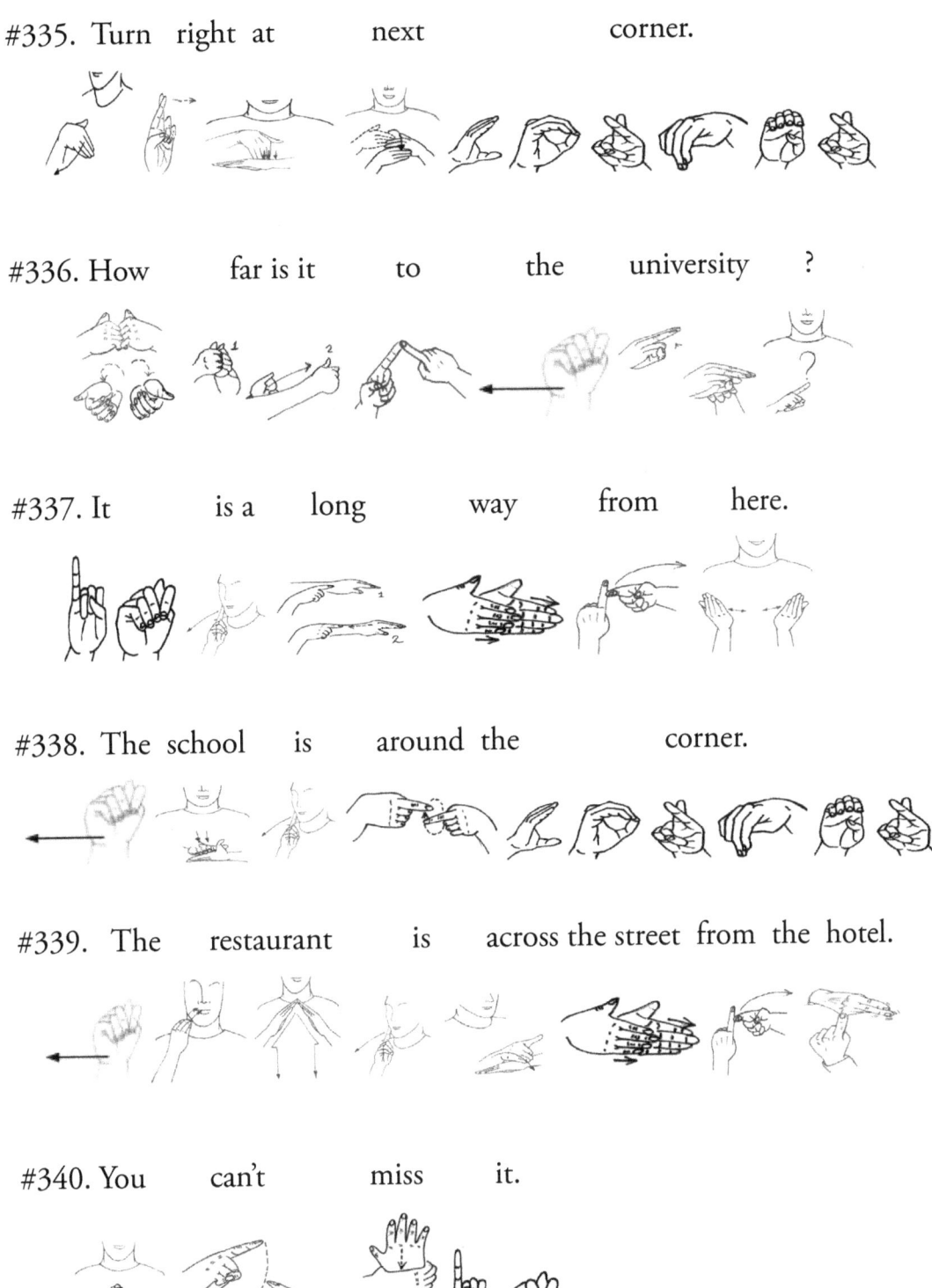

#341. Do you happen to know

Mr. Cooper's telephone ?

#342. Could you tell me where is

nearest telephone ?

#343. Should I go this way, or

that way ?

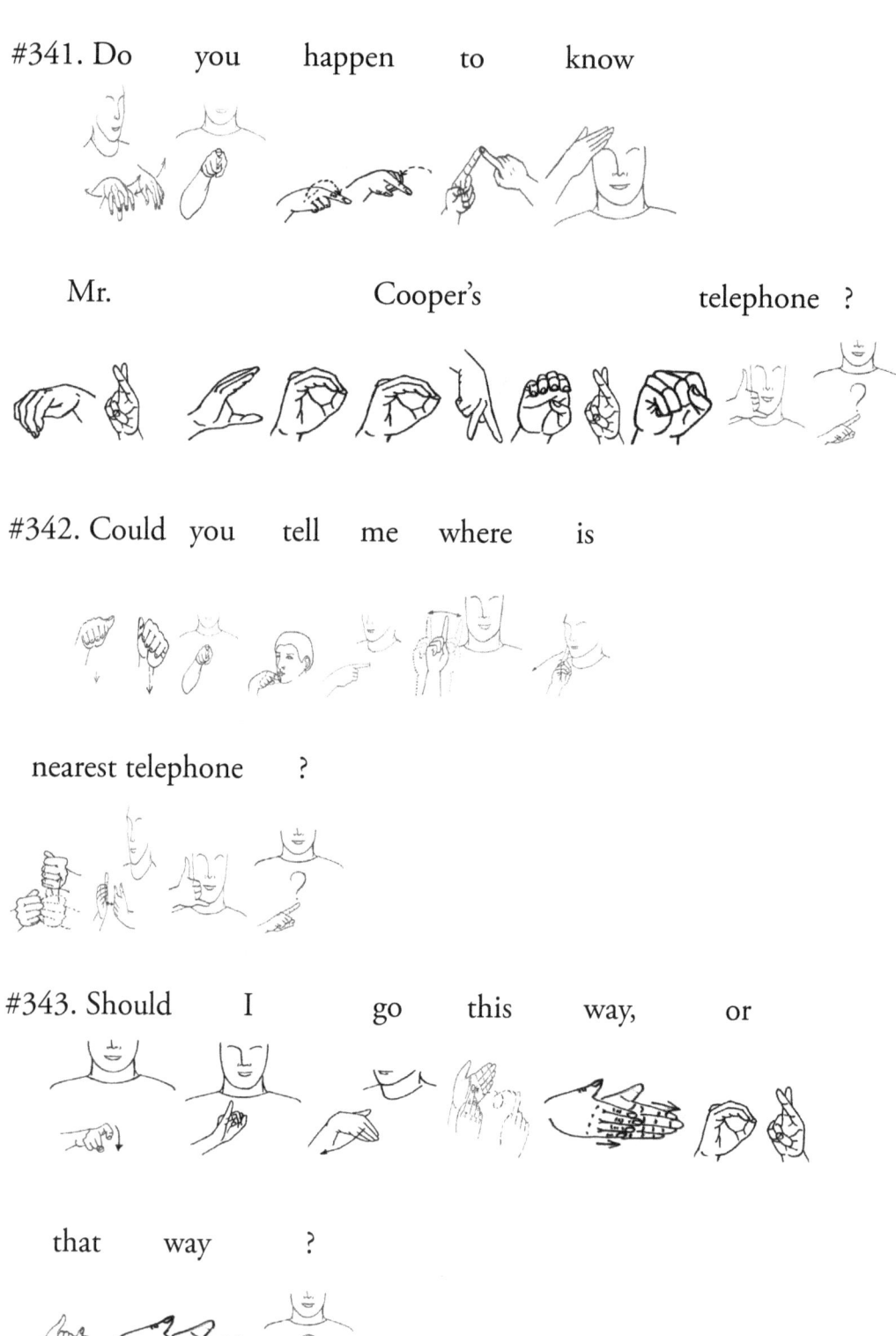

#344.　Go　　　that　　way　　　　for　　　two　　　blocks,

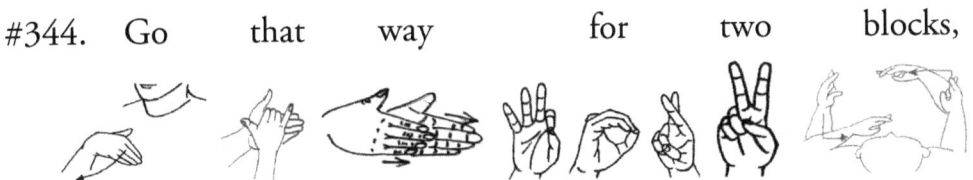

then　　turn left.

#345.　Excuse　　me;　　is　　this　　seat

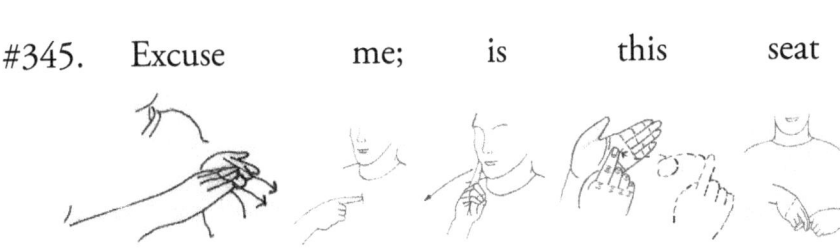

taken　　?

#346.　Are　　you　　married　　?

#347. No,   I'm not   married   I   am   single.

#348. Your   niece   is   engaged,   true   ?

#349. My   sister   has been   engaged   for   two   months.

#350. My grandfather   married in   1921.

#351. When   is   your grandparents' wedding anniversary   ?

#352. How   long   they   been   married   ?

#353. They've   been   married   for   quite a few   years.

#354. Who   did   George

marry   ?

#355. Do   they   have   children   ?

#356. They   had   a baby   last   month.

#357.   My   son   to   get   married   in

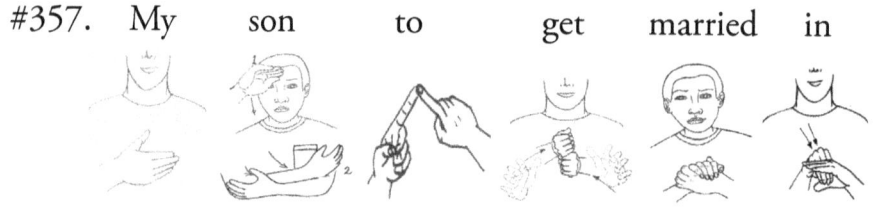

June.

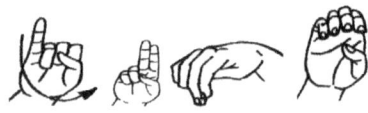

#358. They   don't   know   when   the   wedding

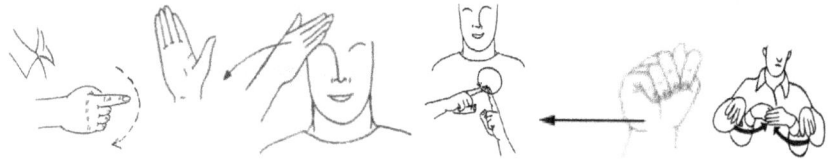

will   be.

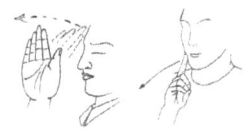

#359. Their   grand   children   grown   now.

#360. She's   widow   Her husband died

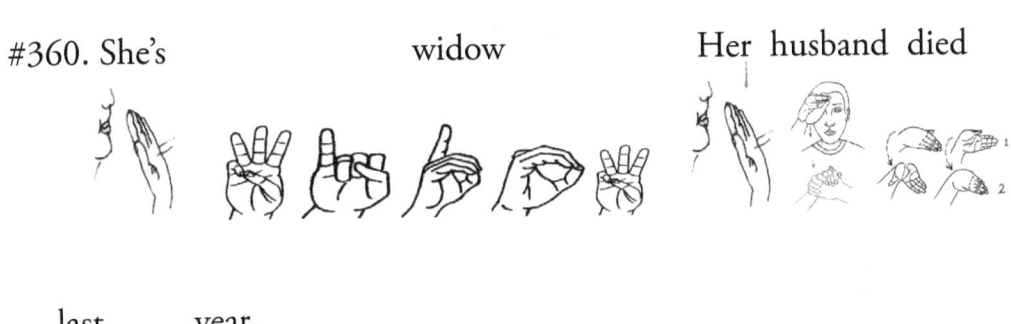

last   year.

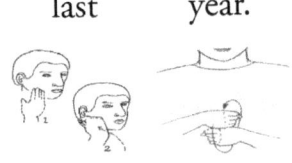

#361. Where did   you   grow up   ?

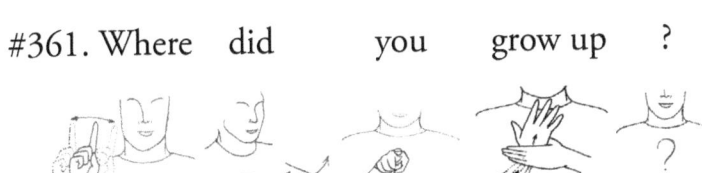

#362. I   grew up   here   in   this   neighborhood.

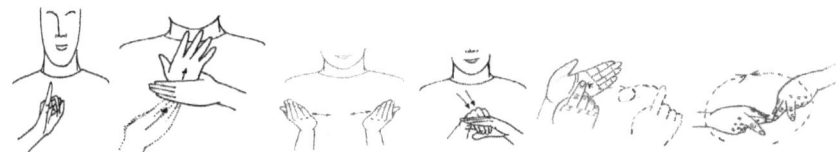

#363. My   friend   spent   his   childhood   in   California.

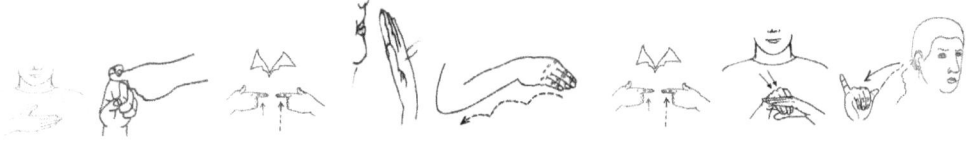

#364   He   lived   in   California until   he   was seventeen.

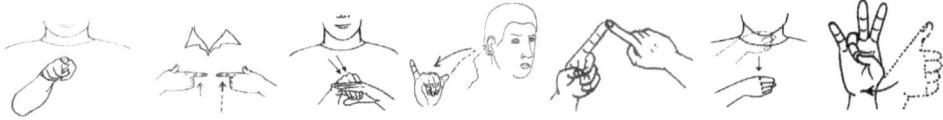

#365. There   have   been   a lot of changes here   in

the last 20   years.

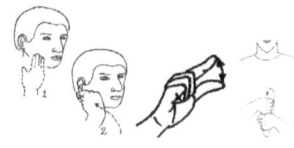

#366. There   was a   grocery store   on the

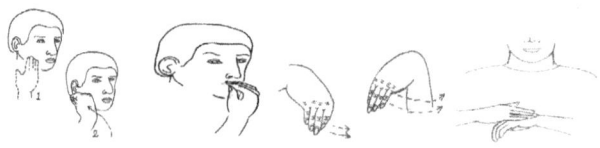

corner.

#367. All of those   houses   were built   in the last ten   years.

#368. They   are   building a new   house   up the street

from   me.

#369. If   you   build   that home,   will   you

spend   forever your life   there   ?

#370. Are   your   neighbors very   friendly   ?

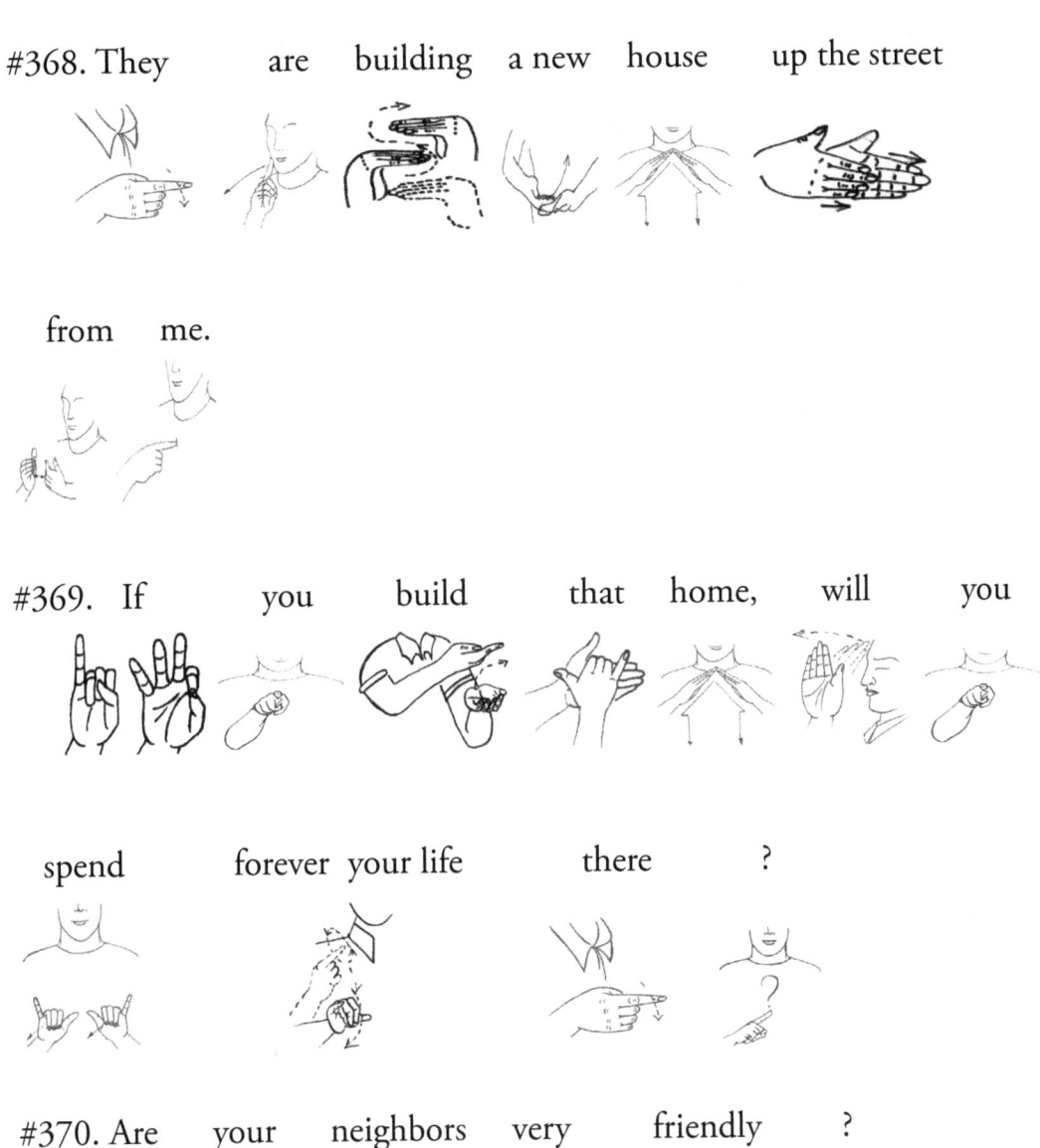

#371. We   know   all   very   good.

#372. A young   married couple   moved   in

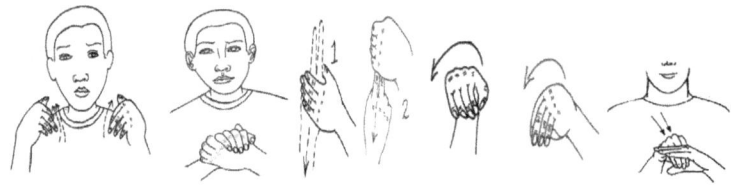

next door   to us.

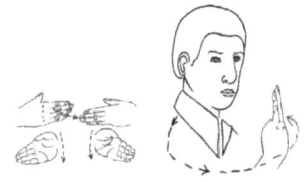

#373. Who bought   that   new   house   on the street

near   you   ?

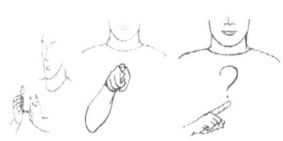

#374. An elderly man rented   the   big   white   house.

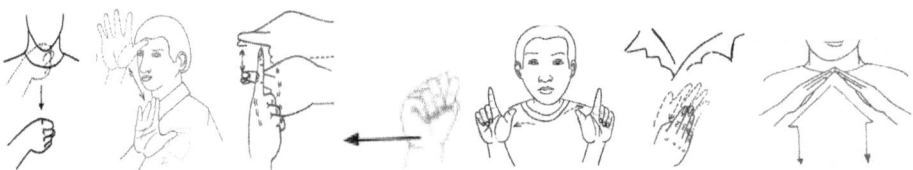

#375. Beautiful trees those   are!

#376. What   time   are   you   wake up

     tomorrow morning   ?

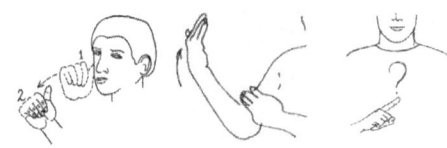

#377.   I   will   wake up   early   and

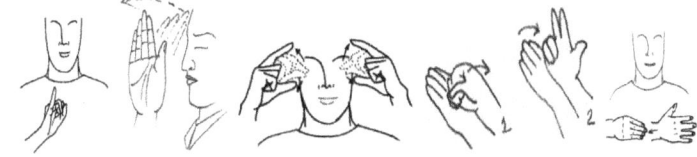

   get up at   6:30.

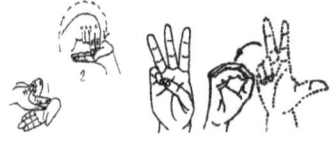

#378. What   will   you   do   then   ?

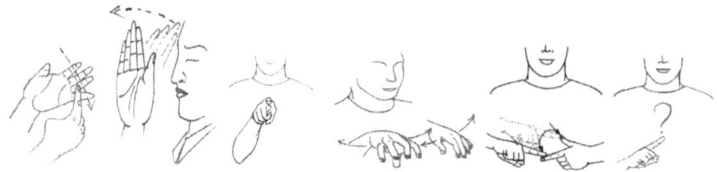

#379. After   I   get dressed, I   will   have   breakfast.

#380. What will   you   have   for   breakfast

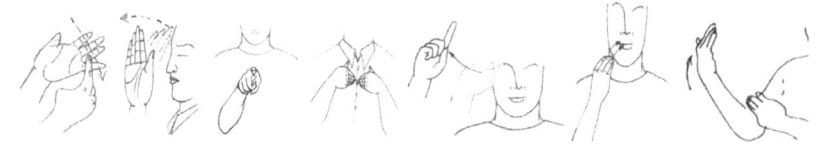

tomorrow   ?

#381. I   will   probably   have   eggs   and   toast

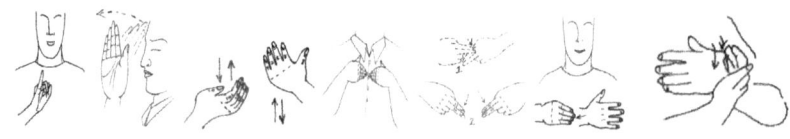

for   breakfast.

#382. After   breakfast,   I   will   get ready to go to work.

#383. I   will   leave the house   at   9:00 and   get

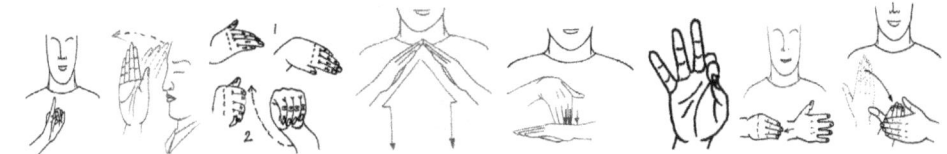

to the office at   9:30.

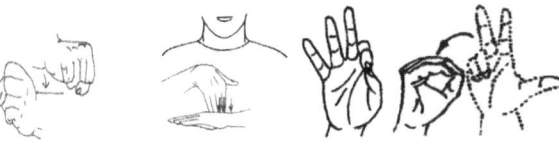

#384. I will   probably   go   out   for   lunch

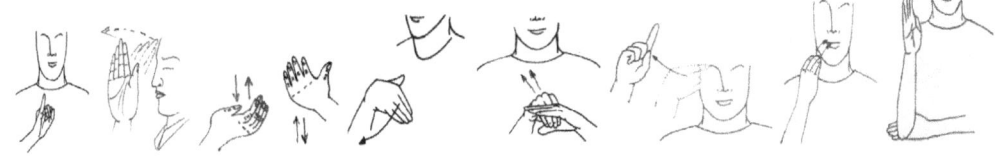

about   12:30

#385. I will finish working at 5:30 and

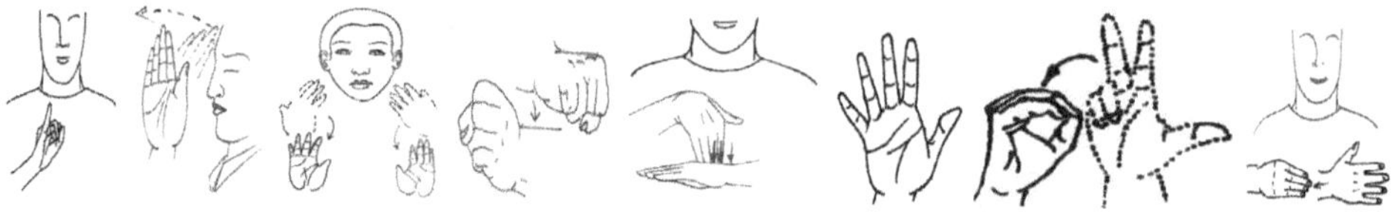

get home by 6 o'clock.

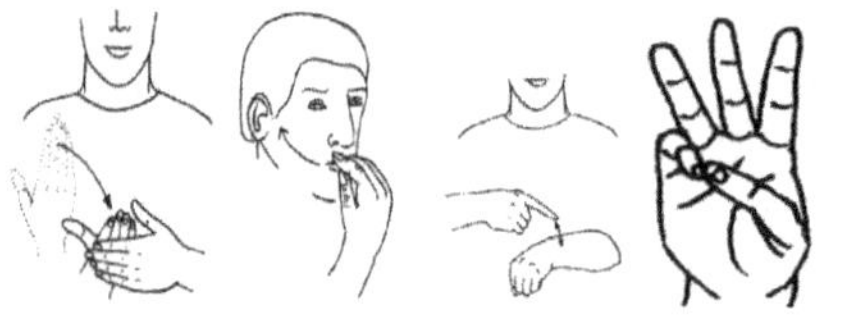

#386. Are you eating dinner at home tomorrow

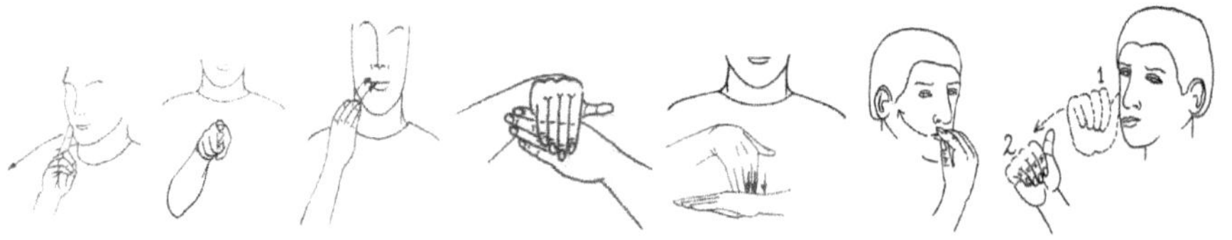

night ?

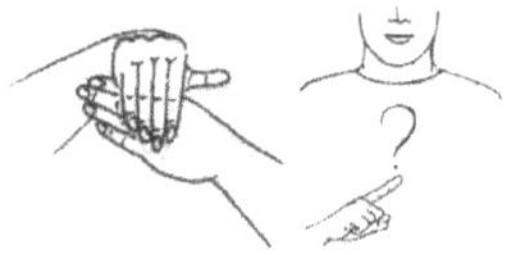

#387. Do you think you will go to

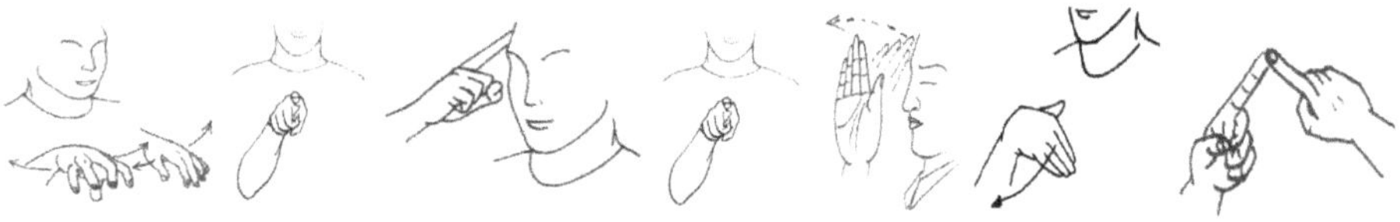

the movies tomorrow night ?

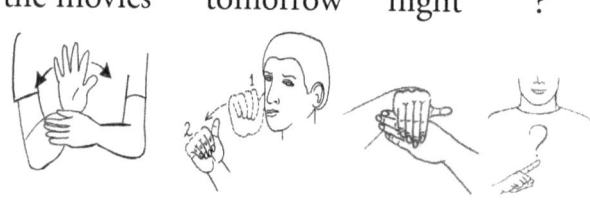

#388. I   will probably   stay home and watch   television.

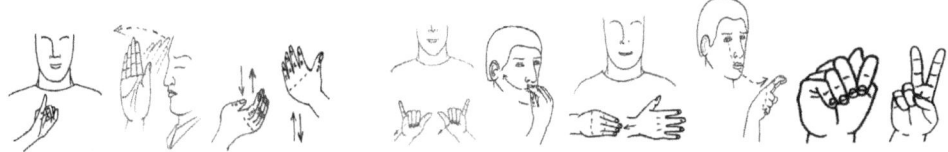

#389. When I   become   sleepy,   I   will probably

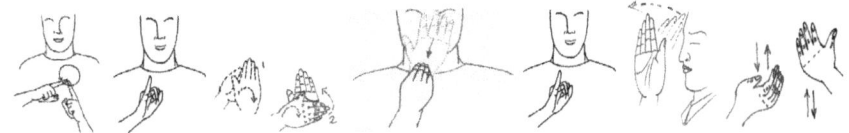

get   ready   for   bed.

#390. Do   you   think   you   can   go   to

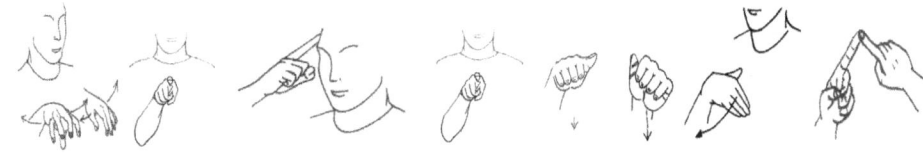

sleep   right away   ?

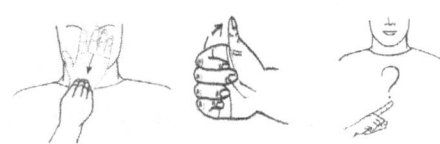

#391. How   is   outside today ?

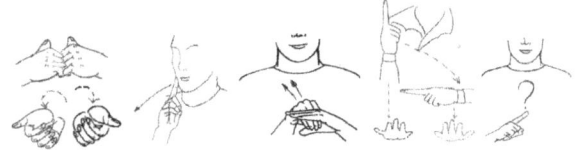

#392. Outside   is   nice   today.

#393. What   was   outside   yesterday   ?

#394. Yesterday it   rained   all   day.

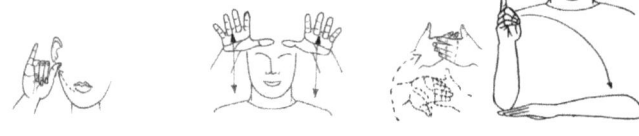

#395. What will   outside   be like tomorrow   ?

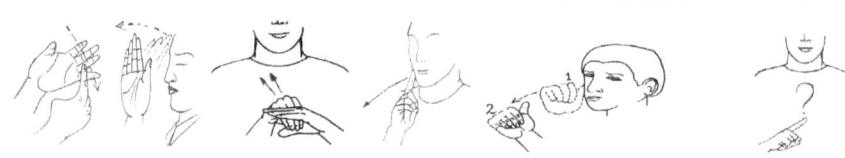

#396. Tomorrow   snow.

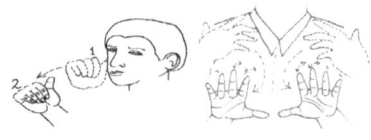

#397. Very   cold   today.

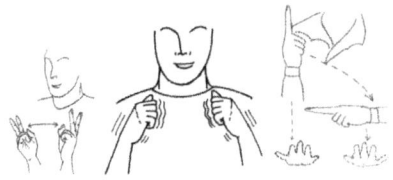

#398. It's   been   cloudy   all   morning.

#399. Is it   raining   now   ?

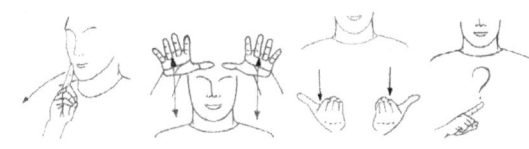

#400. It'll probably   clear up   this   afternoon.

#401. The   days   are   becoming   hotter.

#402. Today   is   the first day   of   spring.

#403. What   is   the temperature   today   ?

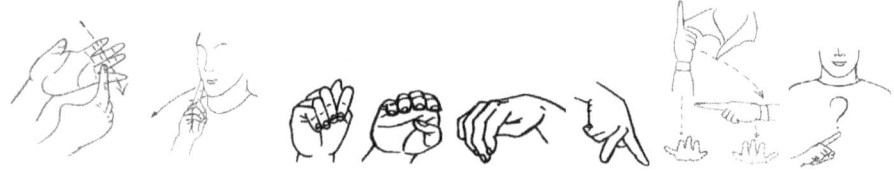

#404. This Afternoon   about   seventy   degrees.

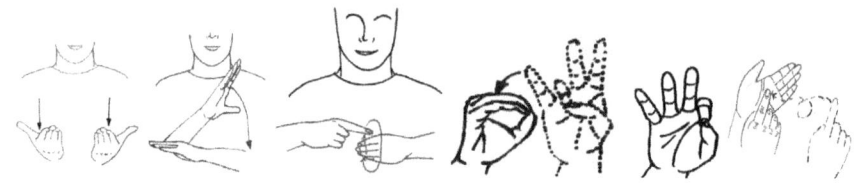

#405. A cool   breeze   this   evening.

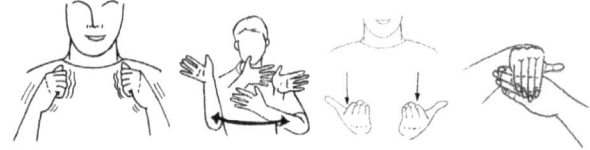

#406. How   are   you   feeling   today   ?

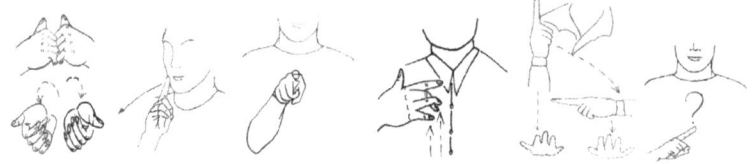

#407. I   don't   feel   very   nice   this   morning.

#408. I   was   sick yesterday,   but   I   am

better   today.

#409. Your   fever   is   gone   ?

But,   I   still   have   a   cough.

#410. My   brother   has   a bad   headache.

#411. Which   of   your   arms   is   sore   ?

#412. My right arm hurts   It   hurts right here

#413. What's the matter   with   you   ?

414. I   have   pain   in   my   back.

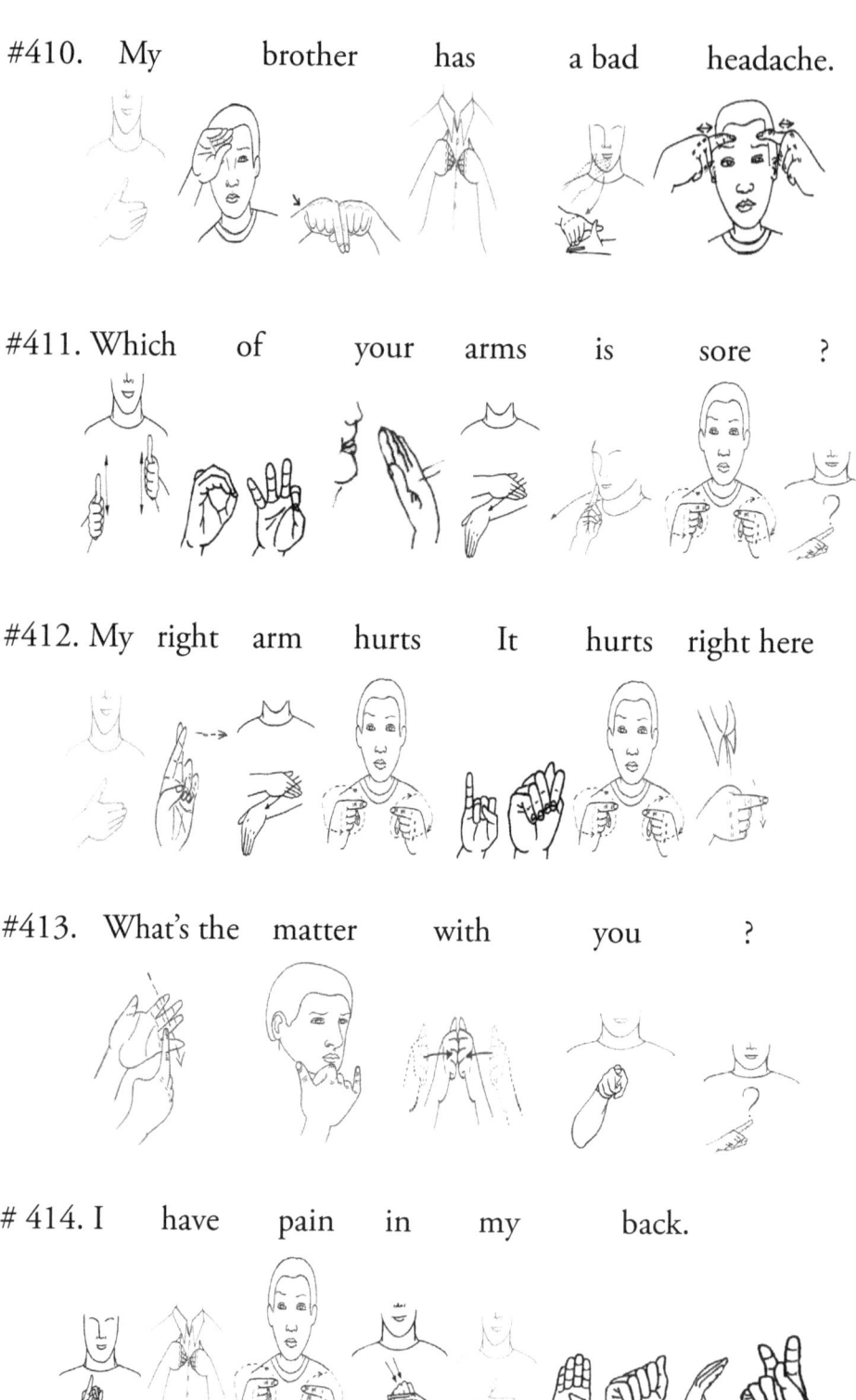

#415. Which   foot   hurts   ?   Is it the   left

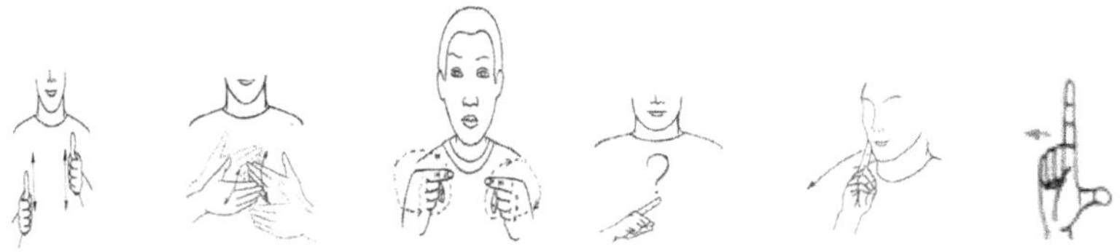

one   ?

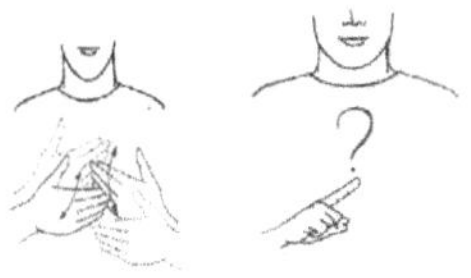

#416. How   did   you   break   your

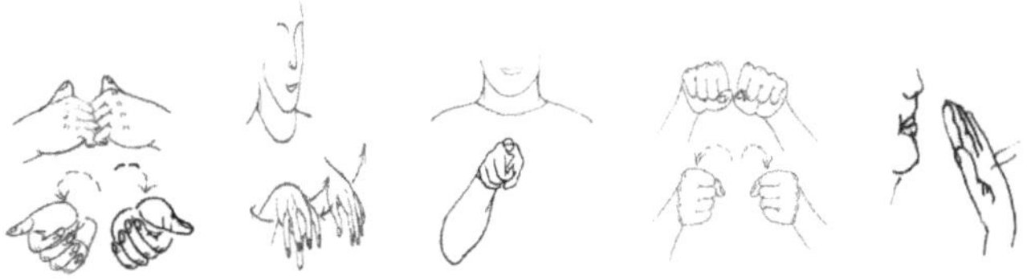

leg   ?

#417. I   slipped on the   stairs   I   broke

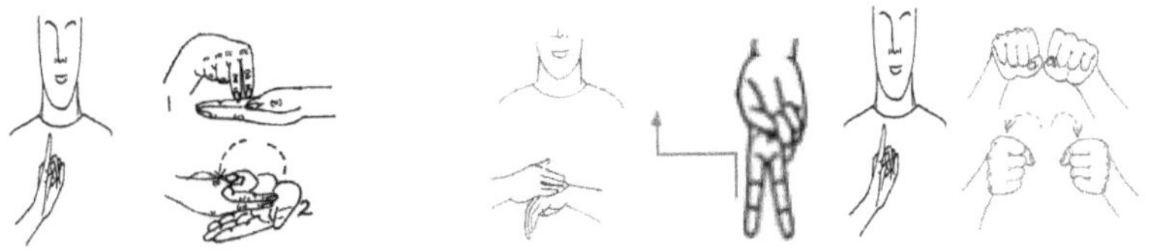

my   leg.

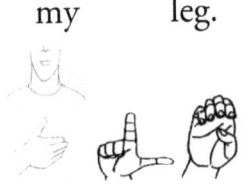

#418. Your right hand is swollen. Does it

hurt ?

#419. It is bleeding. You'd better go

see a doctor about that cut.

#420. I hope you'll be well soon.

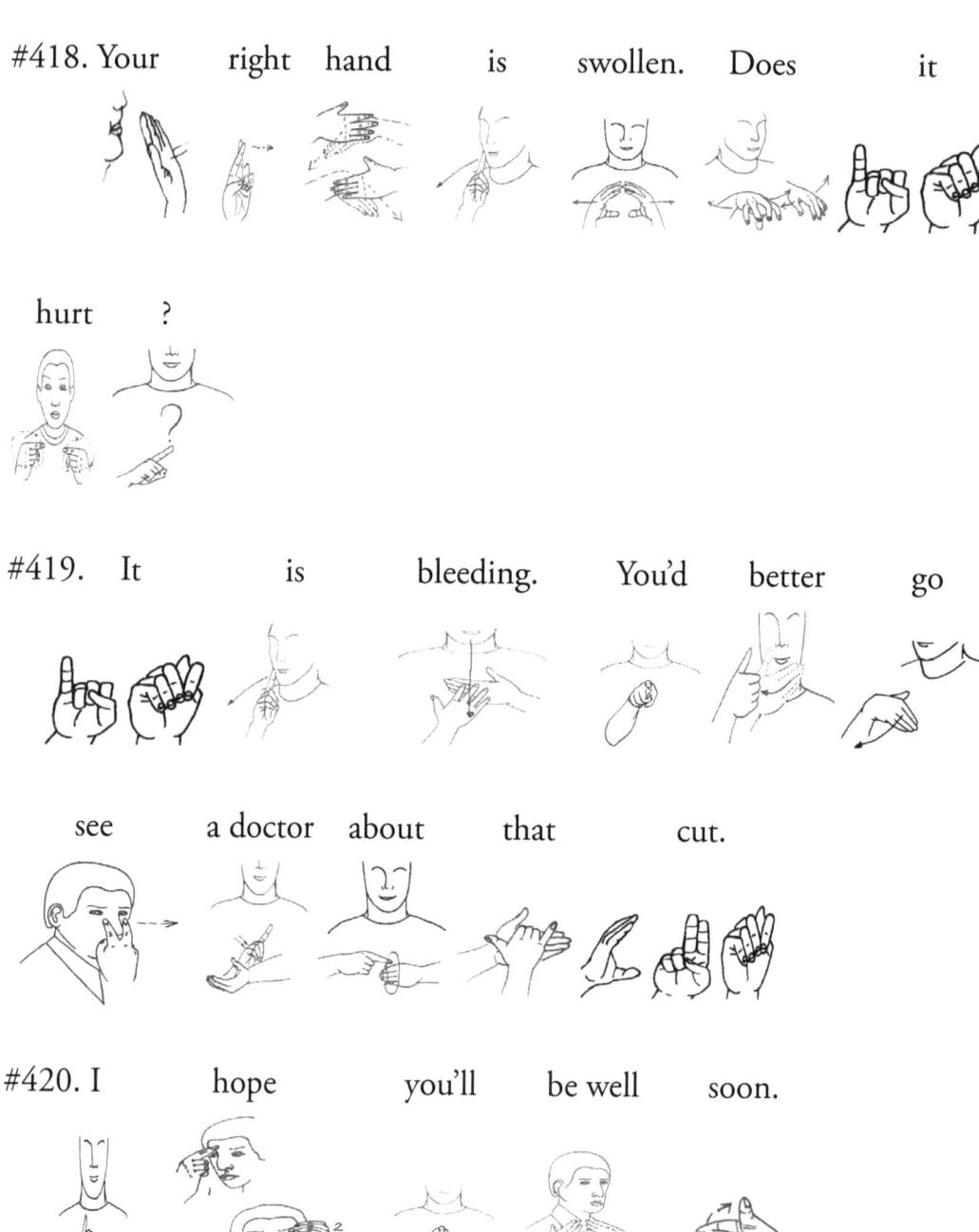

#421. I   get out of bed   about   7 o'clock every morning.

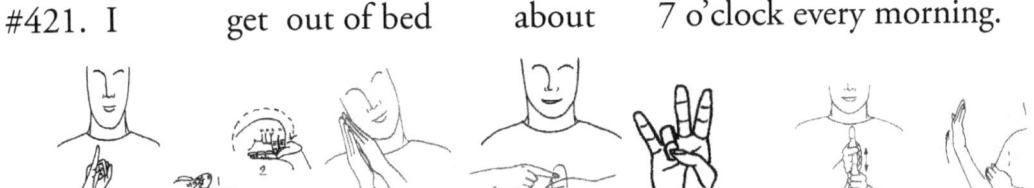

#422. After   getting up,   I   go   to   bathroom   and

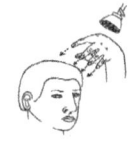

take a shower.

#423. Then,   I   shave,   brush my teeth,

and comb my hair.

#424. After   brushing my teeth,   I   put on my clothes.

   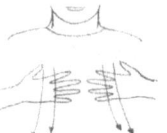

#425. After   that,   I   go   downstairs   to the kitchen

 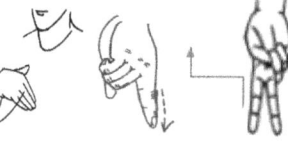  

to   have breakfast.

#426. After eating breakfast, I   go   back   upstairs.

 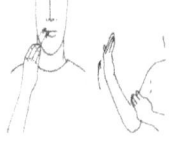   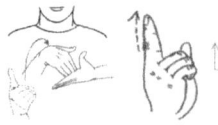 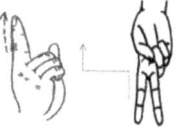

#427. Then,   it's usually   time   to   wake up   my

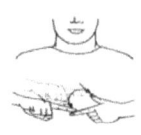 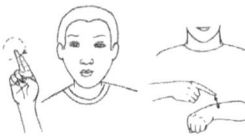  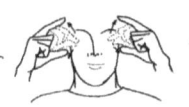 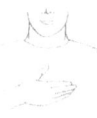

little   brother.

#428. He   can't   dress   himself yet

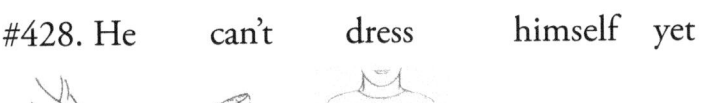

because he's too young

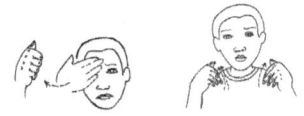

#429. I   wash   his   face   and   hands, then   I

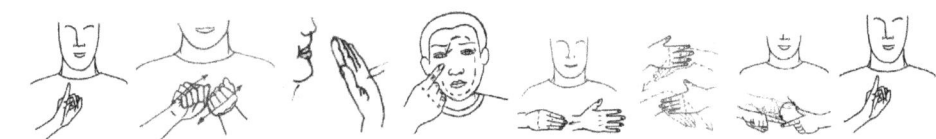

dress   him

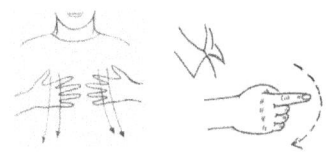

#430. He   tries   to   button

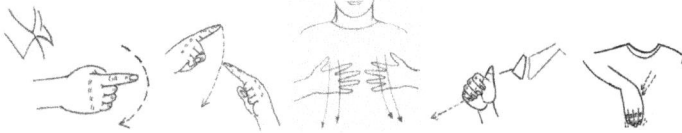

his   shirt,   but   he   can't   do   it.

#431. My little brother bathes before he

goes to bed at night.

#432. He always forgets to wash

behind his ears.

#433. I'm always tired when I come home

from work.

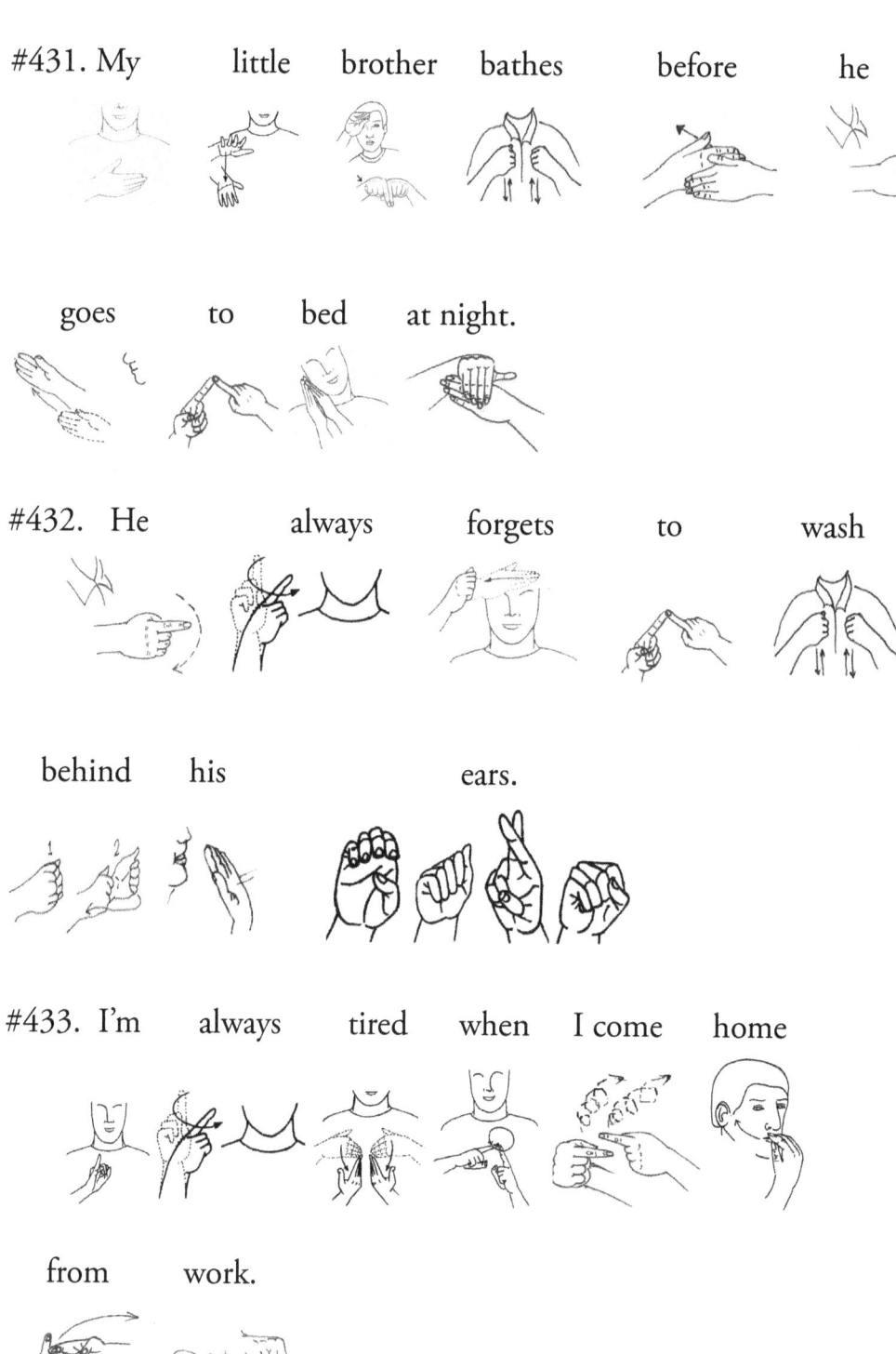

#434. At   bed   time,   I   take off

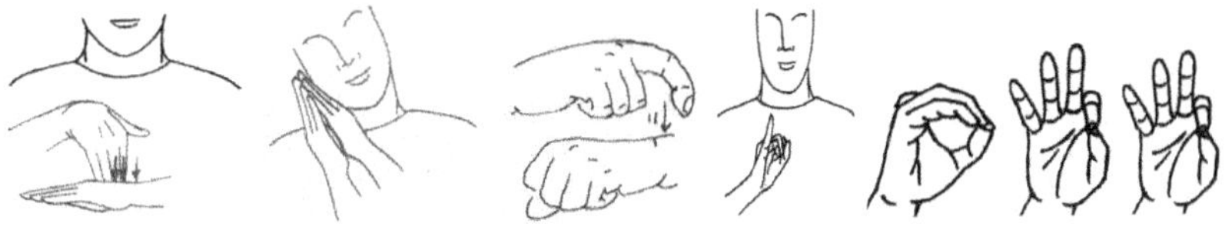

my clothes   and   put on   my   pajamas.

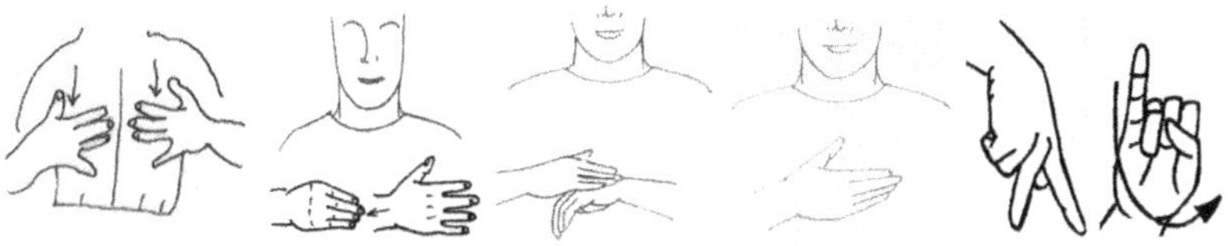

#435. I   get into   bed   about   11:30,   and

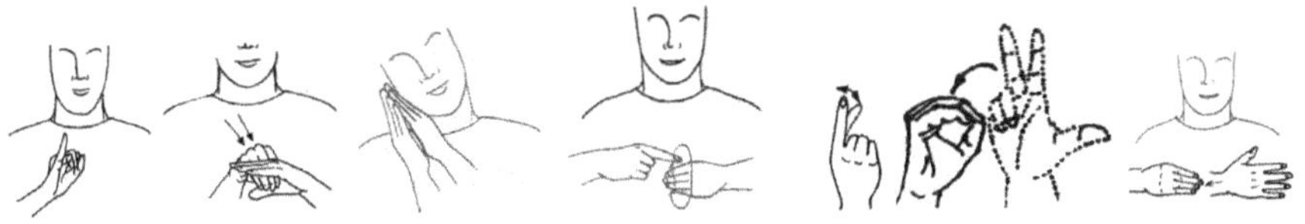

go fast   to sleep

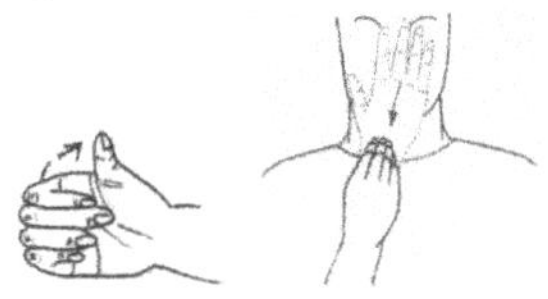

#436. What   do   you   think   ?

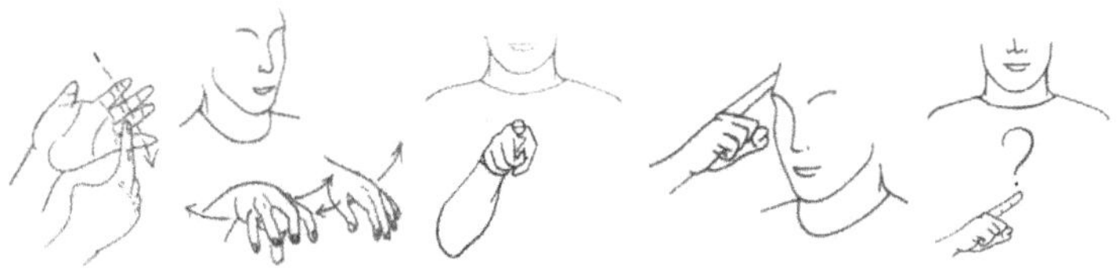

Is   that   right   ?

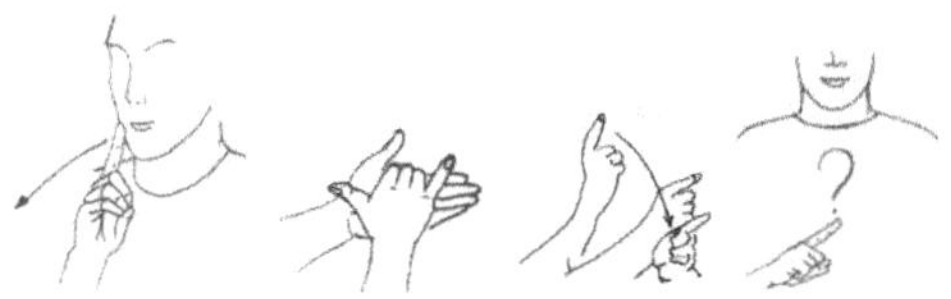

#437. Certainly   you   are   absolutely   right

about   that.

#438. I   think   you   are   mistaken   about   that.

#439.   I   like   hot   weather   best.

#440. Personally,   I   prefer   winter weather.

#441. Do   you   think   it's going to   rain

tomorrow   ?

#442.   I   don't   know   whether   it will rain

or   not

#443. In   my   opinion,   that's   an excellent   idea.

#444. Why   is   Mr.   Cooper

so   tired   ?   Do   you   have   any

idea   ?

#445. He   is   tired   because   he   worked

hard   all   day   today.

#446. What do   you   think   of   my

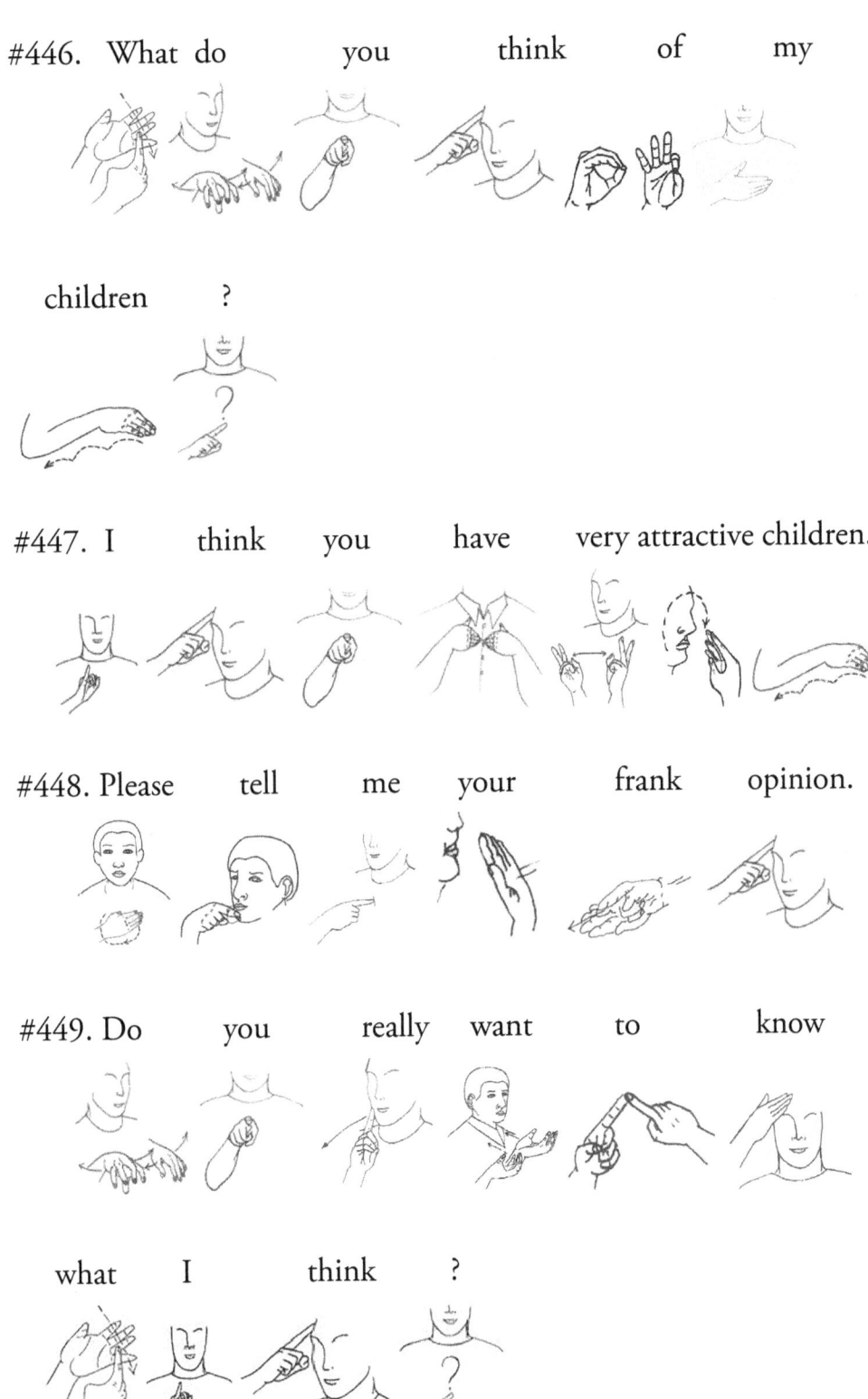

children   ?

#447. I   think   you   have   very attractive children.

#448. Please   tell   me   your   frank   opinion.

#449. Do   you   really   want   to   know

what   I   think   ?

#450.   Of course   I   want   to   know   what   your

opinion   is.

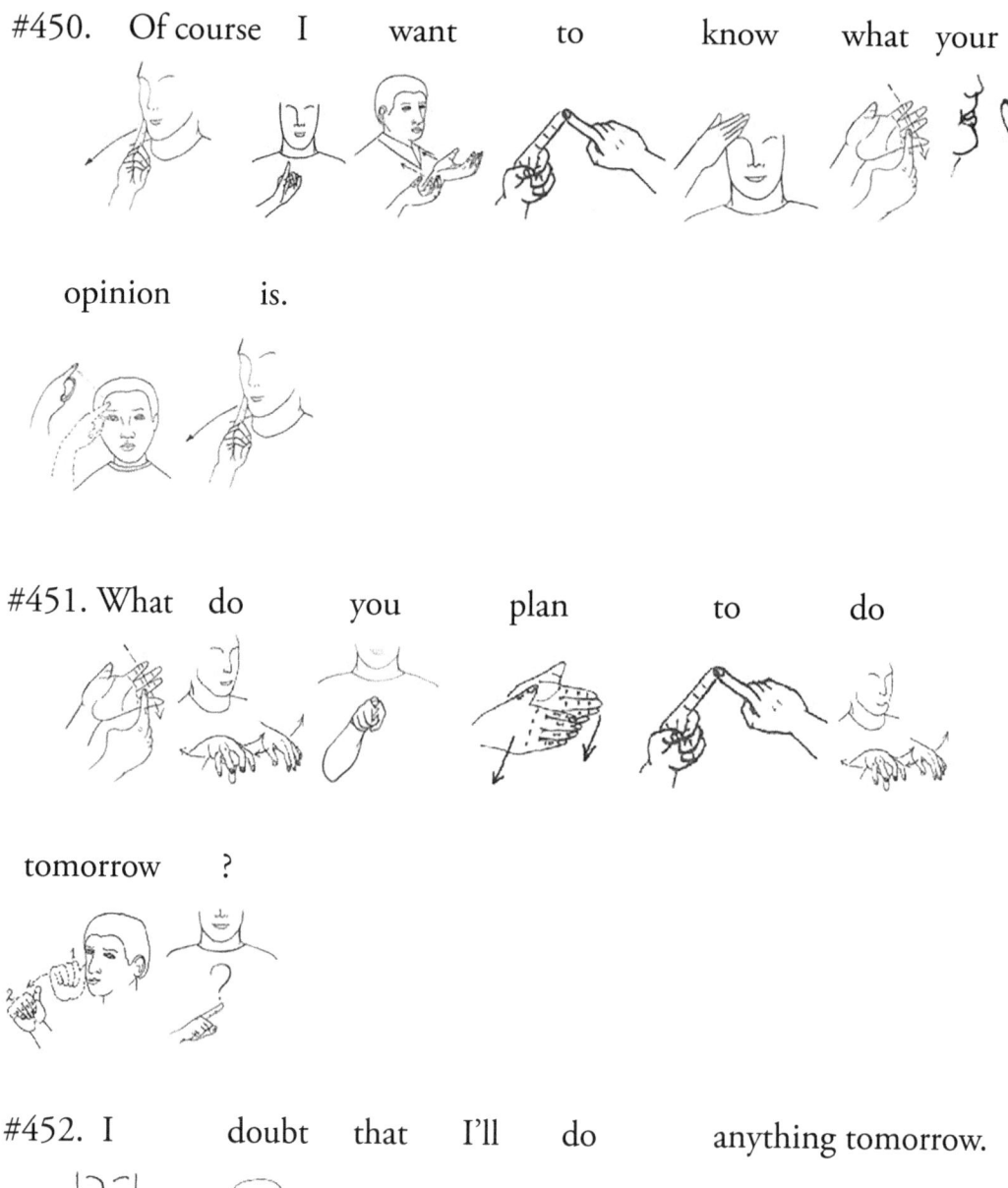

#451. What   do   you   plan   to   do

tomorrow   ?

#452. I   doubt   that   I'll   do   anything tomorrow.

#453. Please   excuse   me   for   a little while.

I   want   to   do   some   thing.

#454. I   imagine   I   will   do   some

work   instead of   going   to   the movies.

#455. Will   it be convenient   for   you   to explain.

your   plans   to   him   ?

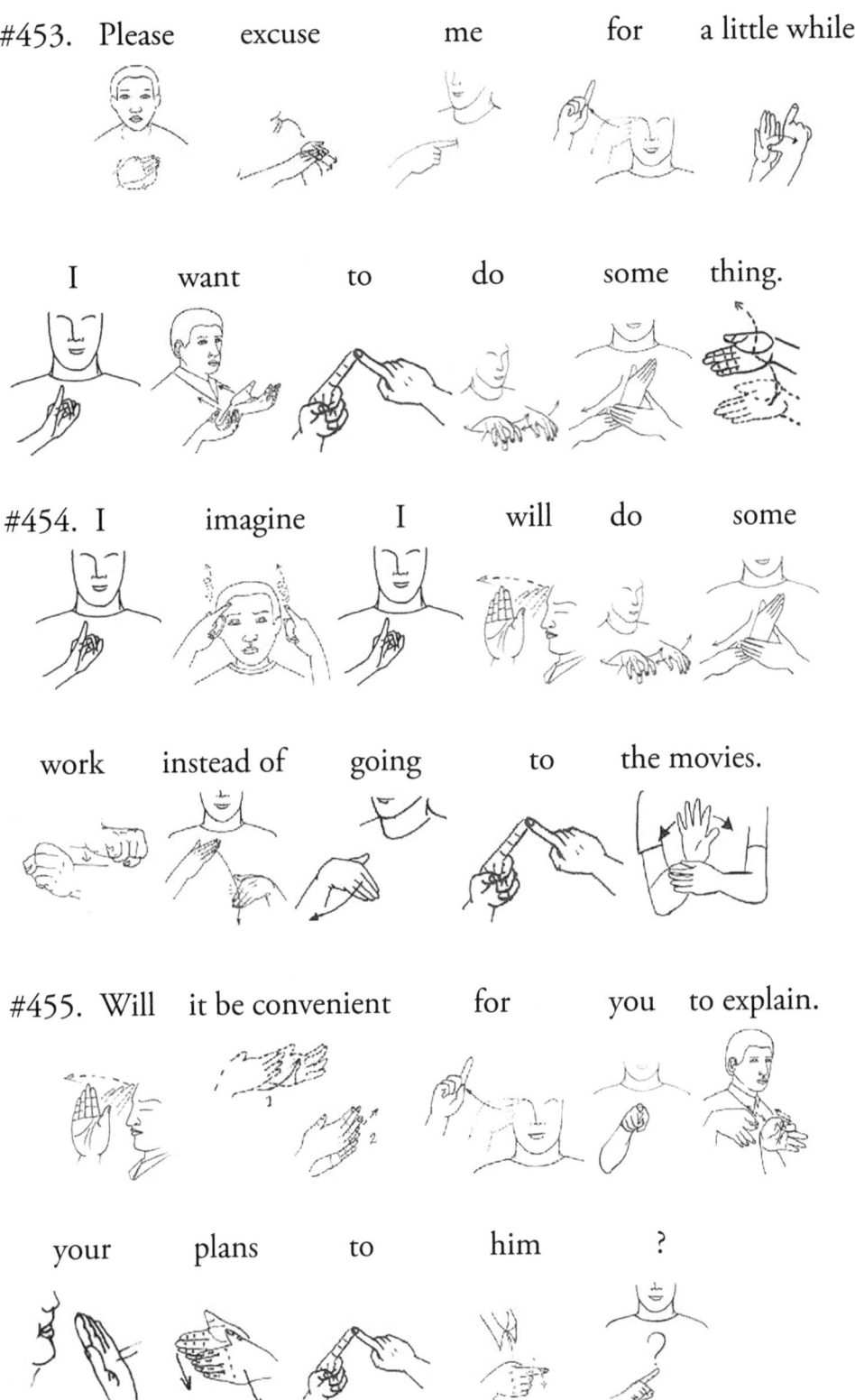

#456. There's   nothing   to   do   because tomorrow

is   a holiday.

#457. What   is   your   brother   planning   to

do   tomorrow ?

#458. He   can't   decide   what   to   do.

#459. It's difficult to   make   a decision   without   knowing

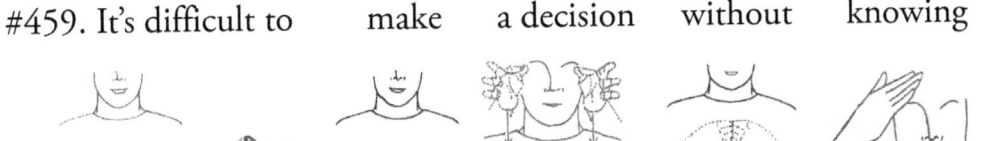

all the   facts.

#460. We   are   trying   to   plan

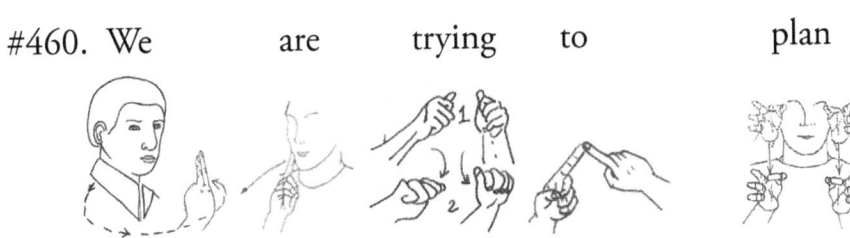

our   future.

#461. That   is   a good   idea.

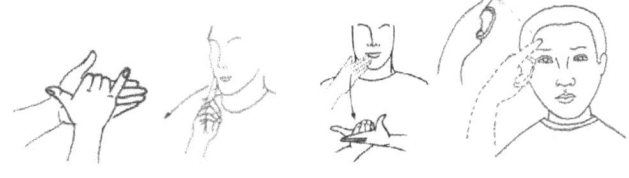

#462.   I   am   hoping   to   stay

a few   days   in   the   mountains.

#463. Would   you   think   about   going   north

this   summer   ?

#464. If   you   will   go   maybe   I

would   like   to   go   with   you.

#465. After you think about it, let me

know what you decide.

#466. I am anxious to know your decision.

#467. I am confident you've made

right choice.

#468. I want to persuade you

to change your mind.

#469. Will you accept my advice ?

#470. What have you decided ?

#471. I have definitely decided to go

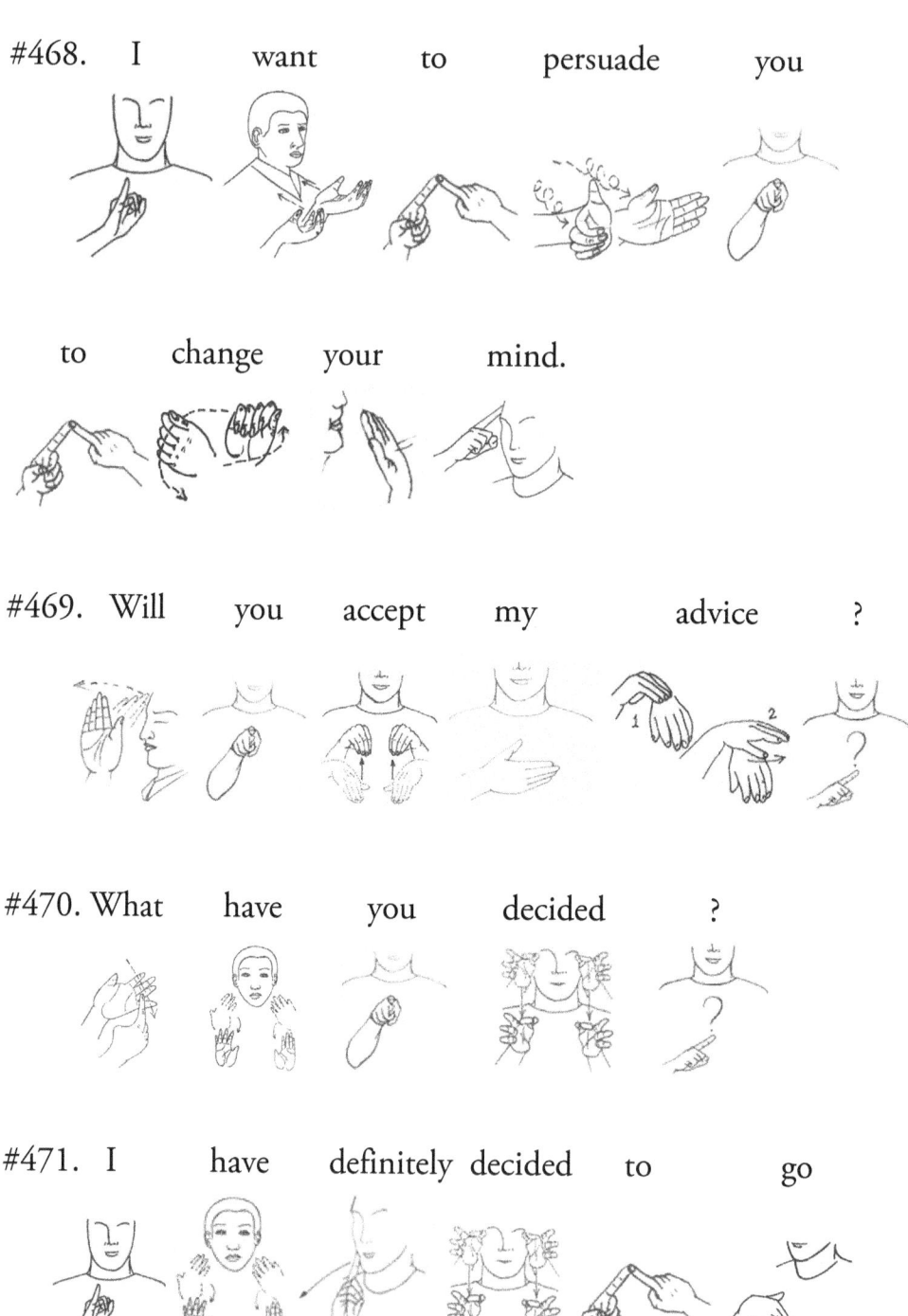

to   California.

#472. He   didn't want   to   say   anything

to   influence   my   decision.

#473. She   refuses   to   make up   her   mind.

#474. I   assume   you   have   decided against   buying a

new   car.

#475. He   took long   time   to   decide.

#476. You   can   go   whenever   you   wish.

#477. We   are   accepting your   plan.

#478. He   knows   it   is   inconvenient,

but   he   wants   to   go   anyway.

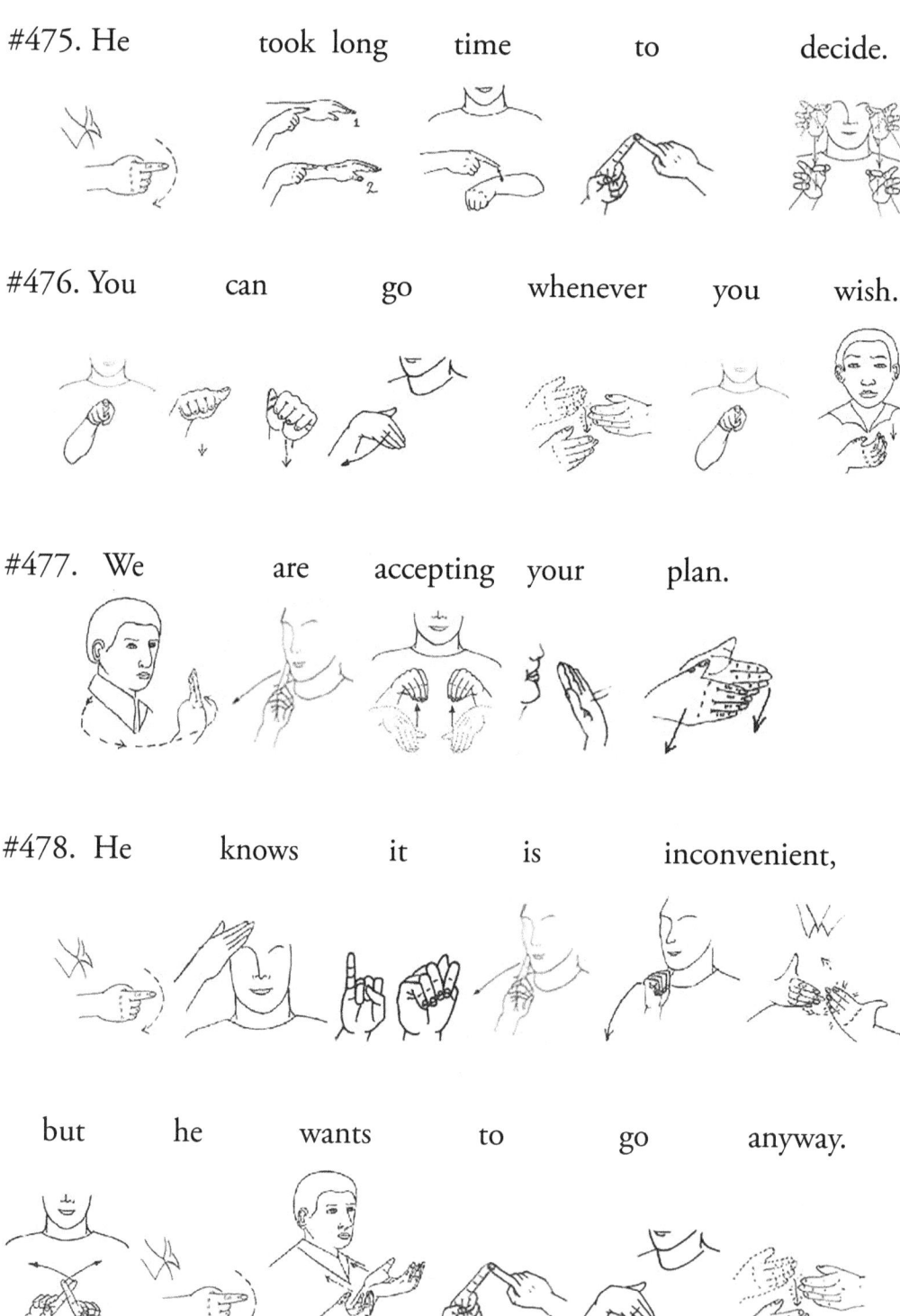

#479. According to Mr. Green,

this is a complicated problem.

#480. She insists that makes no difference.

#481. Are you going to any place this

year ?

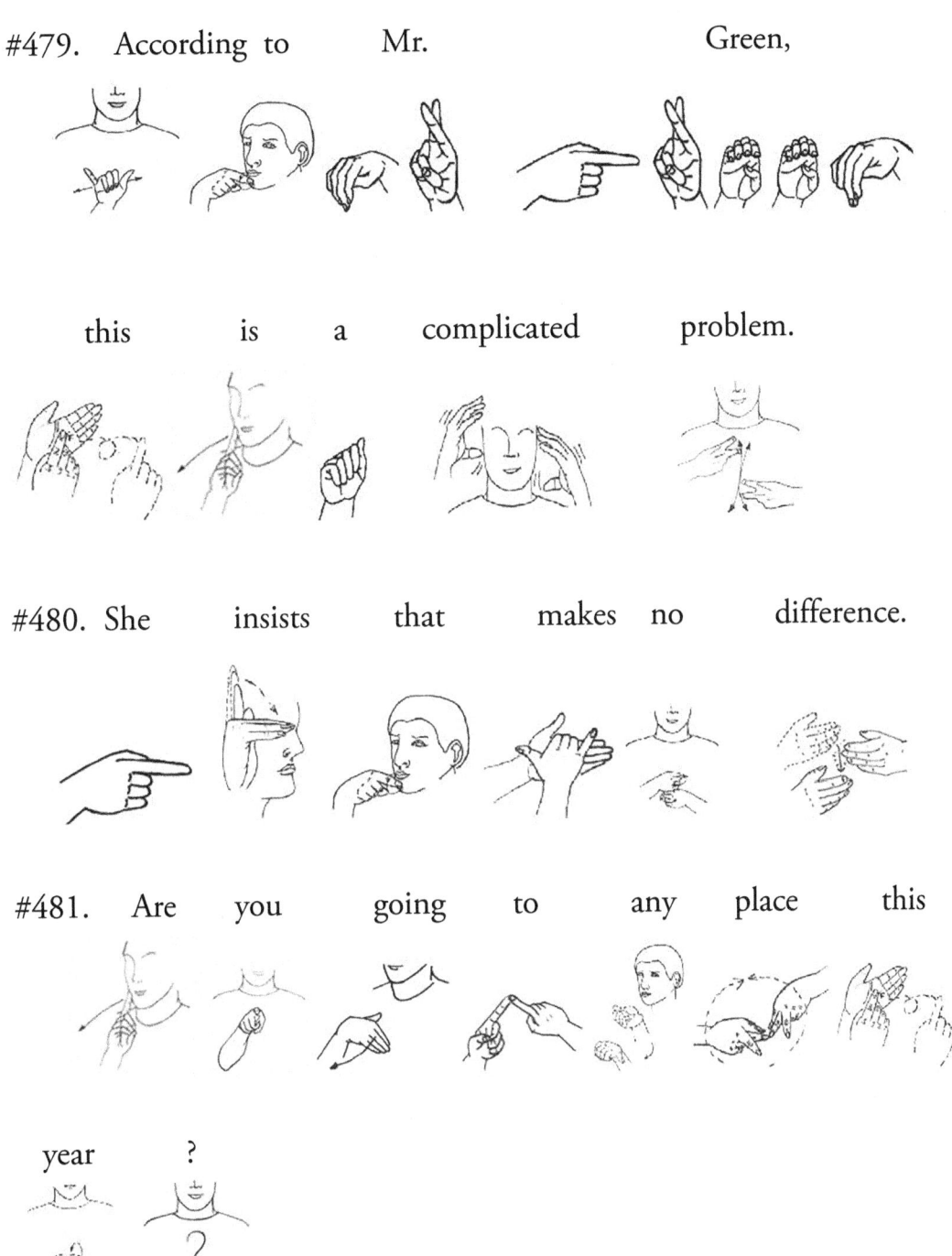

482. If   I   have   enough   money,   I   am

going   to   travel   to   another   country.

#483. How   are   you   going   ?

Are   you   going   by   boat   ?

#484. It   is   more   fast   to   go

by   plane   than   by   boat.

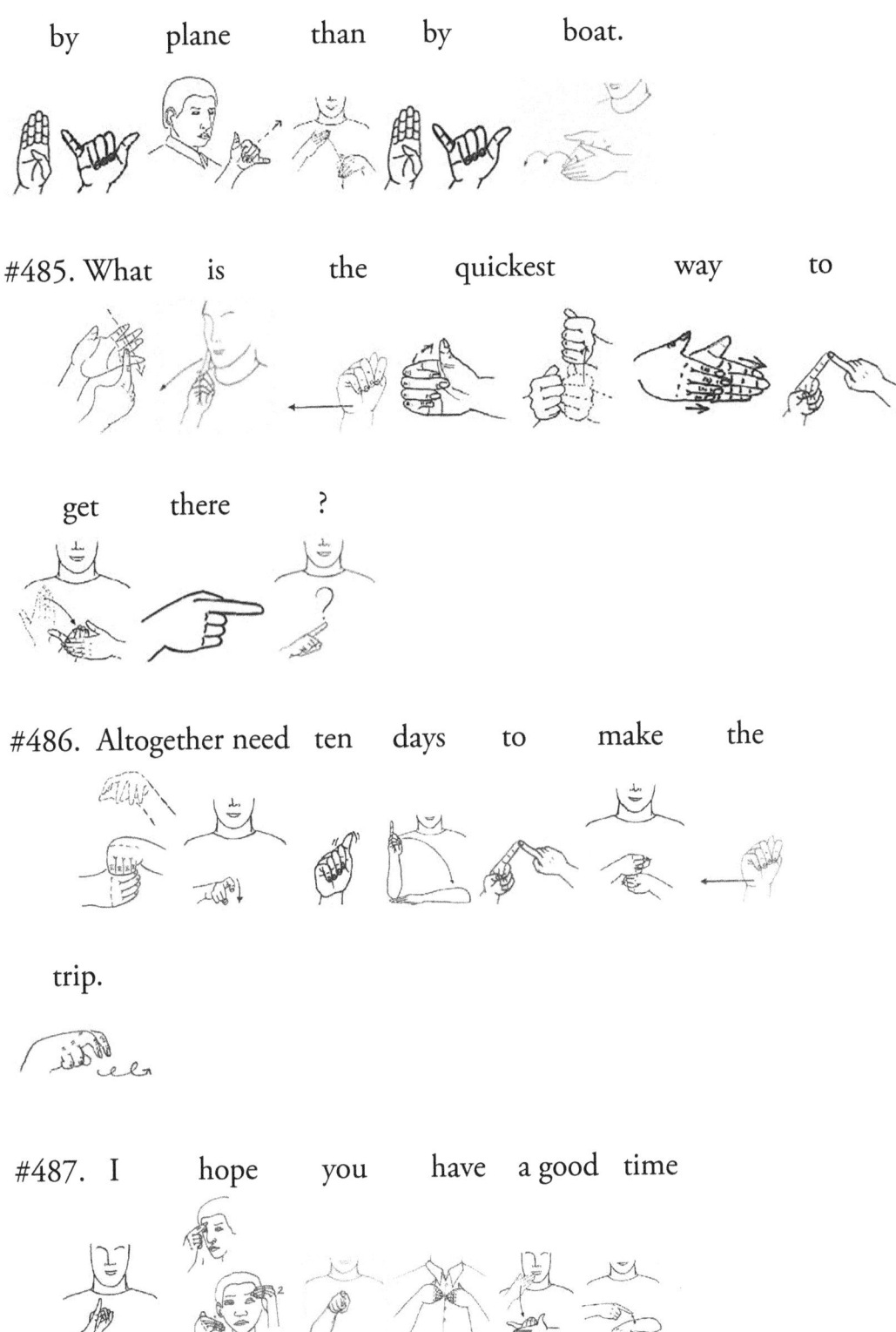

#485. What   is   the   quickest   way   to

get   there   ?

#486. Altogether need   ten   days   to   make   the

trip.

#487. I   hope   you   have   a good   time on   your   trip.

#488.   I   am   leaving   tomorrow,   but   haven't

packed suitcases.

#489.   I   am   going   by   air.

I   like   flying.

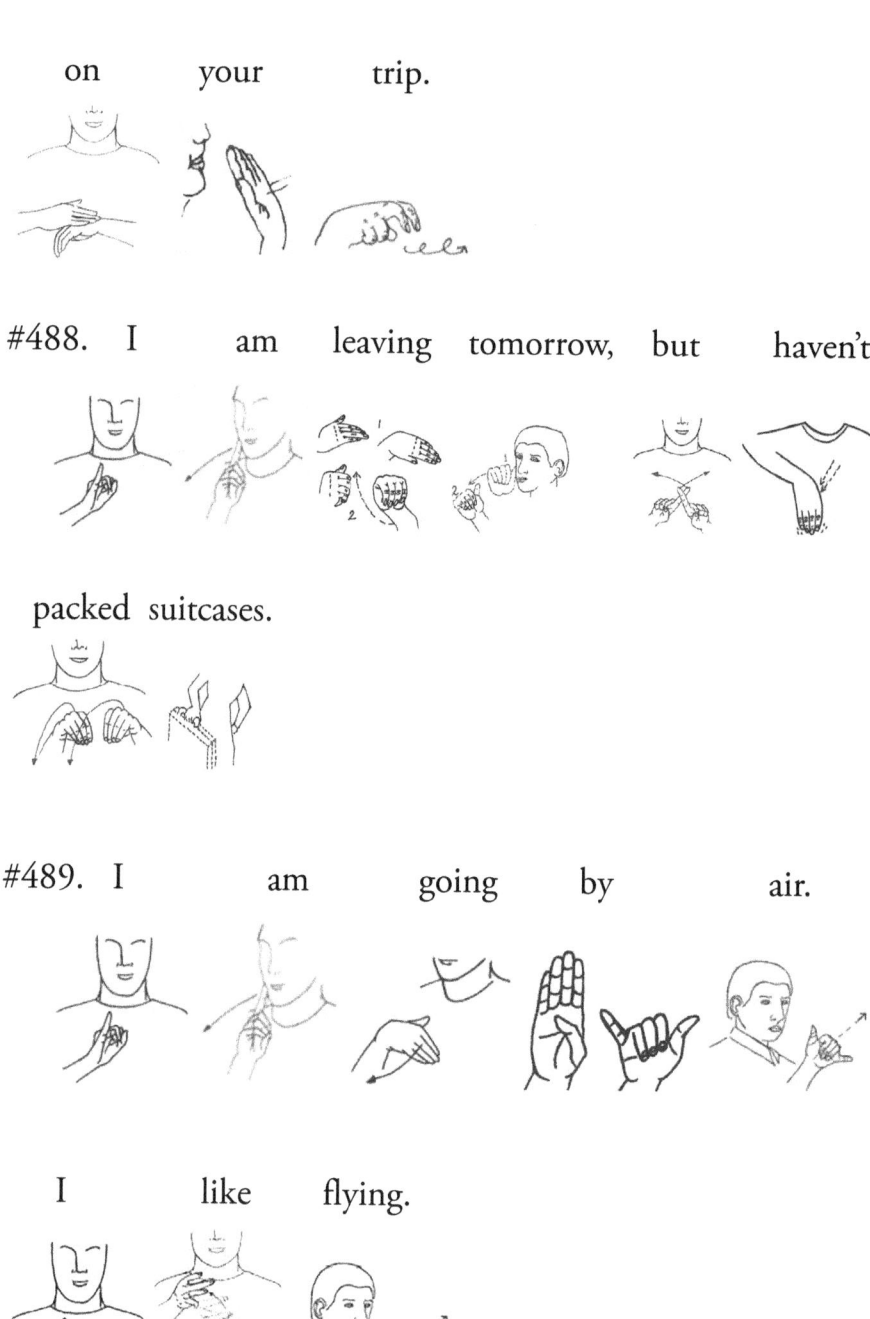

#490. My   brother   took a trip   to   Mexico.

#491. It   was   a six   hour   flight.

#492. How   many   passengers   were on   the   train   ?

#493. His   friend   was   injured   in

an airplane   crash

#494. Would you like to go for

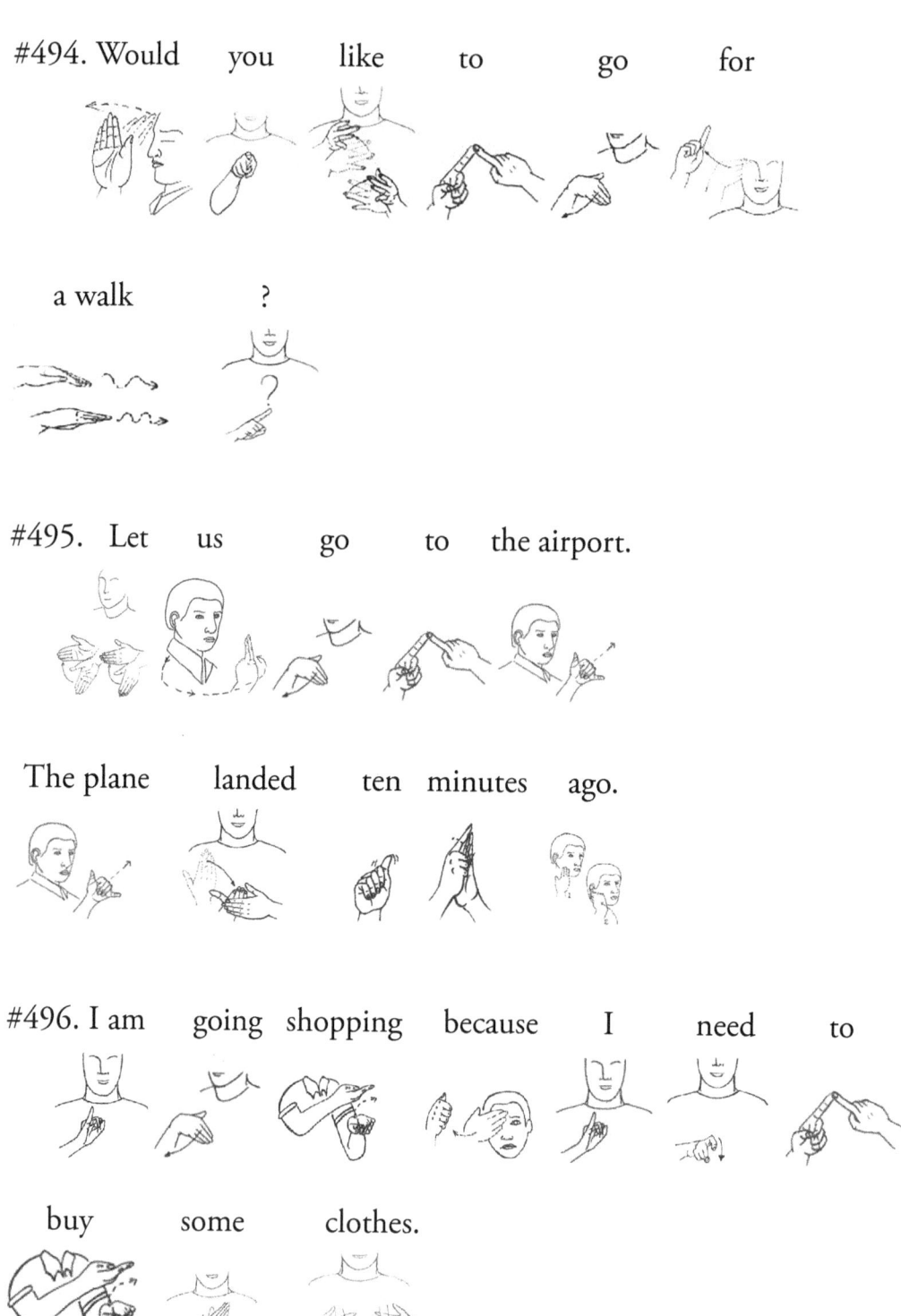

a walk ?

#495. Let us go to the airport.

The plane landed ten minutes ago.

#496. I am going shopping because I need to

buy some clothes.

#497. If   this   shirt   doesn't   fit,   may

I   bring it   back   later   ?

#498. What   size   shoes   do   you

have   ?

#499. That   suit   looks   very   good   on   you.

#500.   This   dress   is   made   of

silk,   isn't it   ?

#501. I   would   like   to   try   on   this   sweater.

#502.   I   am   interested   in   buying

a new   car.

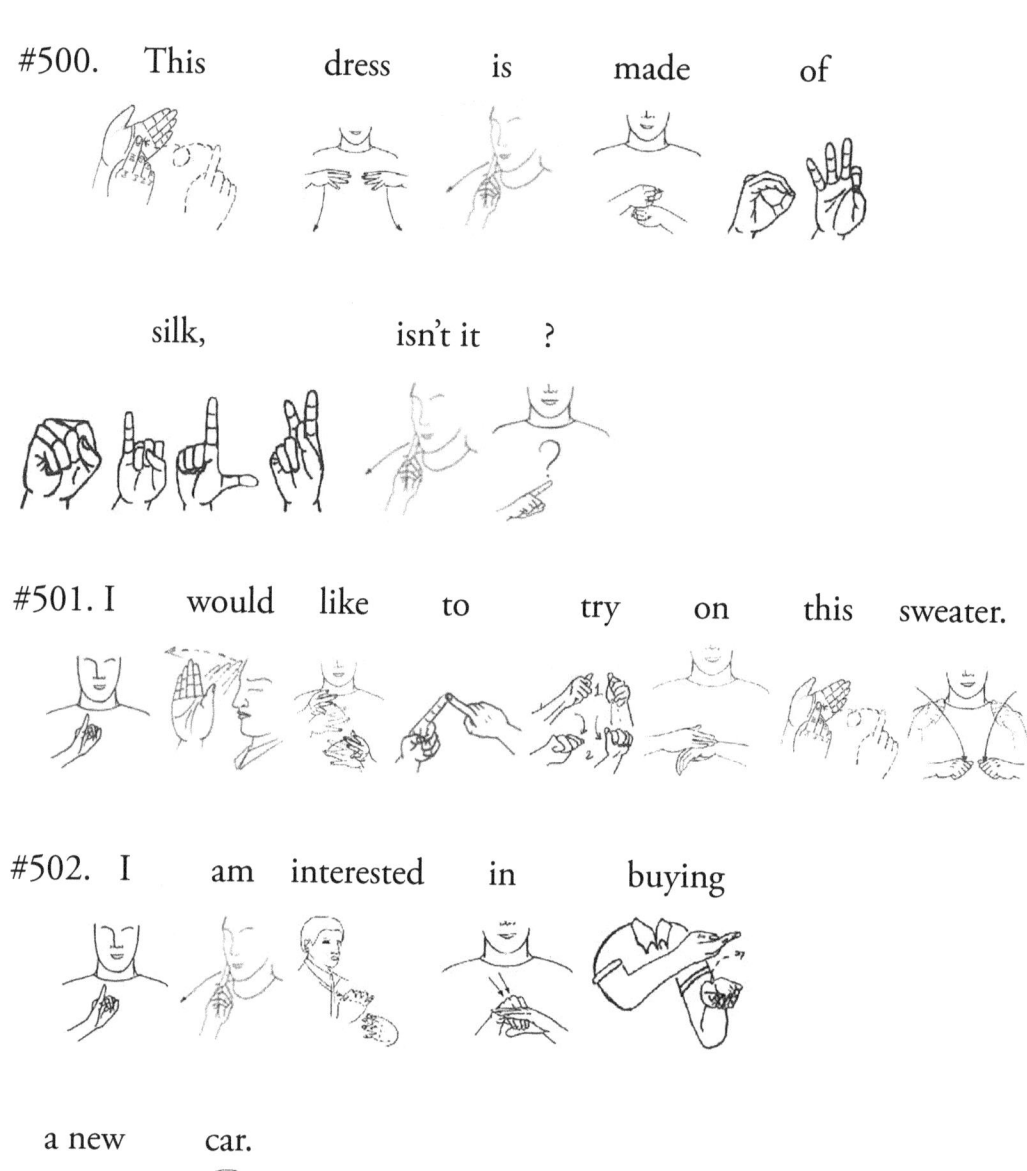

#503. What   is   the price   of   that   electric

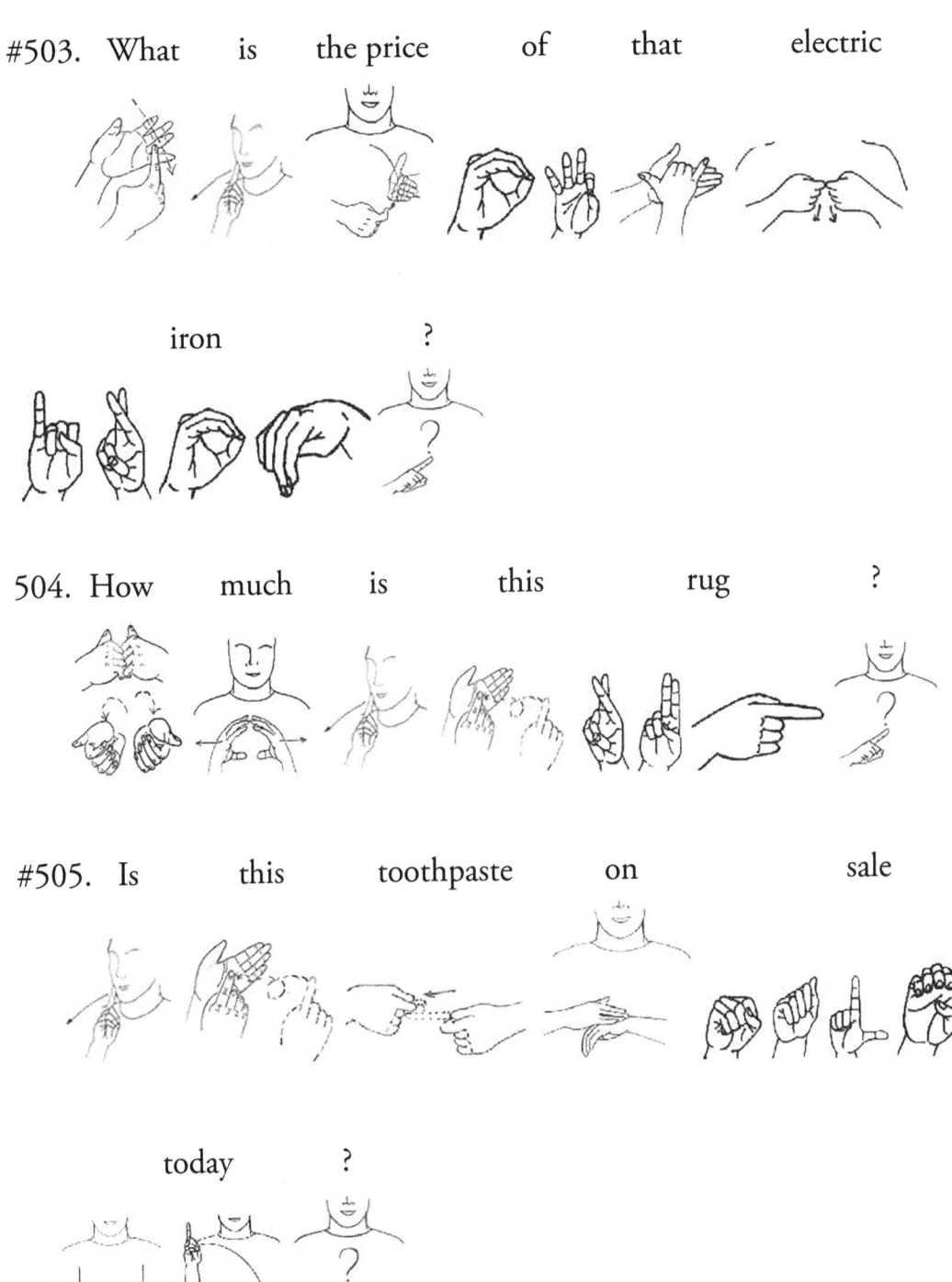

iron   ?

504. How   much   is   this   rug   ?

#505. Is   this   toothpaste   on   sale

today   ?

#506.   That   is   beautiful   leather,   but   it

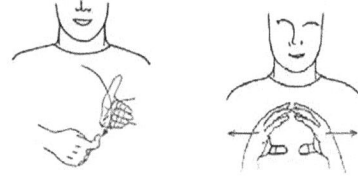

costs   too much.

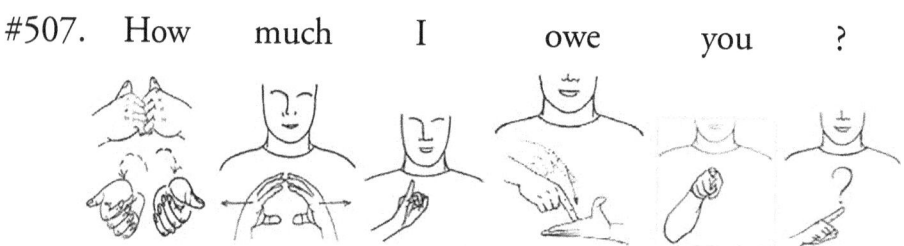

#507.   How   much   I   owe   you   ?

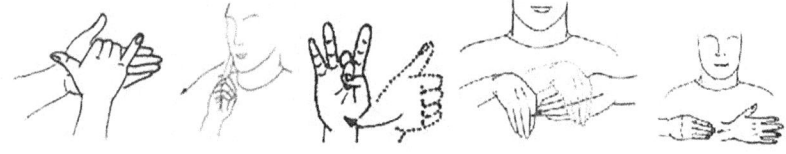

#508.   That   will be   eighteen   dollars   and

cents   seventy-five.

#509. Do   you   have   change   for   twenty

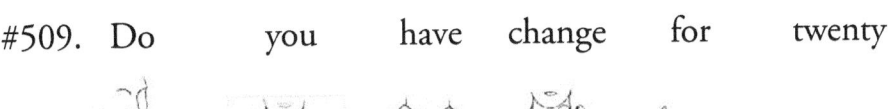

dollar bill   ?

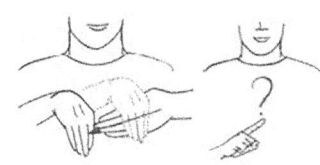

#510. The   sales   person   helped   me   find

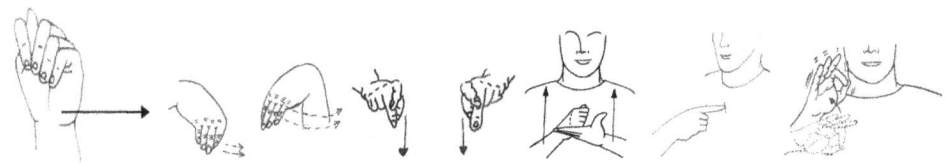

what   I   wanted.

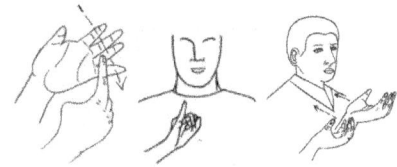

#511. What   would   you   like   to   eat   ?

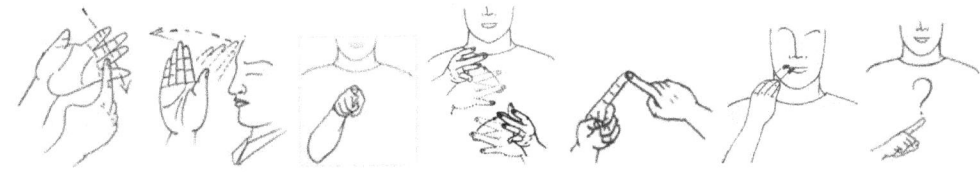

#512. I'd   like   a bowl   of   tomato   soup,   please.

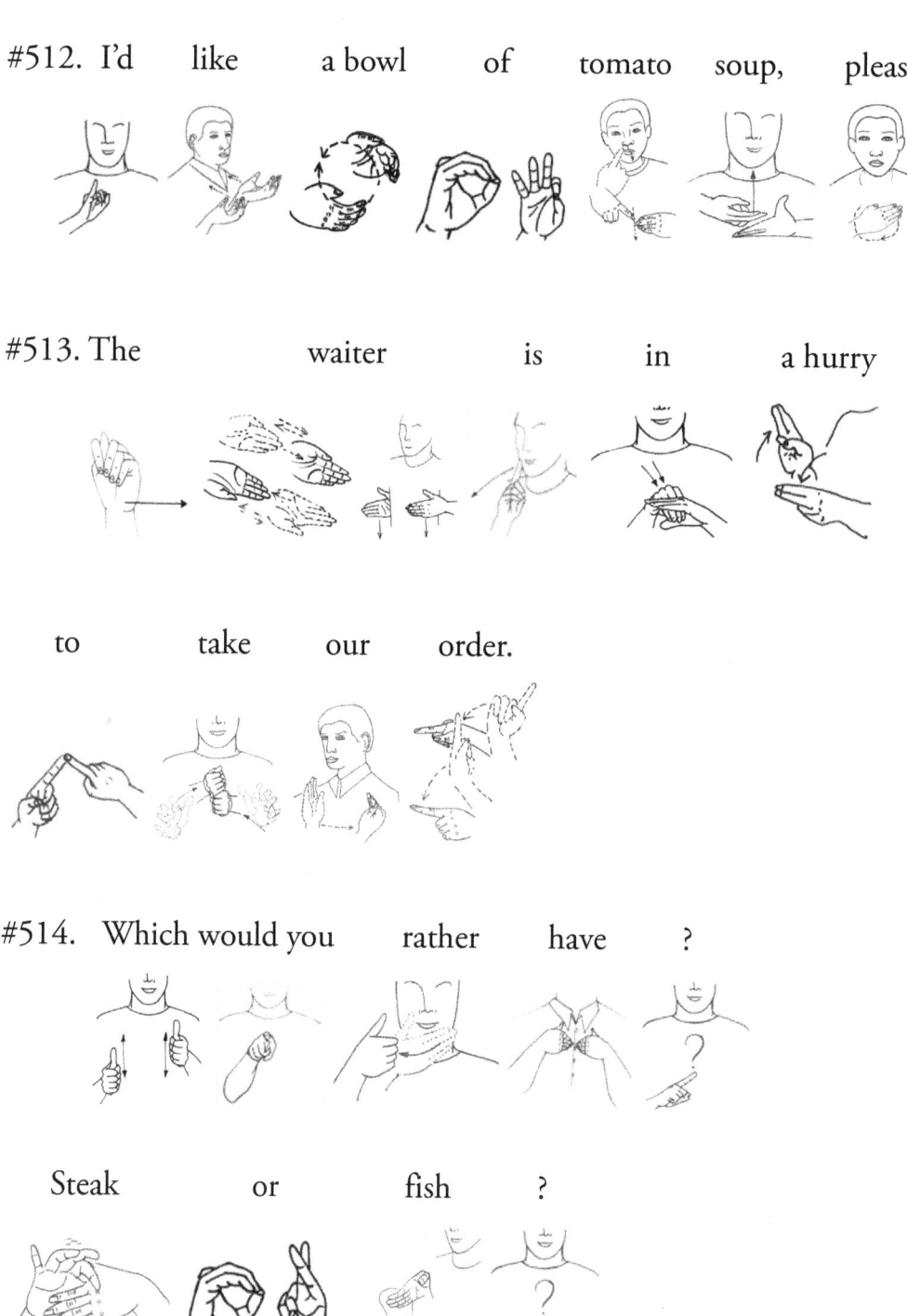

#513. The   waiter   is   in   a hurry

to   take   our   order.

#514.   Which would you   rather   have   ?

Steak   or   fish   ?

#515.   I   want   my   steak   well-done.

#516. What   kinds   vegetables   you   have   ?

#517.   I   will   have   mashed   potatoes

and   beans.

#518. Would   you   please   pass   the salt   ?

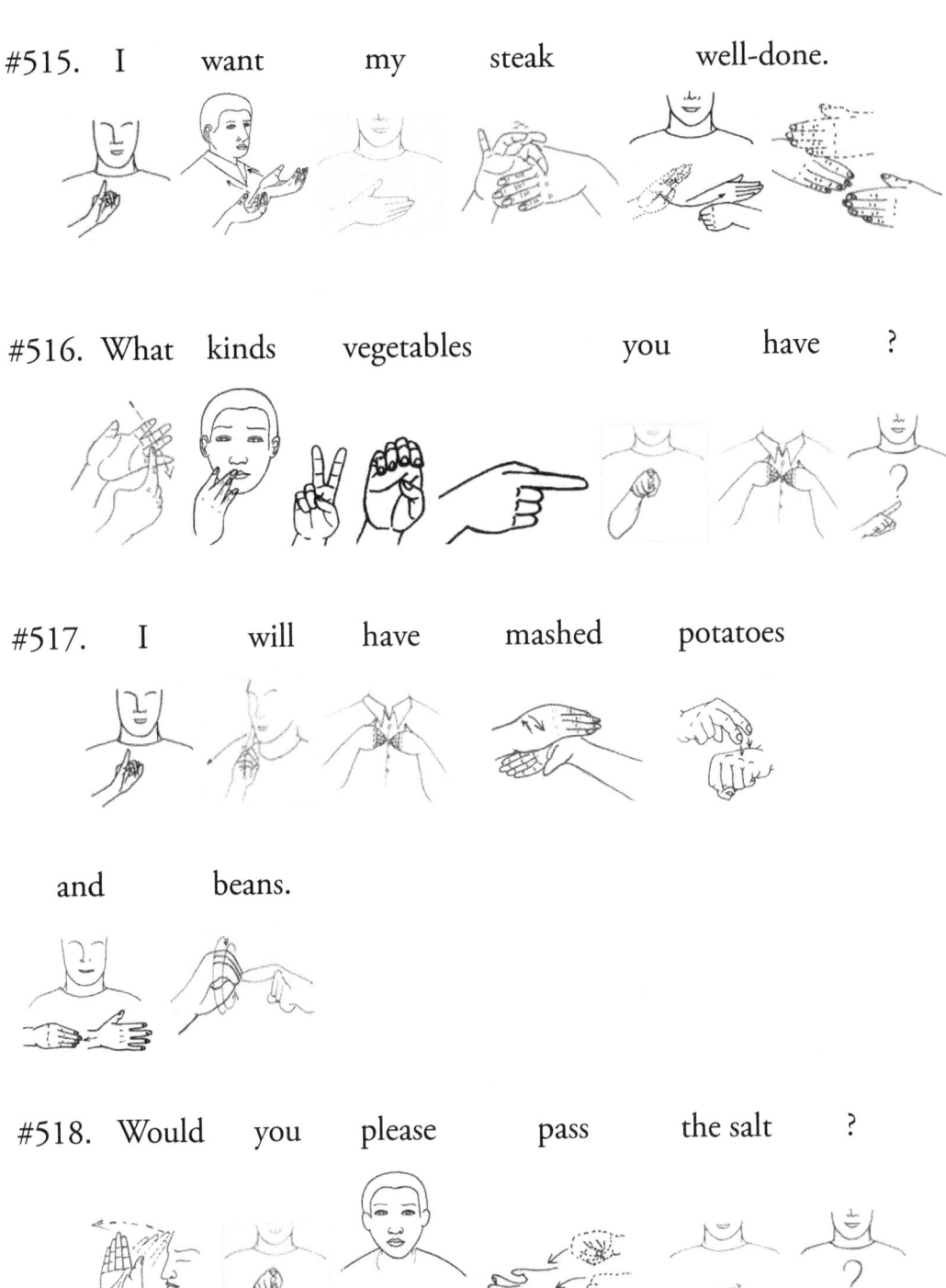

#519. They serve good food in this restaurant.

#520. Are you ready for your dessert

now ?

#521. This knife is dirty Would

you bring me a clean one, please ?

#522. May   I   have   the   check,   please   ?

#523. You   have   your   choice   of   three   flavors

of   ice cream.

#524. We   have   vanilla, chocolate,   and   strawberry.

#525. We   invited   two   guests   to   dinner,

but   they   didn't   come.

#526. How   long   was   the movie   ?

#527. The   feature   started   at   9   o'clock

and   ended   at   11:30.

#528. They   say   the   new   film   is

adventure   story.

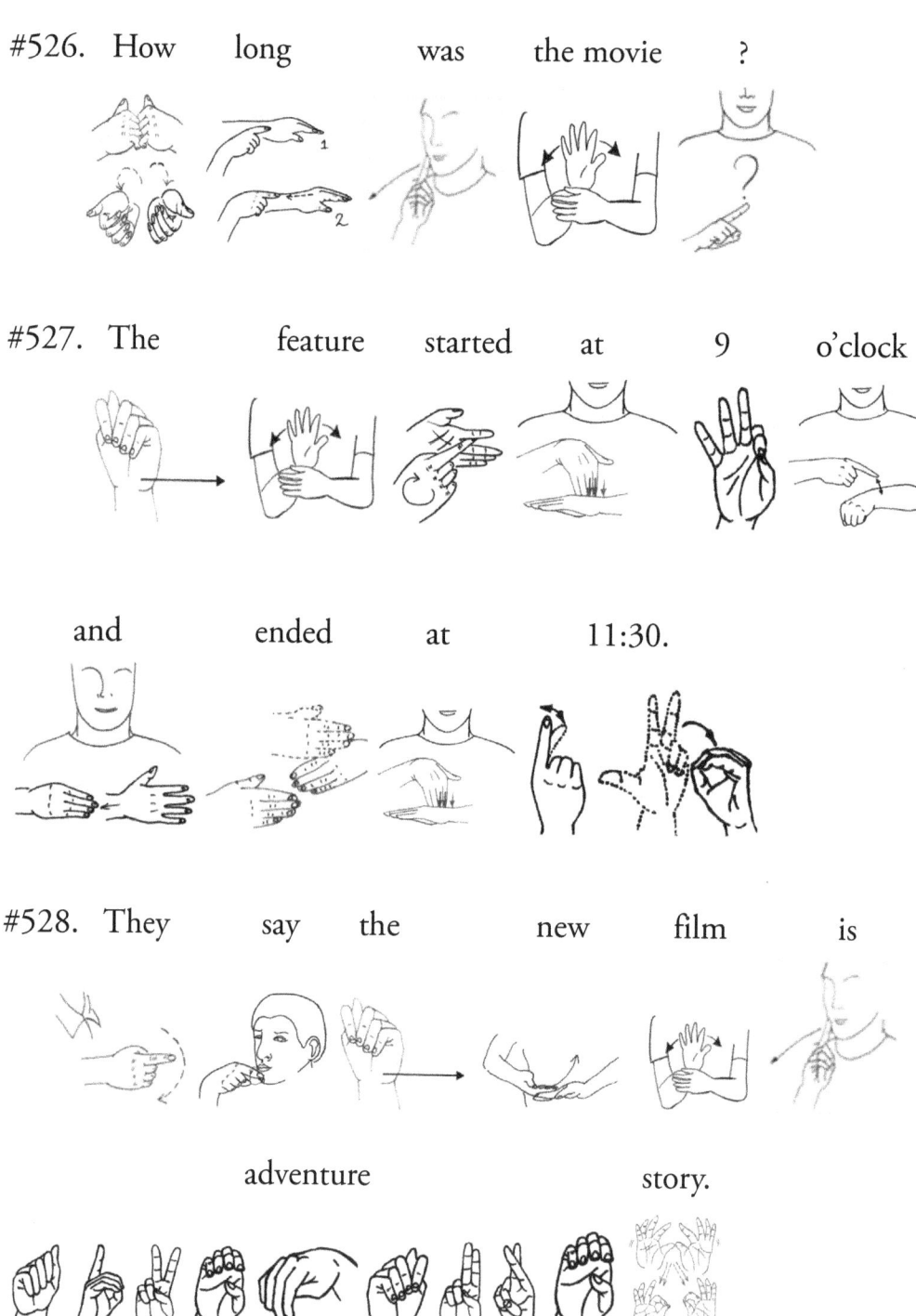

#529. A   group   of   us   went   out   to

the   theater   last   night.

#530. The   new   play   was   good   every

body   enjoyed   it.

#531. By the time   we got there,   play   had already   begun.

#532.   The usher showed   us   to   our   seats.

#533. The   cast   of   the   play   included   a   famous

actor.

#534.   After   the   play   was   over,   we   all

all   wanted   to   get   something   to eat.

#535. There   was   a big   crowd   and   we

had   difficult   time   getting   a taxi.

#536. The   restaurant   filled,   so   we

decided   to go   elsewhere

#537.   My   brother   wants   to   learn   how

to   dance.

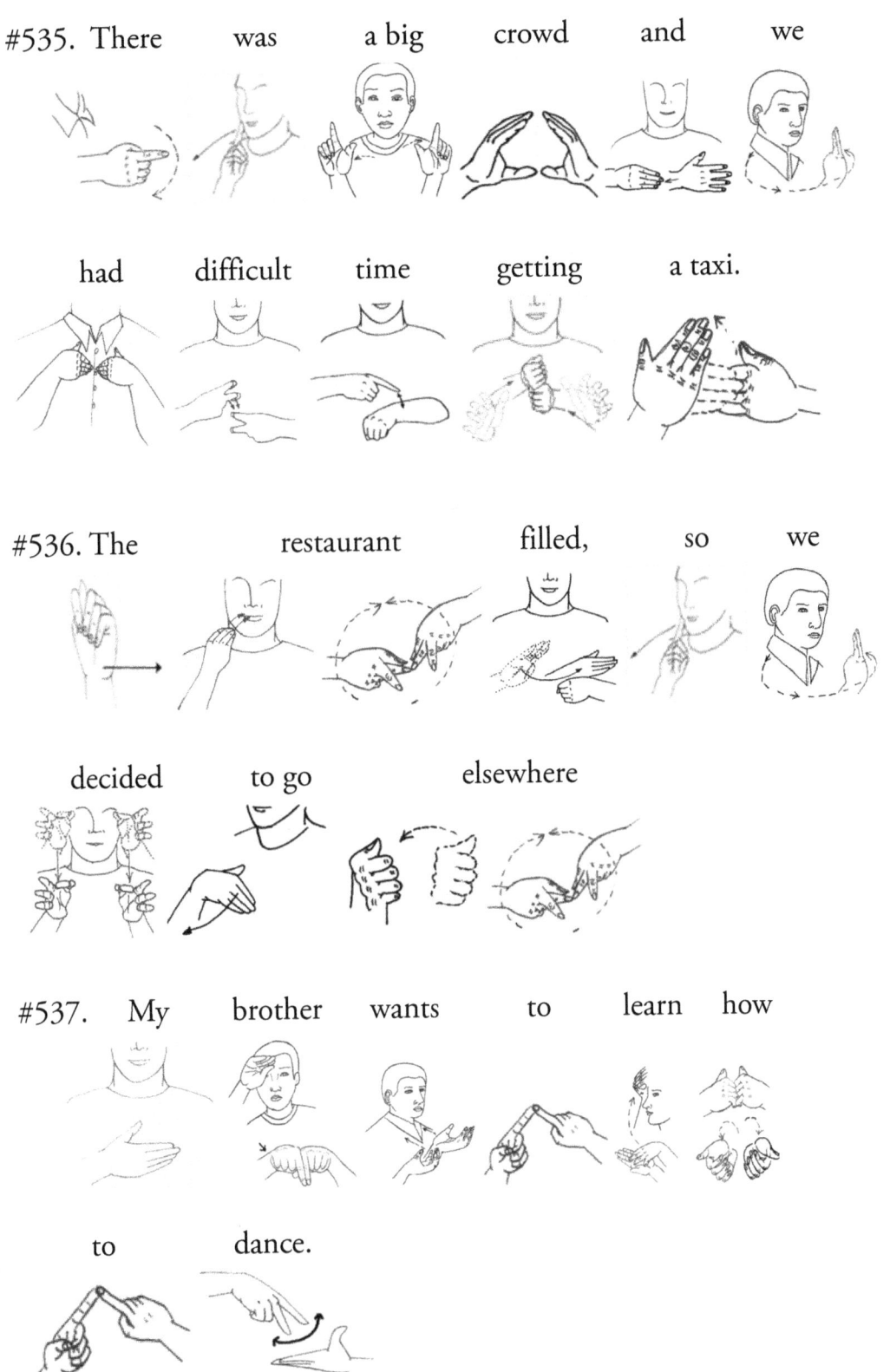

#538. We don't go dancing very often.

#539. Which would you rather do; go

dancing or go to a play ?

#540. I am not accustomed to

going out after dark.

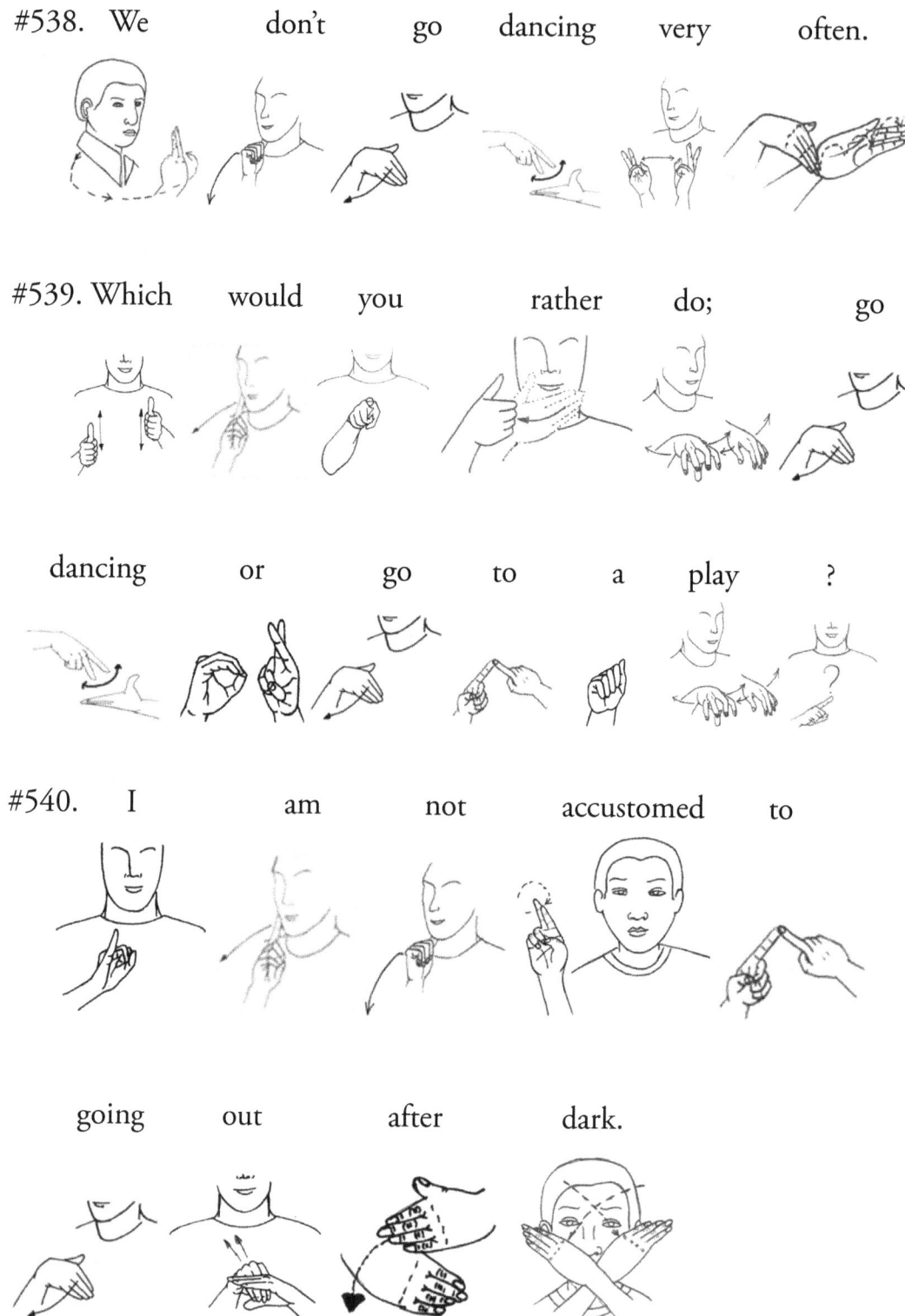

#541. I'd   like   to   make   plan   to

see   Mr.   Cooper.

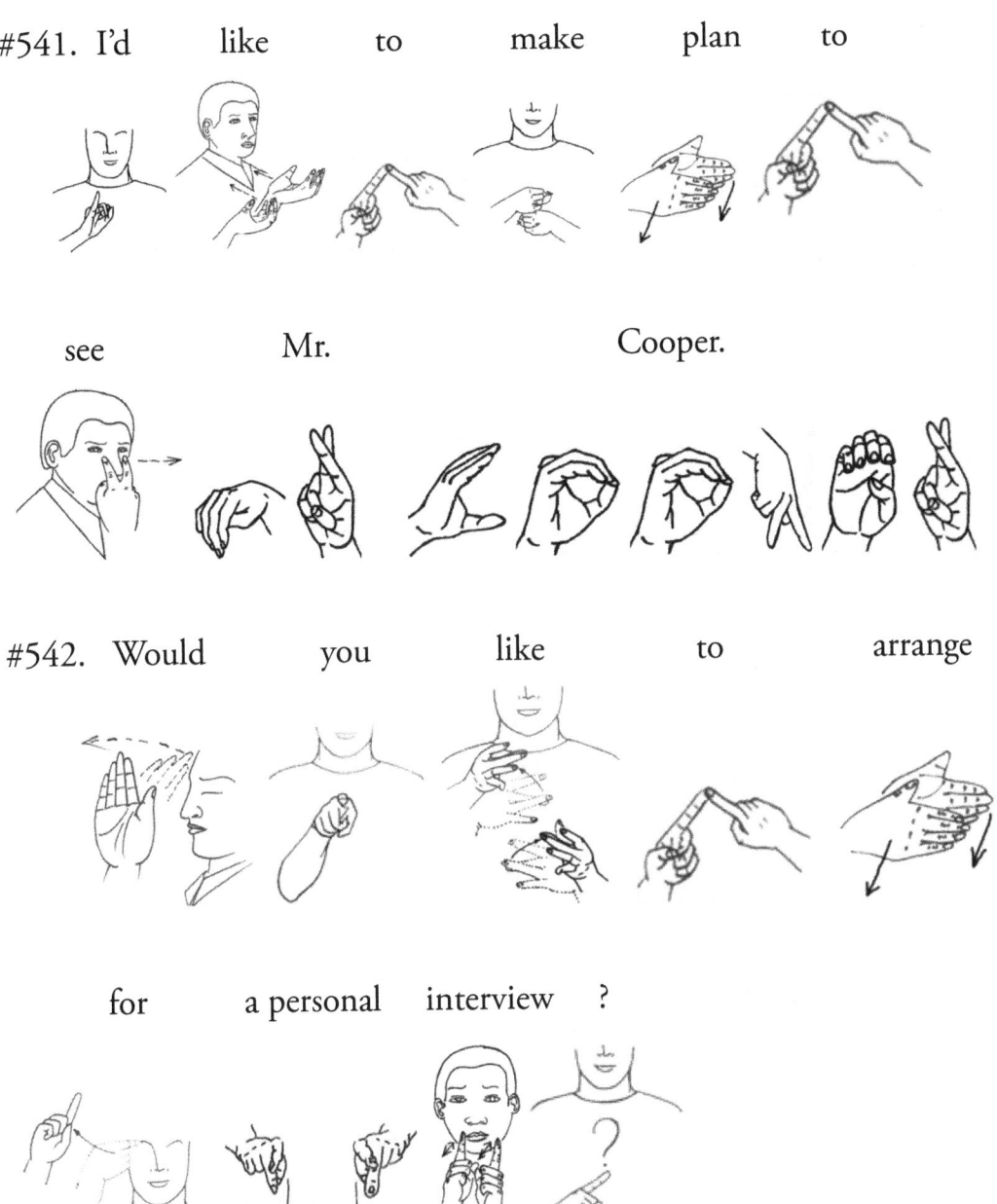

#542. Would   you   like   to   arrange

for   a personal   interview   ?

#543. Your meeting will be next

Thursday at time 10

#544. I can come any day except Thursday.

#545. He wants to change his meeting

from Monday to Wednesday.

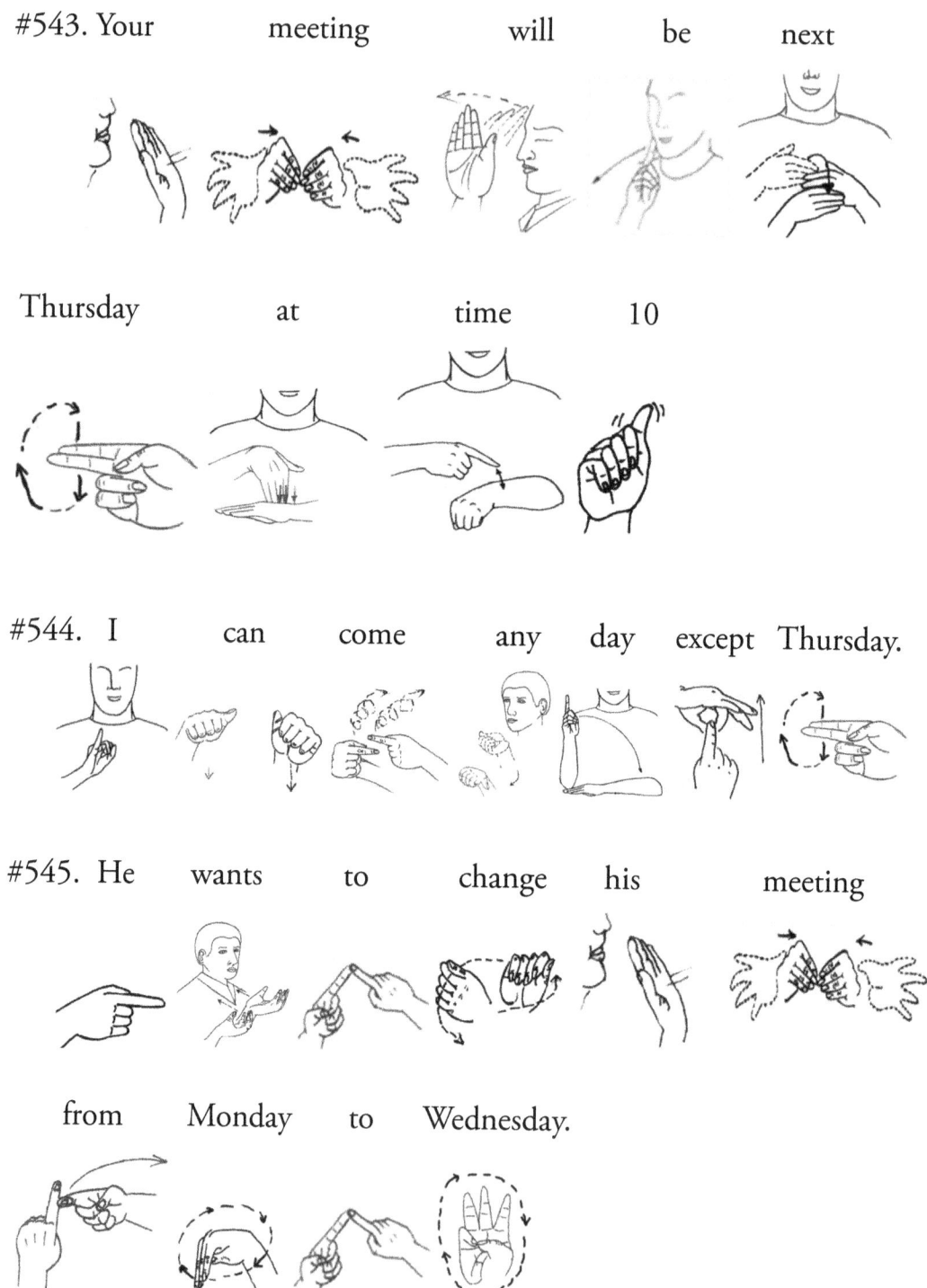

#546. She   did not   call   to   cancel

her   meeting.

#547. I'm   going   to   call   the employment

agency   for   a job.

#548. Please   fill in   this   application.

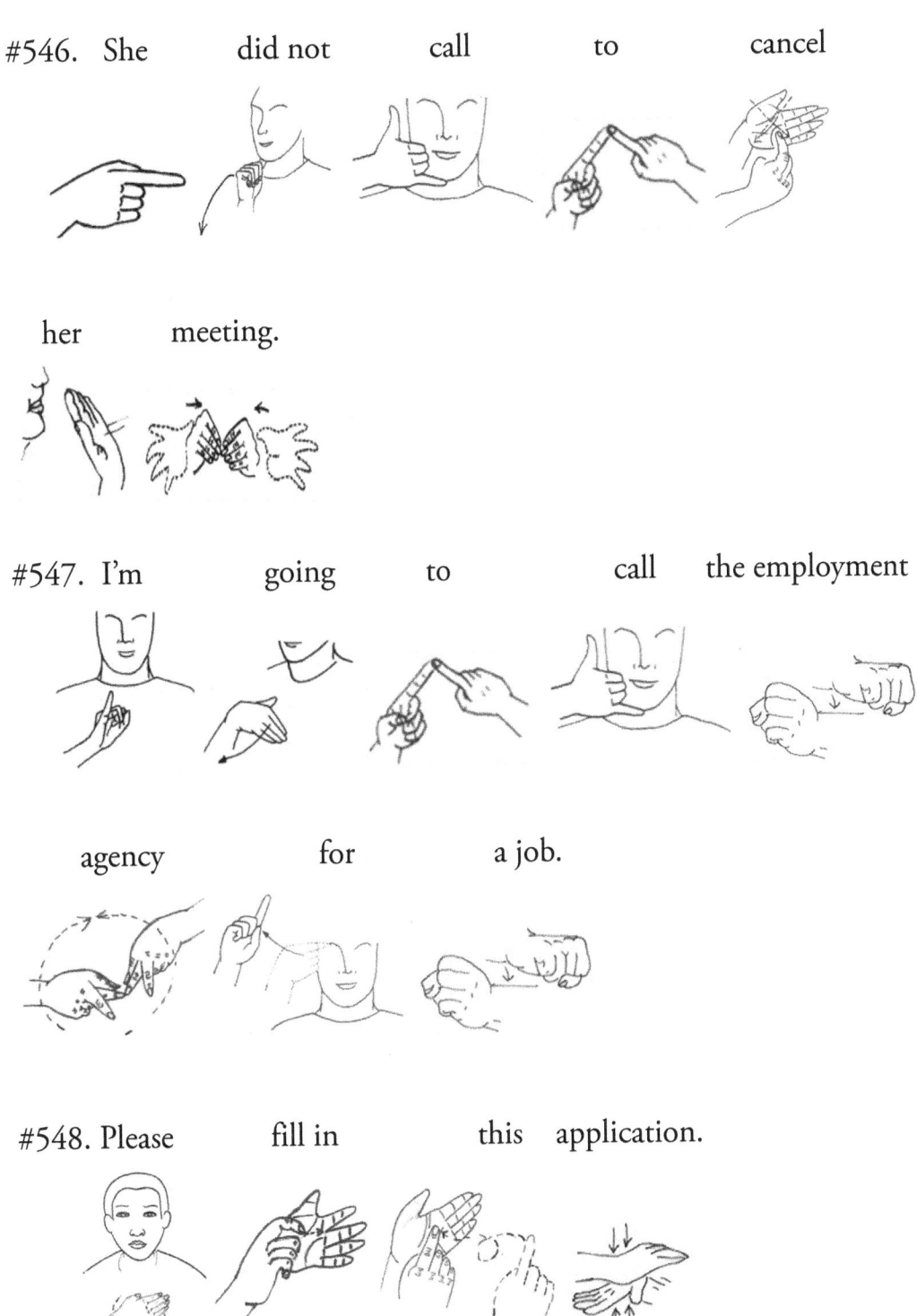

#549. Are   you   looking   for   a permanent position   ?

#550. I   am   calling   plumber

to   come   this   afternoon.

#551. I   couldn't   keep   meeting   because   I was sick.

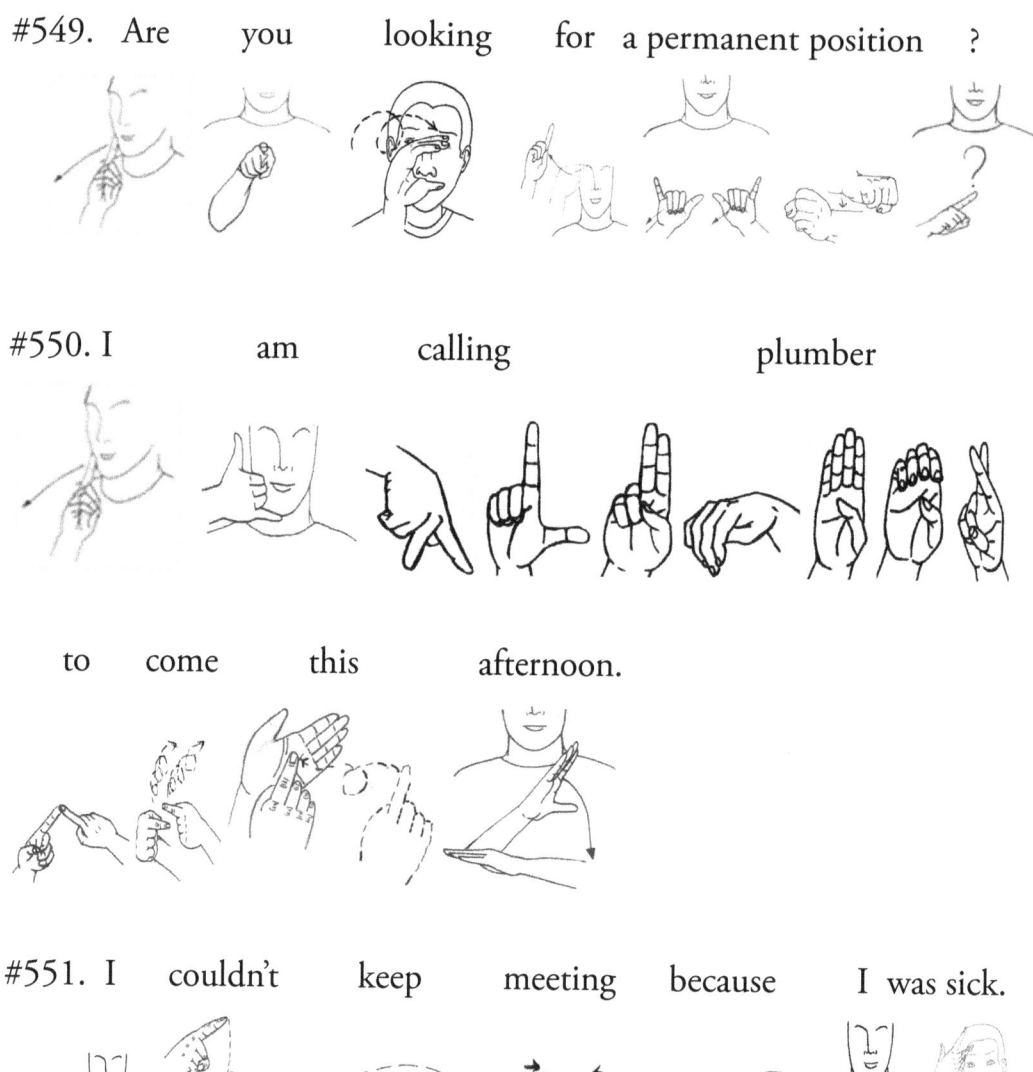

#552.   I   am   a new   employee.

I   was   hired   yesterday.

#553. Please   call   before   you   come,

we   might   not   be home.

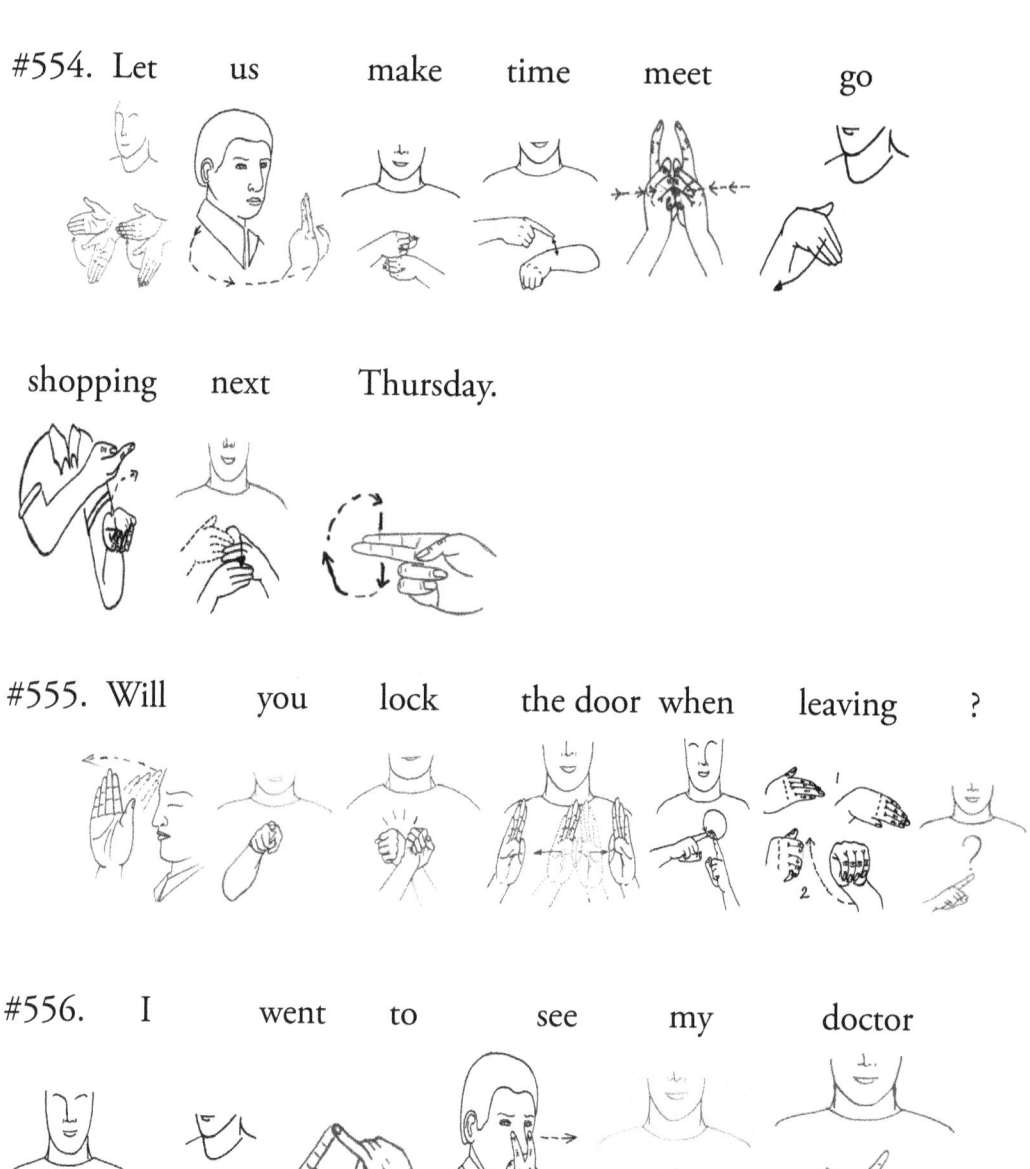

#554. Let   us   make   time   meet   go

shopping   next   Thursday.

#555. Will   you   lock   the door   when   leaving   ?

#556.   I   went   to   see   my   doctor

for   a check-up   yesterday.

#557. The doctor discovered   I'm   a little overweight.

#558. He   gave   me   chest   X-ray

and   took   my   blood   pressure.

#559. He   told   me   take pills   every   four   hours.

#560. Do   you   think   the patient can   be   cured   ?

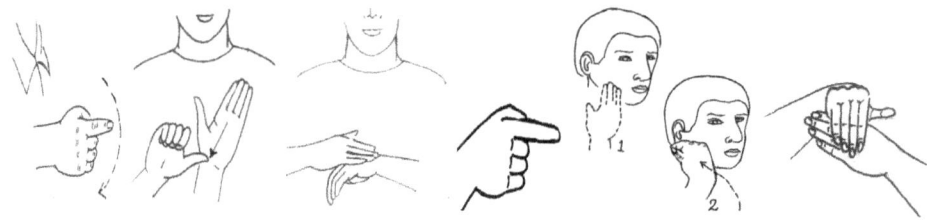

#561. They   operated   on   him   last   night.

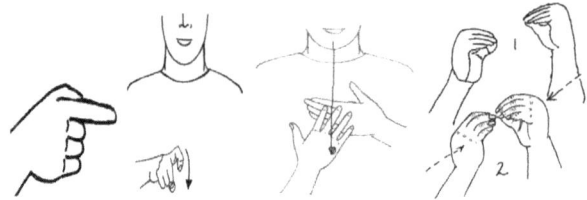

#562. He   needed   a blood   transfusion.

#563. My   uncle   had   a heart attack   last   year.

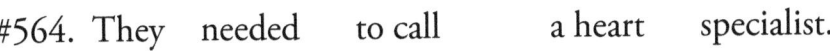

#564. They needed   to call   a heart   specialist.

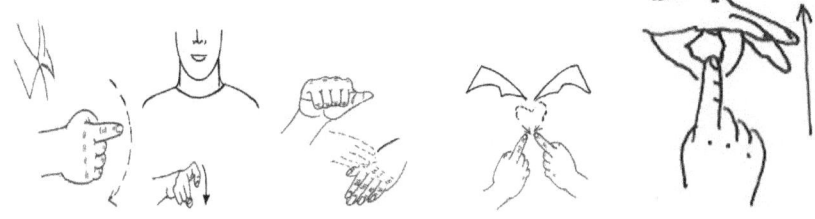

#565. What   did   the doctor   say   ?

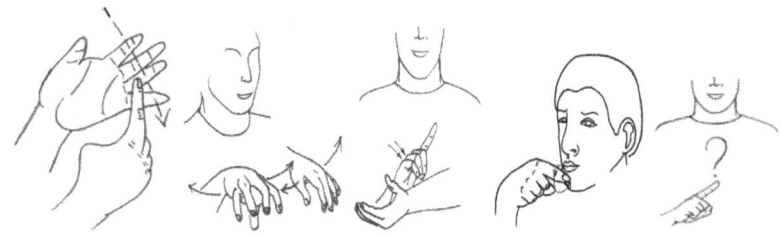

#566. The doctor advised   me   to   get   plenty

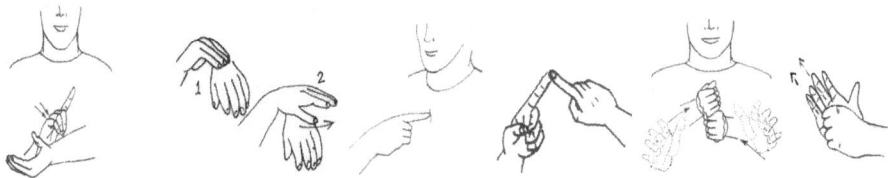

of exercise.

#567. The doctor said I look pale.

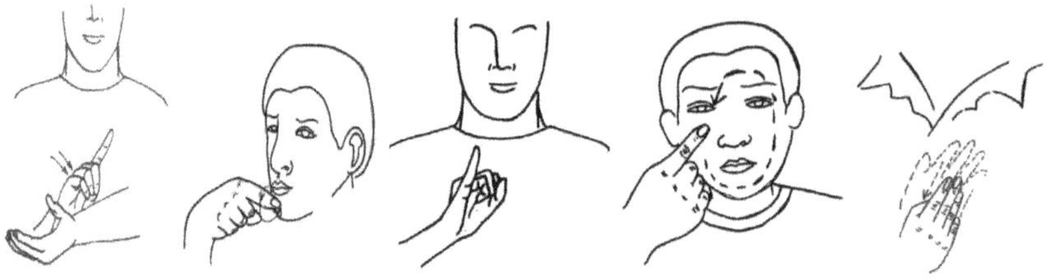

#568. If I want to be healthy

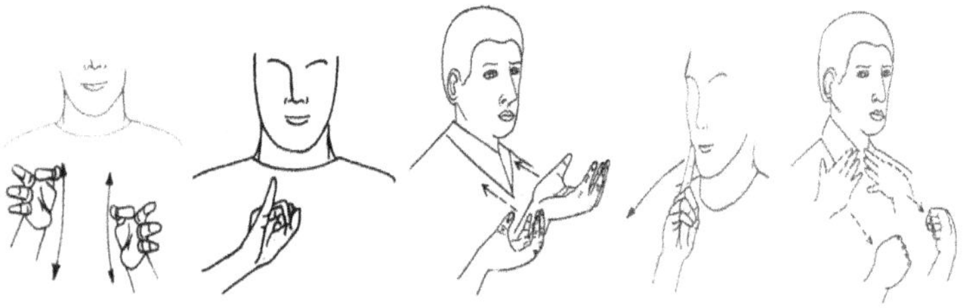

I need stop cigarettes.

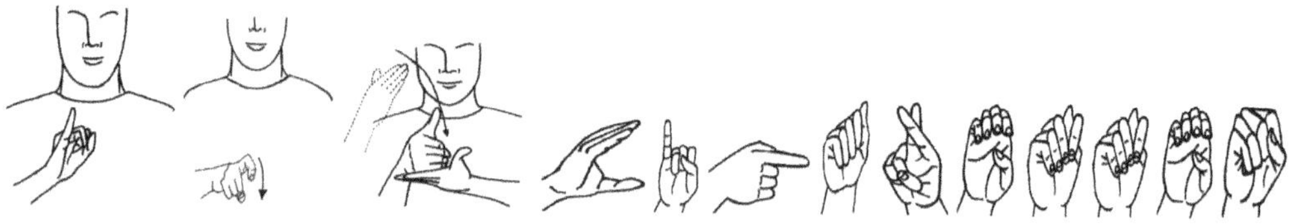

#569. The physician said smoking is harmful to my health.

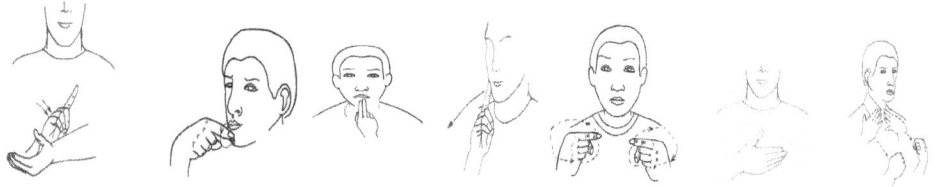

#570. It's   mosquito bite.   There's nothing to worry   about.

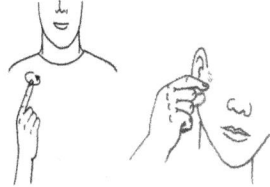 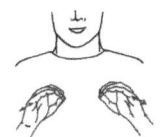  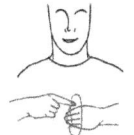

#571. Telephone wants   you.

#572. What   dial to   phone operator   ?

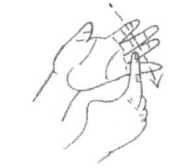   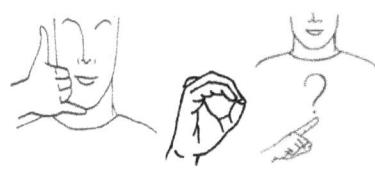

#573. I   want   to make   a long distance   call.

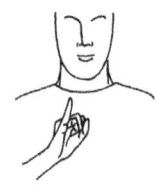  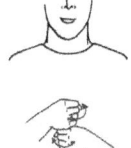  

#574. Pick up   the receiver   and   deposit a coin   in the slot.

  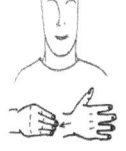 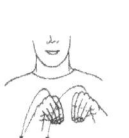 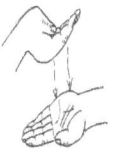 

#575.   I   tried   to call   Mr.   Cooper,

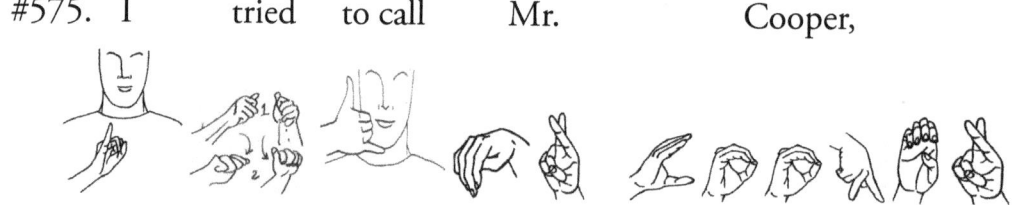

but   the line was busy.

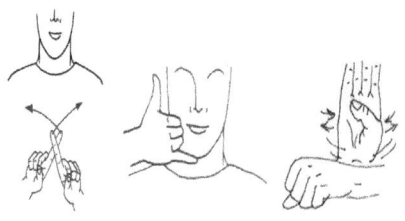

#576. You   must   wrong called.

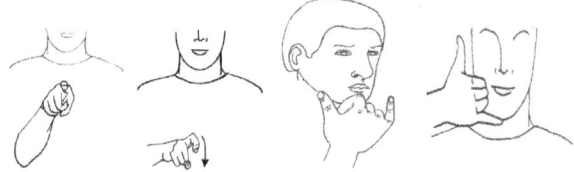

#577. I   dialed   the right, but   nobody   answered.

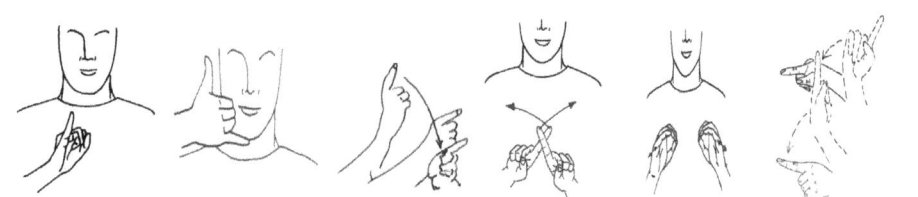

#578. Telephone is ringing.   Would   you

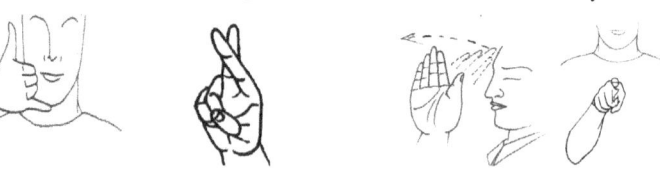

answer it, please   ?

#579. Would   you   like   to   leave   a message   ?

#580. Who   is   this   ?   I   don't   recognize   your   voice.

#581. Would   you   please   tell   Mr.

Cooper   I   called   ?

#582.   Is   this   5   4   0   9   3   ?

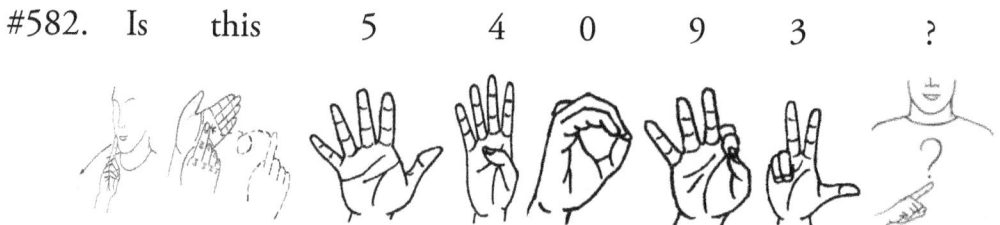

#583.   I   must   hang up   now.

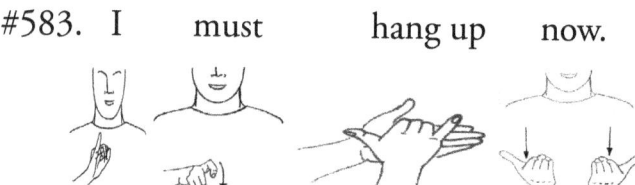

#584.   I   can't   hear   you.

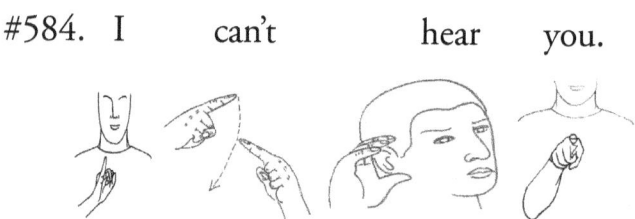

#585.   Would   you   mind   calling   back   tomorrow ?

#586.   How   long   since   you've   heard

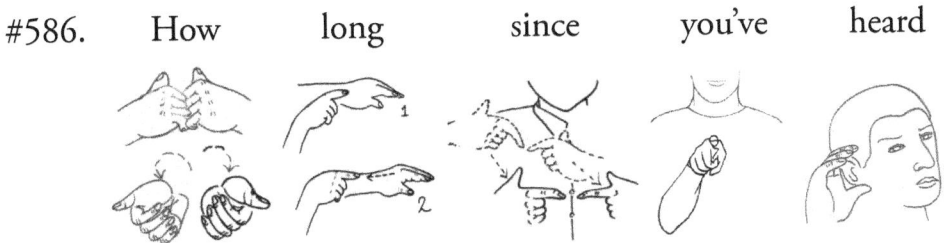

from   your   uncle?

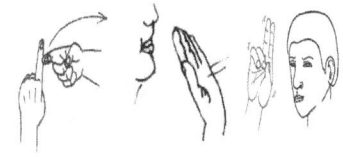

#587. When was the last   time   he   wrote   you   ?

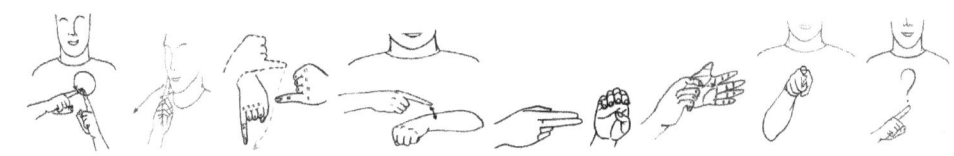

#588. I   can't   recall   how   long   it's been.

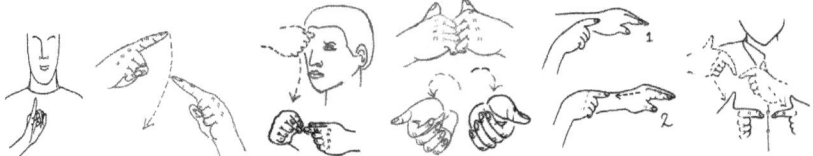

#589. I'm   always   disappointed   when   I   don't   get

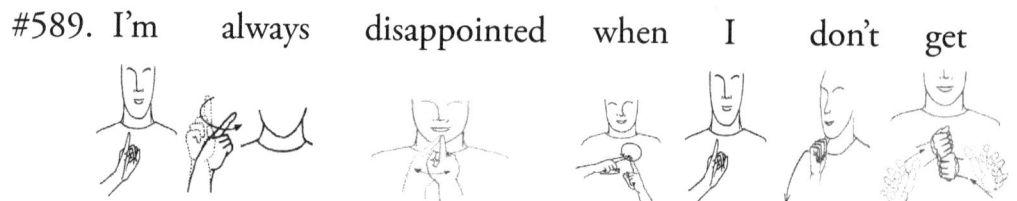

any   mail.

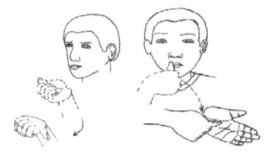

#590. I   feel   guilty   because   I   haven't

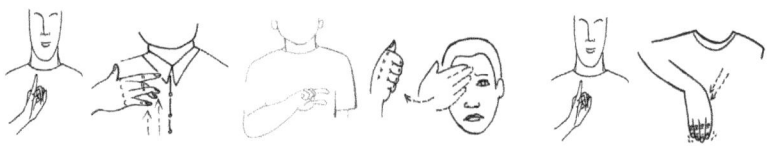

written   her.

#591. What time   is the mail   delivered   on

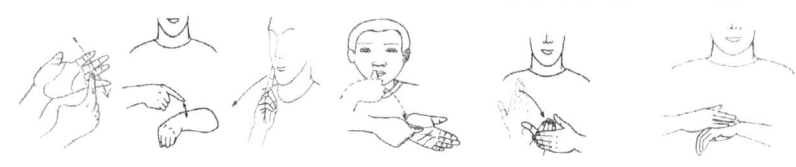

Saturday   ?

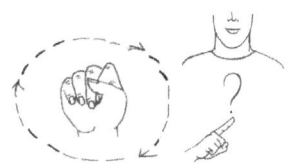

#592. The   postman   always   comes at   3   o'clock.

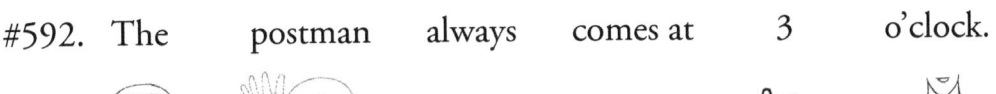

#593. I   wrote   to   my   uncle   last   night.

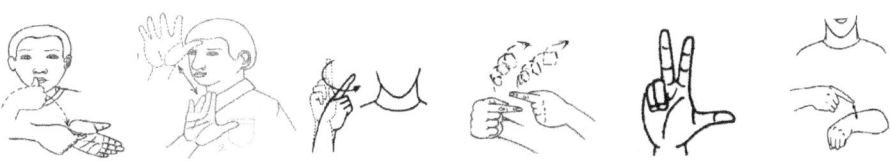

#594. I   enclosed some photographs   in   my   letter.

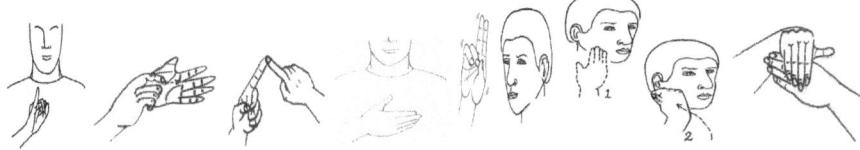

#595. I   didn't   know   whether   to   send   letter

airmail   or   not.

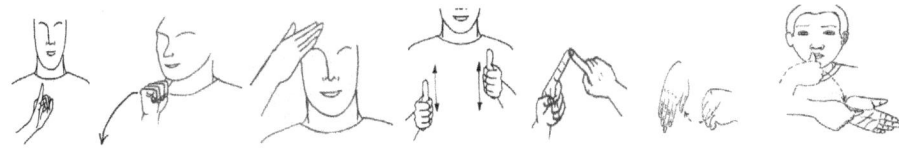

#596. How   long   for   a letter   to get   to California   ?

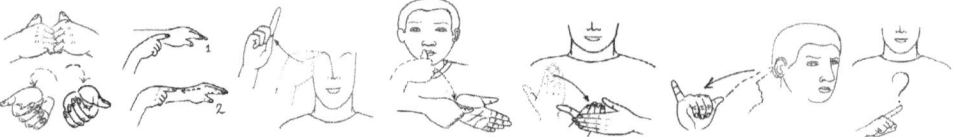

#597. Don't forget   to put   on   stamps   before you   mail it.

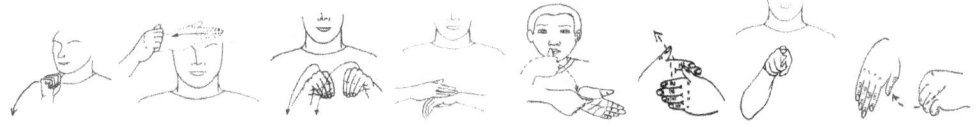

#598.   He   went   to   the post office to mail   a letter.

599.   I   dropped   the letter   in   mail   box.

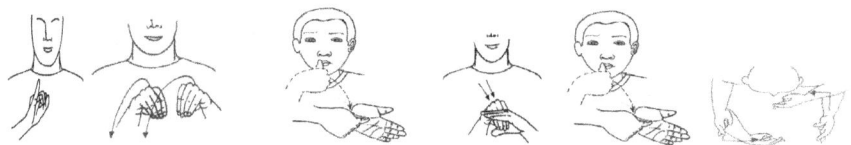

#600. Did   you   write   and   sign   the letter   ?

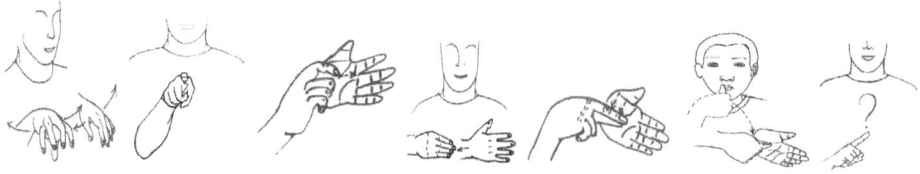

#601. A strange thing   happened   to   me   this   morning.

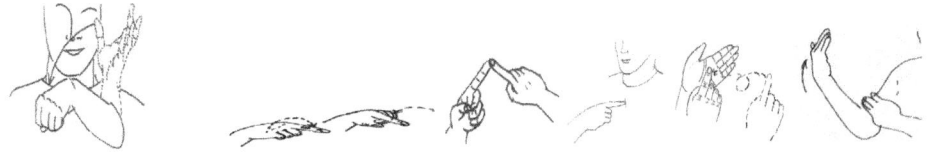

#602. I was   crossing the   street   and   was almost   hit

by a   car.

#603.   I   jumped back in   time to   not be   hit.

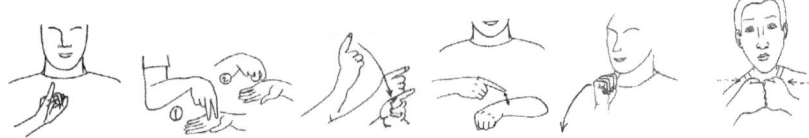

#604. It was a terrible experience,   and   I   won't   forget it.

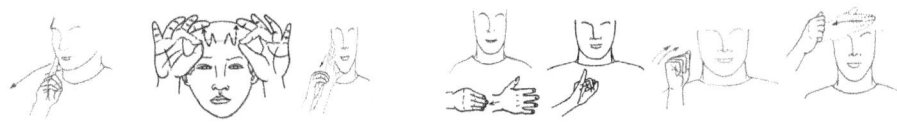

#605. Yesterday   was such a beautiful day   we   decided   to

go for a   drive.

#606. We   prepared a   picnic   lunch

by the river.

#607. After a while, we   found a   shady   place

under   some   trees.

#608. On the way   home,   we   had a   flat   tire.

#609. After   dark   we   arrived home,   and

we   were all   tired.

#610. I   wish you would   explain more about   your   trip.

#611. Did   I   tell you   about   my

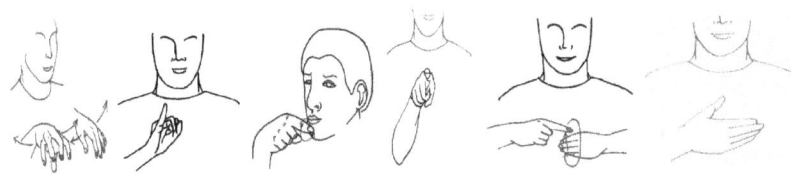

travel   experience   ?

#612. We   used to   have   a lot   of fun   when

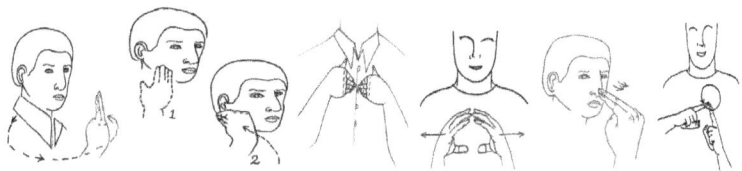

we were   that   age.

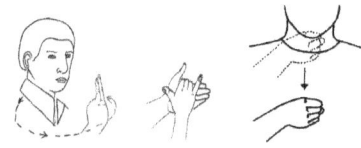

#613. I   can't   recall   exactly   what   happened.

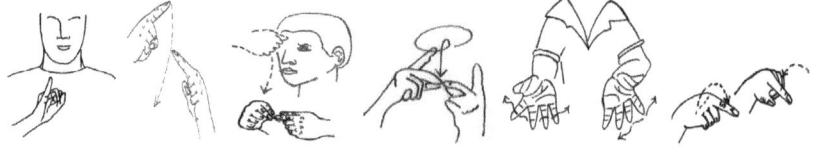

#614. I   never   realized   some   day   I   would

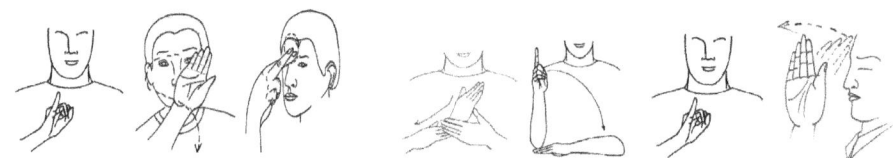

be   living   in   New York.

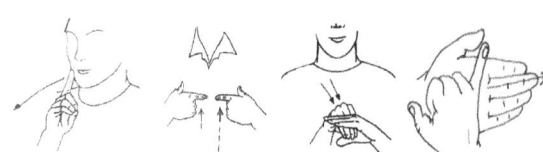

#615. We   never   imagined   John   would

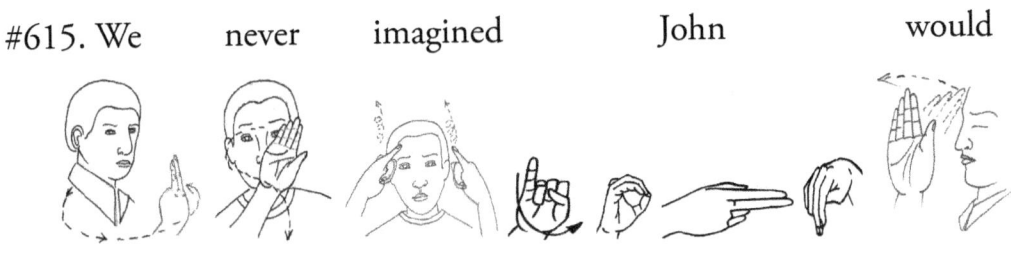

become a   doctor.

#616. We're looking   for a house   to   rent   for the summer.

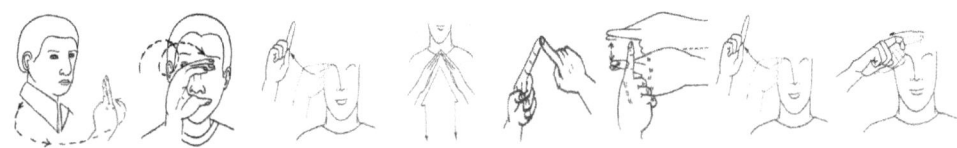

#617. Are   you   trying   to   find   a   furniture

house   ?

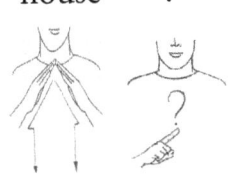

#618. This   split-level   house   is   for   rent.

It   is   a bargain.

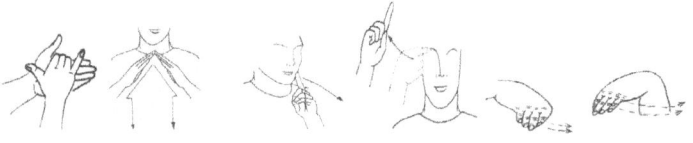

#619. That house   is   for   sale.

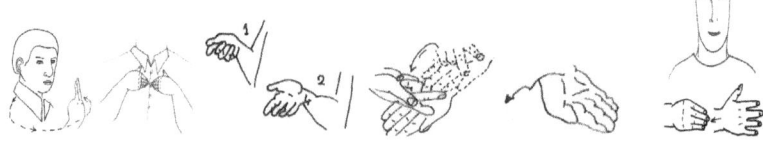

#620. We   have   a few   kitchen   things   and

a dining room   set.

#621. This   is an   interesting floor   plan.   Please   show

me   the   basement.

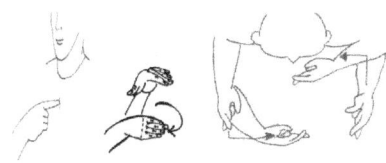

#622.   The front   steps   need   to be fixed.

#623.   We   need   to   get   a bed   and

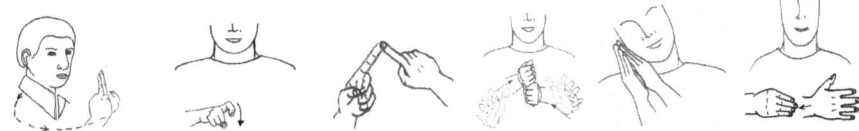

a dresser   for the bedroom.

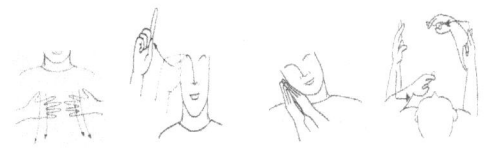

#624.   Does the back   door   have   a lock   ?

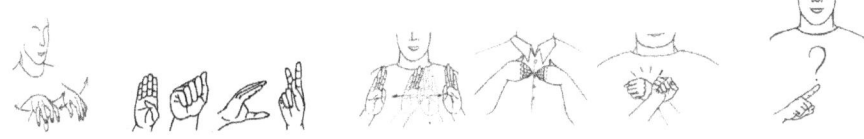

#625. They've   already   turned on the electricity.

 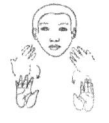 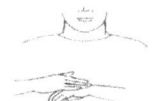 

The house   is   ready.

#626.   I   am   worried   about   the appearance   of

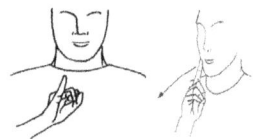  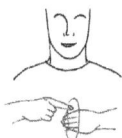 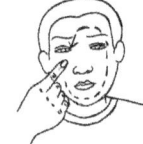 

the floor.

#627.   If   you   want   a towel,   look   in

   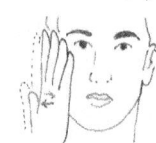  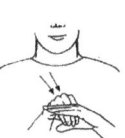

that   closet.

 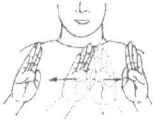

 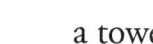 

#628. What style furniture do you have ?

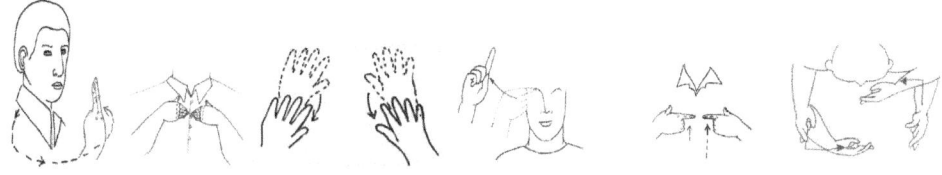

#629. We have drapes for the living room.

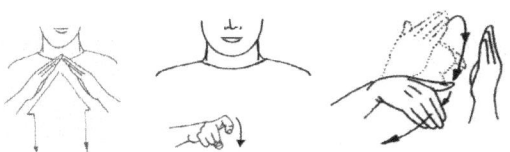

#630. The house needs painting.

#631. What are you planning to wear

today ?

#632.   I   am   planning to   wear   my

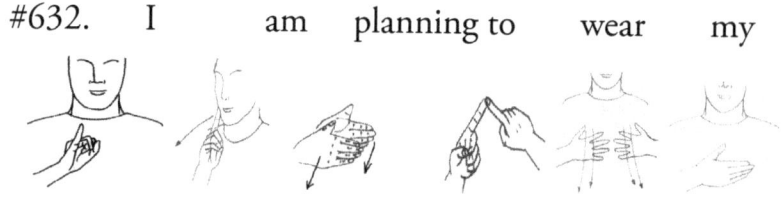

blue   suit.

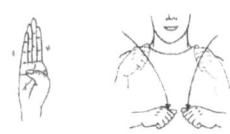

#633. I   have   two   suits   to   send

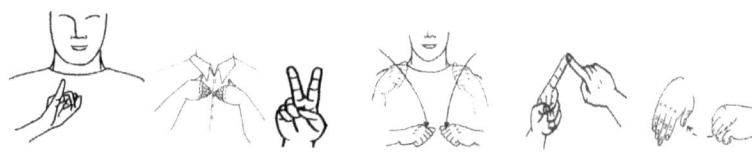

to   the cleaners.

#634. I   have   some   shirts   to   send   to the laundry.

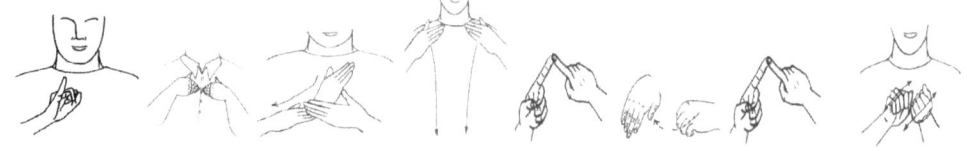

#635. You ought to have that coat cleaned.

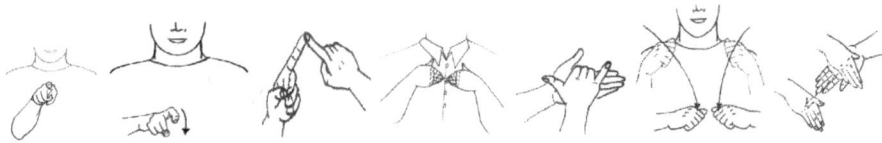

#636. I've got to have this shirt washed.

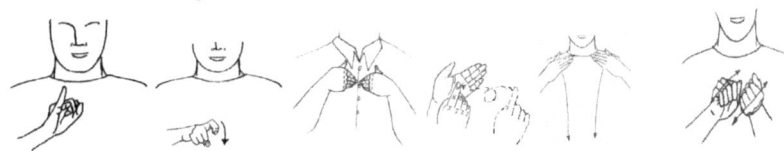

#637. All my suits are dirty.

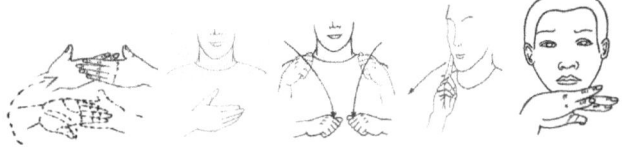

#638. You'd better wear a light jacket it's

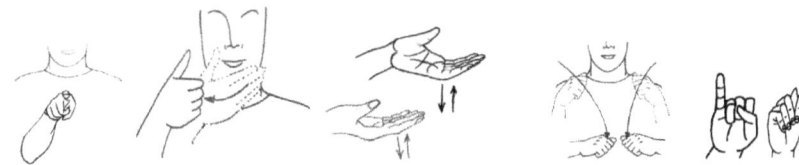

chilly today.

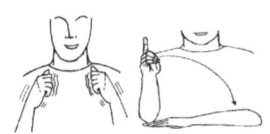

#639. This   dress   doesn't   fit   me

any   more.

#640.   I   guess   I   have   grown   out

of   these   trousers.

#641. These   shoes   are   worn-out.

They've   lasted   a long   time.

#642.   I   can't   use   this   coat.

#643. Why   don't you   get   dressed   now   ?

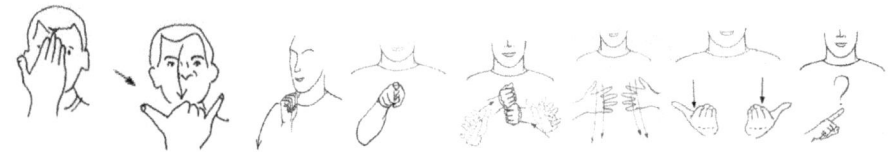

Put on   your   work   clothes.

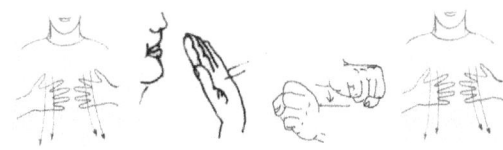

#644. My   brother   came   in,   changed   his

clothes,   and   went   out   again.

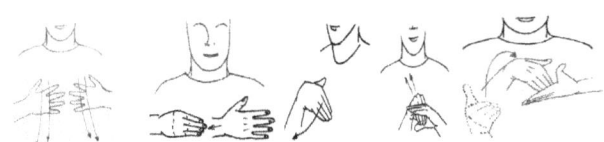

#645.   I   didn't   notice   your   new   hat.

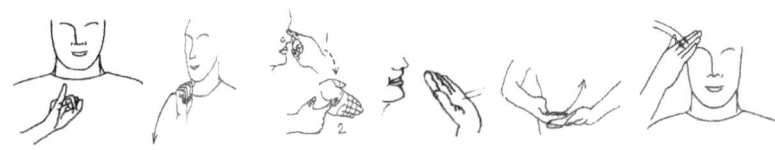

#646. You   have   your   idea,   and   I

have   mine.

#647. Your   approach   is   a different   way   than

I   do.

#648. I   won't   argue   with   you,   but

I   think   you   are   not   fair.

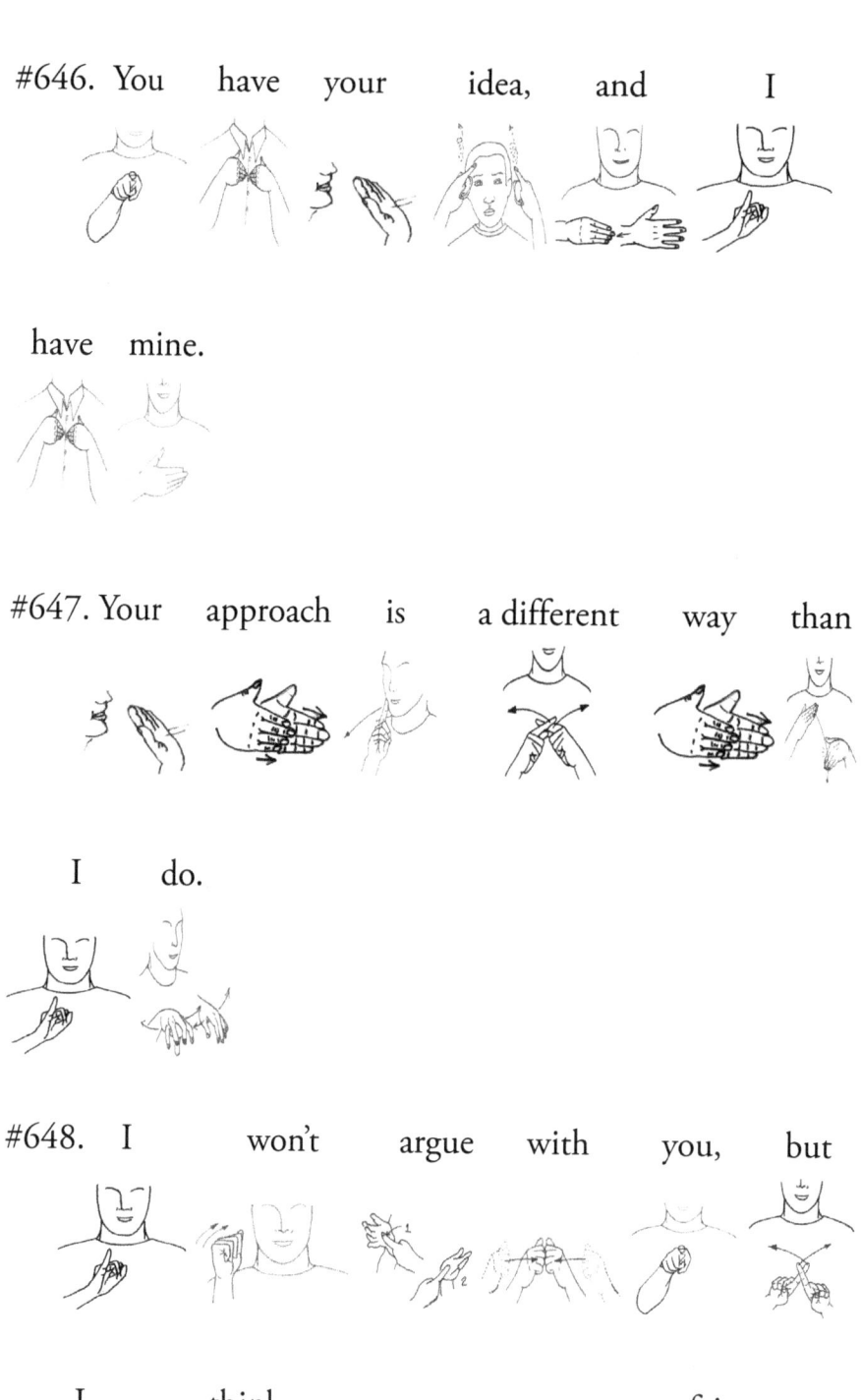

#649. That   is   an opposite   way   of   thought.

#650. He   does   have   a lot   of strange   ideas.

#651. I   don't see   any   point   in discussing   further.

#652. What   other   do   I   have   ?

#653.   Everyone   does   have   his own   opinion.

#654. There are   always   two   sides   to   every   thing.

#655. We   have   opposite   views   on   this.

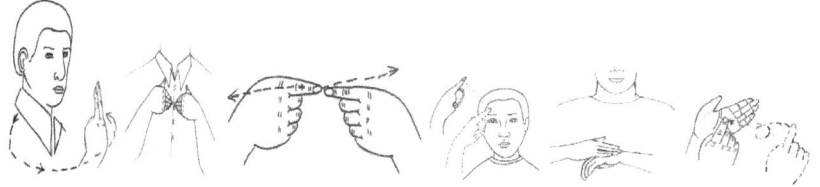

#656. Please   forgive   me   I   didn't   mean   to

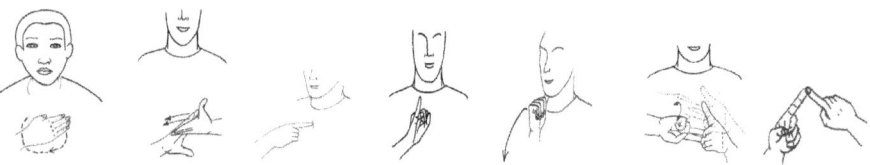

start an   argument.

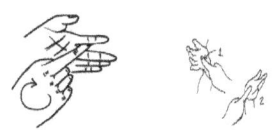

#657. I   must   know   your   opinion   Do   you   agree

with   me   ?

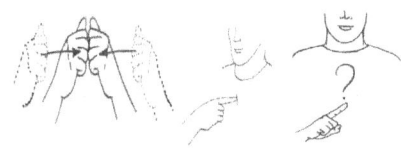

#658. What   is   your   idea   ?

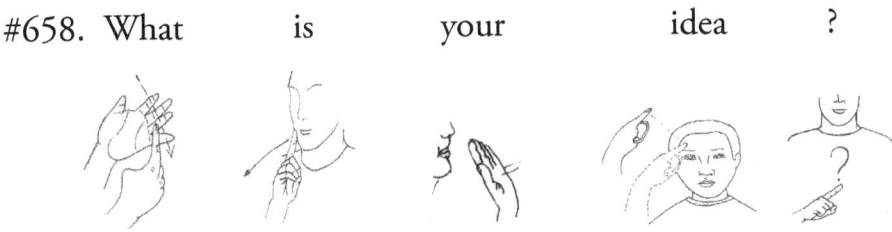

#659. Our   ideas   are   not so far   apart.

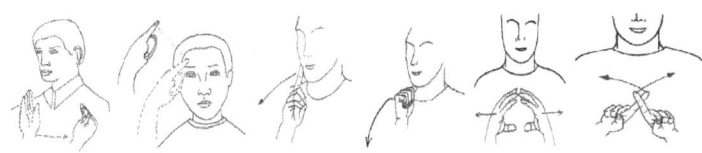

#660. We   can   resolve   our differences.

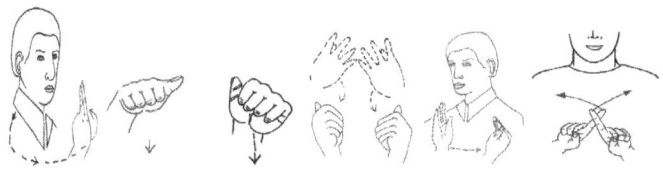

#661. If it   doesn't   rain   tomorrow,   I   think

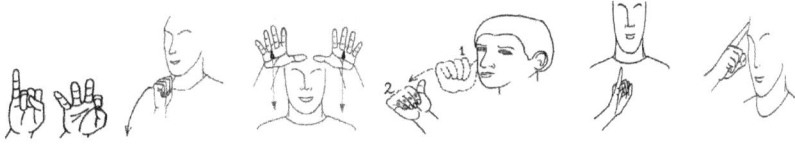

I'll   go   shopping.

#662. Maybe we'll go, but depending on the weather.

#663. If I have time tomorrow, I think

I'll get a haircut.

#664. I must remember to ask the barber

not to make my cut too short.

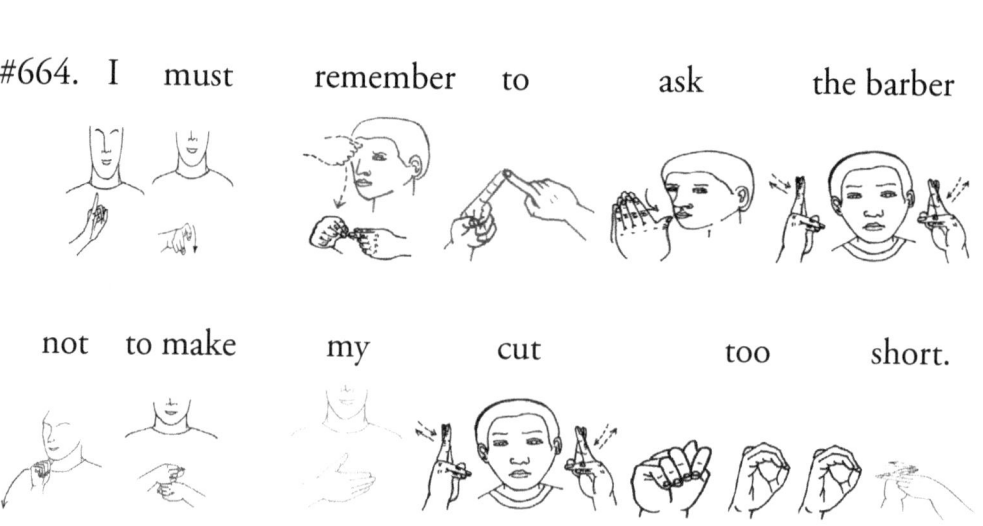

#665. My   son   wants   to   be   a policeman when

he grows   up.

#666. If   I   finish   my   work ,

I   will   leave   for   New York   Monday

#667. Suppose   you   couldn't   go   on   the trip,

how   would   you   feel   ?

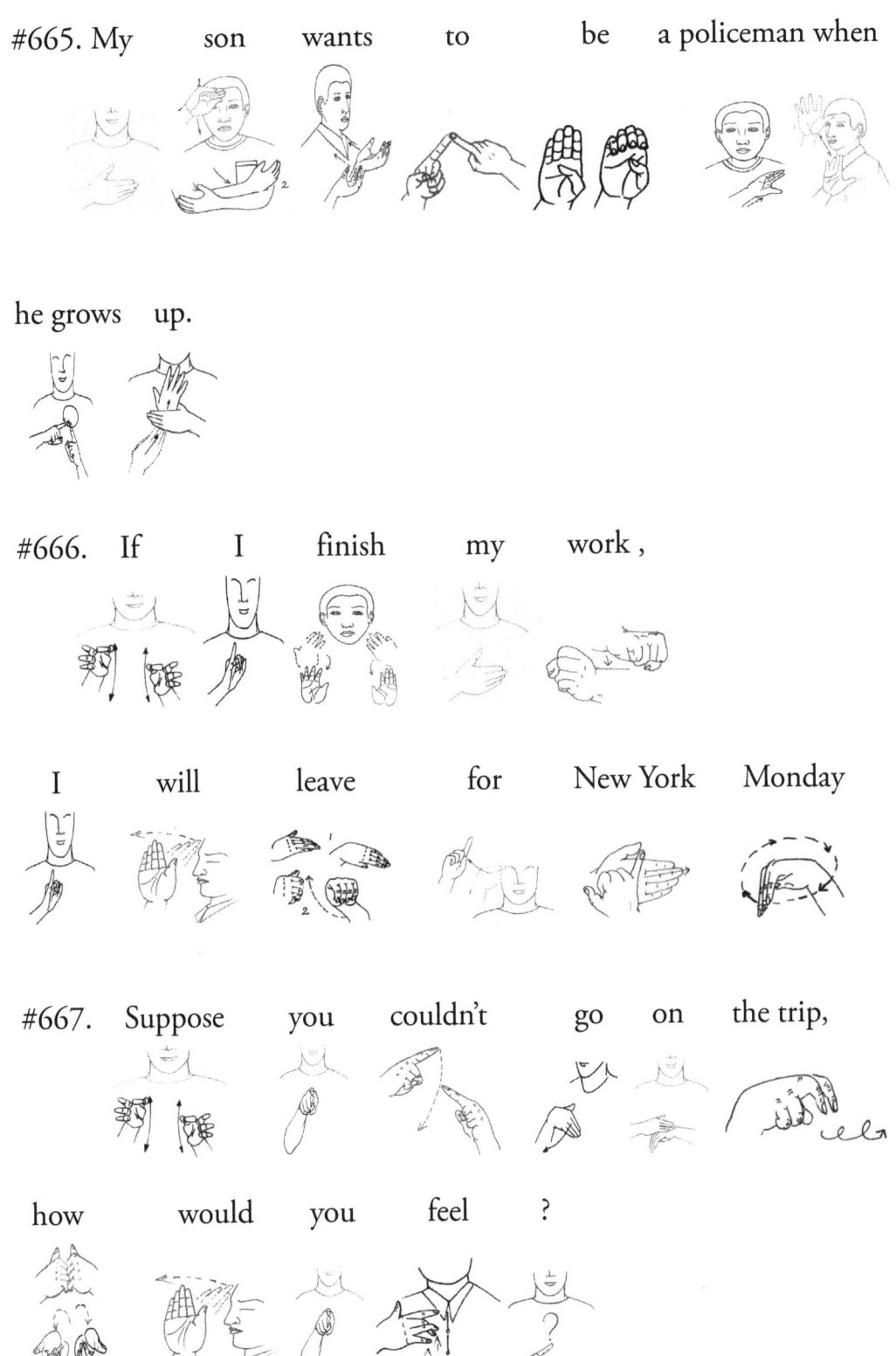

#668. What   would   you   say   if   I   say

I   couldn't   go   with   you   ?

#669.   If   I   buy   that   Car

I'll   have   to   borrow   some   money.

#670. If   I   went   with   you,   I 'd   have   to be

back   by   six o'clock.

#671. One of these days,   I'd   like   to   take

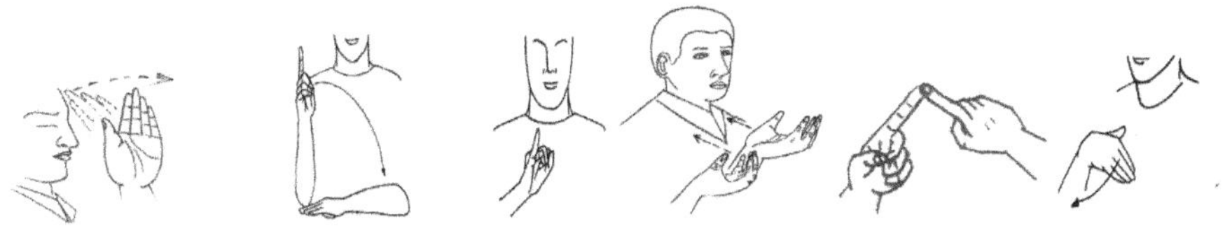

a vacation.

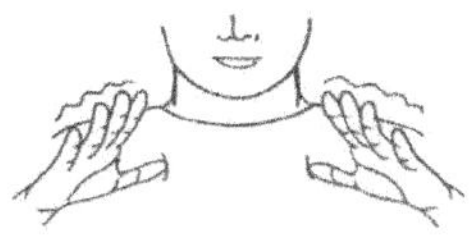

#672. Soon,   I   want   to   change   jobs.

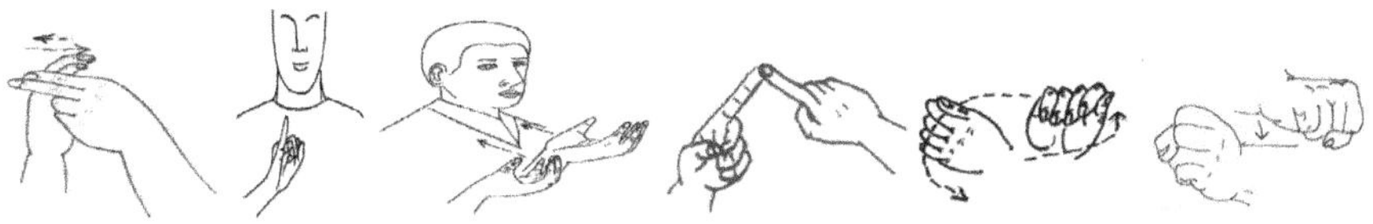

#673. Maybe   he   won't   be able to be

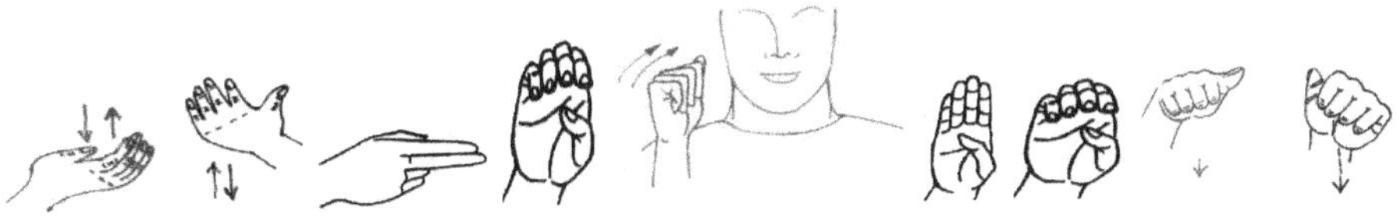

home for Christmas.

#674. We   may be   able   to   help   you

in some   way.

#675. If   you   attend the banquet,   what would you

wear   ?

#676. If   you   did not study,   what   would   you

have done   ?

#677. I would have gone on the

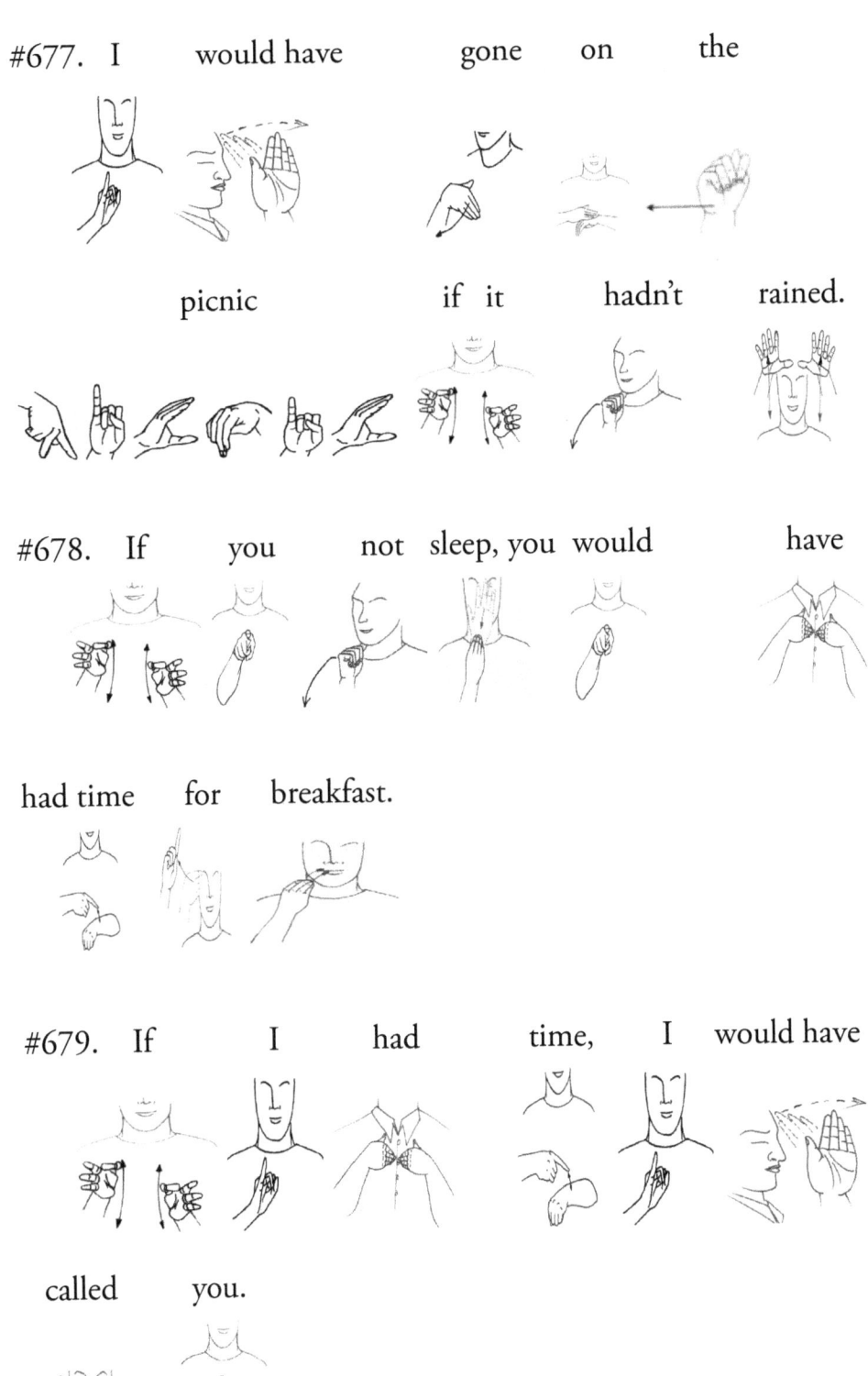

picnic if it hadn't rained.

#678. If you not sleep, you would have

had time for breakfast.

#679. If I had time, I would have

called you.

#680. Would he have seen you if you

waved ?

#681. If   he   had enough money,

he   would have bought that house.

#682. I wish `you had called me back the next day

as I had asked you.

#683. If   you   hadn't fallen,   you   wouldn't brake

your   leg.

#684. If   I   knew   you   wanted   to   go,

I   would   have   called   you.

#685. If   I   known   you   didn't   have   a key,

I   would   not have   locked   the door.

#686.   She   would   have gone   with   me,   but

she   didn't   have   time.

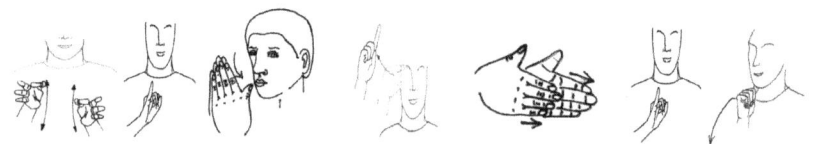

#687. If   I   had asked   for   directions,   I   wouldn't

be lost

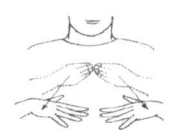

#688. If   we   could   taken   a vacation,

we   might   not have   wanted   to   go.

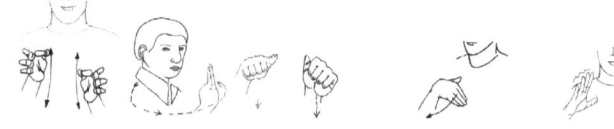

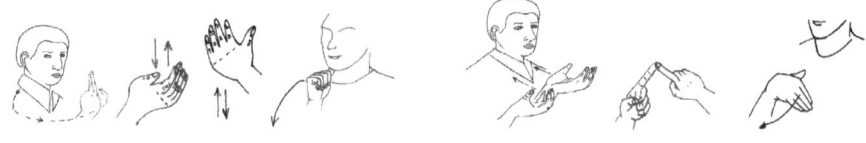

#689.   Every   thing   would have been all right   if

you   hadn't   said   that.

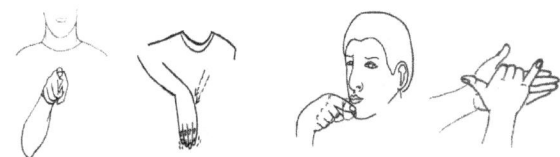

#690. I   wish   we   hadn't given in so   easily.

#691. What is it you don't   like   about   winter

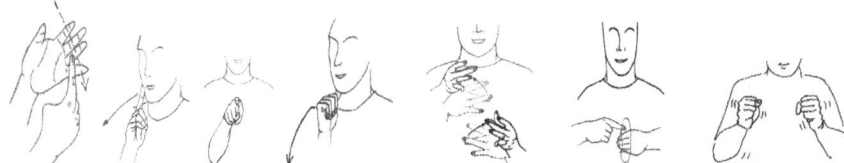

weather   ?

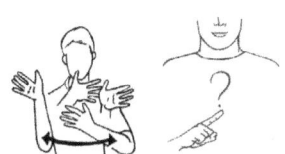

#692.   I   don't like it   when the   weather   becomes

real   cold.

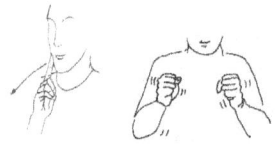

#693.   I   can't   stand   summer   weather.

#694. The   thing   I   don't   like   about   driving   is

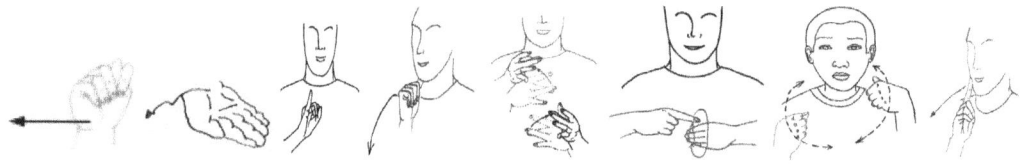

all the   traffic   on   the   road.

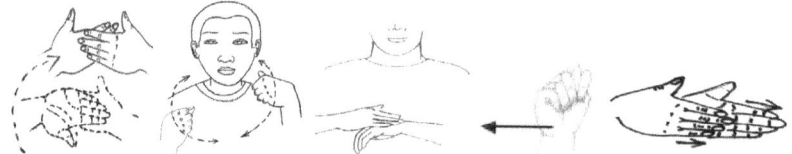

#695. He doesn't   like the   idea   of   going

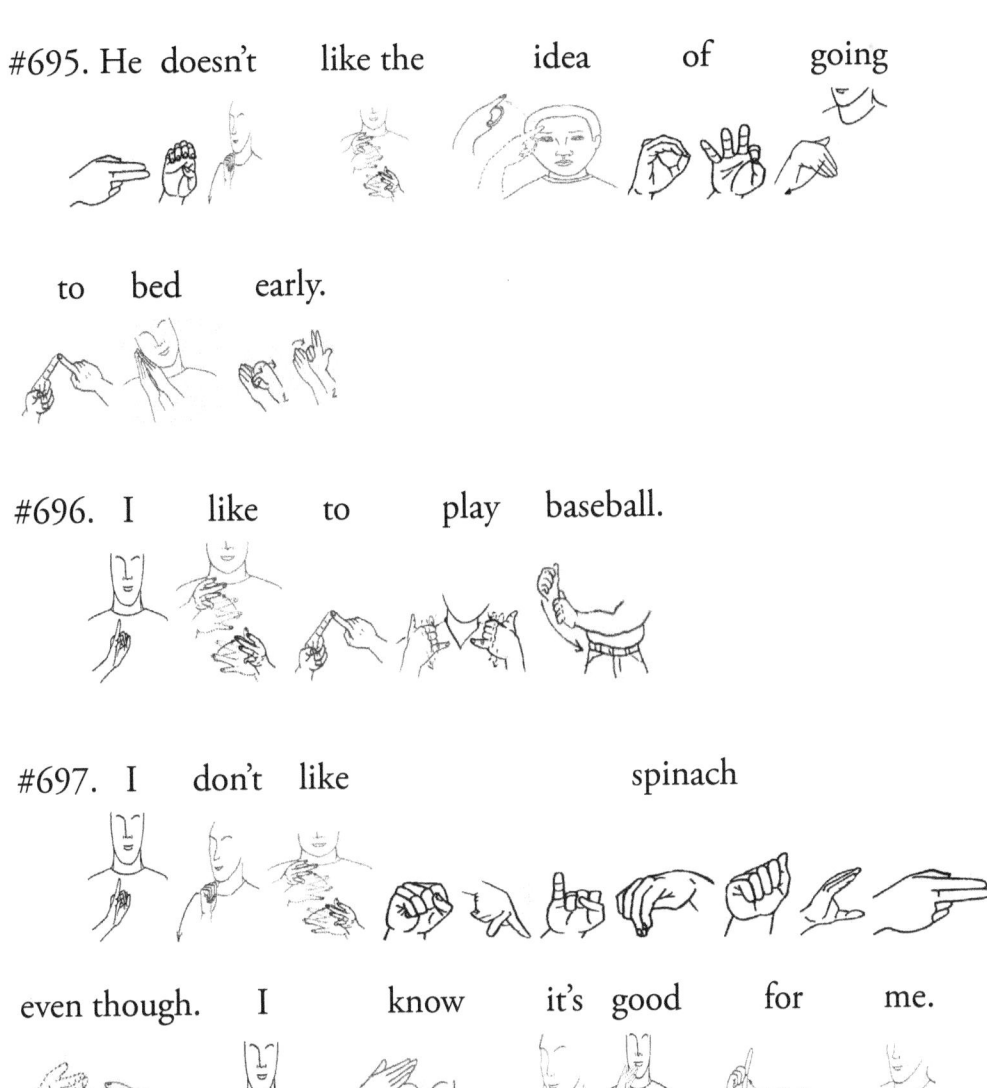

to   bed   early.

#696. I   like   to   play   baseball.

#697. I   don't like   spinach

even though.   I   know   it's good   for   me.

#698. I   am   afraid   you're being too   particular

about   your   food.

#699.   He   always finds fault   1with   everything.

#700.   She   doesn't   do   anything

I   say.